With Love From Karen...

In her teen years and as she grows into womanhood . . . a lovely girl for whom every day remains a wondrous gift, filled with seemingly insurmountable challenges and miraculous triumphs . . .

"Funny things, awesome things, painful things and wonderful things have happened to Karen and the Killilea family in the past eleven years . . . But there is more laughter than tears . . . and a super-abundance of faith, wisdom, warmth, and friends."
—LOUISVILLE COURIER-JOURNAL

"If you are not profoundly stirred; if you are not inspired with new hope and spirit and determination, you are without heart." —CAMDEN COURIER-POST

With Love from Karen

MARIE KILLILEA

Published by
Dell Publishing Co., Inc.
1 Dag Hammarskjold Plaza
New York, New York 10017

Dedication: to my husband

Laurel-Leaf Library ® TM 766734, Dell Publishing Co., Inc.

ISBN: 0-440-99615-5

RL: 7.0

Reprinted by arrangement with Prentice-Hall, Inc.

Printed in the United States of America

First Laurel-Leaf printing—August 1980

ACKNOWLEDGMENT : I would be grossly unjust were I not to acknowledge the assistance of Dorothy Haigney, Rett Kelly, eight loving and lovable Mc-Eneaneys, and Kathy Cassidy who, because I am ear-minded rather than eye-minded, read me every word that I had writ, made valuable suggestions with rare perspicacity and humor, and was generous with trans-fusions of encouragement.

foreword

There are files in our study, files in our bedroom, files in our attic and files in our cellar. The burden of these files is the inspiration for this book and its title,

With Love from Karen

With love *to* Karen and her family, have been sent to date, over 27,000 letters from all kinds of people, all over the world. They had one query in common: "What has happened to Karen and her family since *Karen* was published?" We decided, when the avalanche started, that under no circumstances could such warm, personal letters be answered with a form letter, so we undertook to answer each one personally. We have written over 14,000 responses and deeply regret that family circumstances make it impossible for us to continue a correspondence so cherished. It is my fervent hope that each writer will consider this book a personal reply, written with tender appreciation and thankfulness.

Writing a sequel to your own family story may appear to be an undertaking of slight dimensions. And so it is, if one has been scrupulous in the recording of episodes, incidents, weather, names, dates, places, flora and fauna. We have been most scrupulous and as a consequence all we have to do is work from an outline based on indexed cards, based on notes gleaned from scraps of paper filed in bureau drawers, pocketbooks, desks, coat pockets, the glove compartment of the car, prayer books, medicine chests, spice rack and bedside tables. To support a better understanding of the value of such notes I cite two examples:

Morris Who's Whistling Bird
Gaban—red shoes—black—NO!

Obviously from here on it's clear sailing.

It's been an exciting search, a sort of Treasure Hunt during which I have found cancelled checks from twenty years ago, a royalty check from Holland for $1.38 (I could have used that), three wills (if I have time before surgery I write a will), a fire insurance policy on our first apartment dated August, 1933, the grocery list for my husband when I was coming home from the hospital with our first born and other memorabilia preserved, or misplaced, neither interpretation reflecting too kindly on the author.

I have also found the records of large excitements, small heroisms, difficulties leavened by saving humor, the solutions of "hopeless" problems, and the certification that there is no such thing as a dull day.

Ah! Must Thou char the wood ere Thou canst limn with it?

—Francis Thompson

chapter one

The house was spacious and shabby and it had that air of pitiful loneliness peculiar to neglected houses built almost a century ago. It was elevated above its neighbors, set cater-corner on a plot hedged in by high, untrimmed privet. Its three stories were topped by two chimneys and an assortment of cupolas. Around it great oaks, elms and maples stood protectively, helping to preserve the dignity of the Victorian era when houses were built in which children could romp or curl up on window seats on a rainy afternoon. There was a wide porch around the bay front, and a story above, a widow's walk from which one could scan the shore of Long Island, five miles across the Sound, and pick out Execution Light, that infamous Tory prison of Revolutionary days, standing harsh and solitary on its island of rock.

A small breeze brought us the smell of salt and whispered among the still leaves of rhododendron and laurel. High above seagulls swirled and floated like lazy snowflakes.

This was the end of years of searching for a house that offered all we wanted in a home—proximity to the water, trees, a porch, ten large rooms, a farm kitchen complete with coal stove, fireplaces and, most important of all, a room on the ground floor with its own private entrance and bath for our twelve year old daughter, Karen.

We stood gazing with varied emotions at the dingy, peeling façade. Karen, who has cerebral palsy, balancing on her crutches, leaning a little against the side of Shanty, her big red Irish Setter. "We" also included: my husband, Jimmy, our adopted twenty-two year old daughter, Gloria, a friend, Russ Lea, our fifteen-year old Marie, Joe Bardinella, slender, handsome, just a year older than Marie, and our son Rory, a mercurial seven.

Looking back I marvel that our gratification, anticipation and excitement were undimmed by the enormous job of repair and restoration that faced us, for our hideously beautiful (well-mortgaged) house had been undisturbed by workman or painter for many, many years and our present financial state dictated that we should do most of the work ourselves. Perhaps our placid acceptance of the situation stemmed from the fact that we had always done our own painting, papering and plumbing, and our children had practically been weaned on paint brushes and turpentine. Our friends Russ and Joe had started later but were quickly trained and had become invaluable. Russ, a towering six feet three inches, was ideal for hanging wallpaper, while Joe painted expertly and was equally valuable when I needed advice on design and color. So, for that matter, was Rory.

In September we installed our equipment, donned what was to be our uniform for the next three and a half months —sneakers, old dungarees, old shirts, painters' caps, and began work. Word of our mad purchase was noised about and friends dropped in to gawk with mingled awe and amazement. We proudly showed the plot plans for the house, signed by one Frank E. Towle, dated, August 1873, at which time there were only 36 states in the Union. The country was then in the throes of Reconstruction; the telephone had not yet been invented; and 14 million buffalo still roamed the Plain States.

In all these years, there had been only three changes of ownership, and we discovered that one summer Mary Pickford had lived in it.

A few people with vision enthused over "possibilities"; others were guarded in their remarks. One friend, who loved us especially, walked through the house in what rapidly became a somnambulistic state. She positively blanched at the festoons of wires, like a Rube Goldberg contraption, that reached all sections of the kitchen from one outlet set directly in the middle of the ceiling. She grew glummer and glummer as she proceeded from one stained dark brown room to the next. (I think originally, say a quarter of a century ago, they had been "buff.") To distract herself from the depressing dinginess she walked to a window to find solace in the view but quickly withdrew as she saw that the putty had broken off around the panes and the frames were weather-rotted. She was appalled by the plumbing which did not boast one foot of copper and positively staggered when she discovered one bathroom had a deep tin tub, painted a violent blue and set in wainscoting, and a toilet with a water box hanging on the wall like a metastasized mushroom, eight feet above the floor. What she couldn't know was that both were to become a status symbol for our seven-year old for no child in the neighborhood (and very few adults) had ever seen the like. This was too much for our friend and she left us in tears. Her letter the following week said in part: "I know Jim Meighan, who is an authority on real estate, says the worst house on the block is a good investment, *but did you have to buy the worst house in Westchester?*"

I felt I should take time from painting, and everything needed *three* coats, to write a condolence letter in which I assured her that before we bought the house we had Morford Downes, builder extraordinary, go over every inch. He examined it from cellar to attic and at intervals jabbed an evil-looking penknife into the wood in the most obscure places. I assured my friend that Morf had found the house sound and sturdy and if we decided not to buy it, he would —as an investment.

I think the Smithsonian Institute would have been interested in the furnace. It was hard to find a heating engineer who was. As the weather grew colder and repairs to the furnace were proceeding at a lame snail's pace, we added to our uniforms woolen underwear, socks, heavy sweaters, gloves and ski caps with ear flaps. How lucky we were, we told each other through chattering teeth, to have the fireplaces and the coal stove.

Early in December, we dismantled our scaffolding, collected our paint cans, cleaned our brushes, capped our turpentine and paste, burned tons of newspaper, washed fifty-nine windows, scraped the last of the plaster drippings off the floors, cleaned from attic to cellar, started the furnace—kept it going—lost of chilblains, borrowed Sherburne's truck and moved in.

The pulsing beauty of the carillon, spilled over water, rocks, trees, roof tops, and rose to melt the cold, dark stillness stretched tightly above:

"Joy To The World!"

Happily, Russ, on leave from the Air Force, could be with us this Christmas Eve. He and Jimmy were hanging the tiny ornament at the top of the tree while Glo, Marie, Joe and Rory strung tinsel through the wide lower branches. Karen, using Shanty as a back rest, sat on the floor surrounded by more than a dozen large boxes from which she carefully took the ornaments and unwrapped them.

I glanced at the clock and sent Rory, protesting, to get ready for bed.

When he was pajama-d he came back into the living room for night prayers. I went to the crèche and picked up a lamb. It was Rory's. According to the virtue displayed during the day, the lamb advanced to the stable, it being my son's pious hope to be good enough to have his lamb by the manger on Christmas Eve. "Well—you've made it," I told him, placing the figure and banishing any doubts I might in justice entertain. Rory cheered in most unliturgical glee and Karen praised him with all the patronage of her twelve years.

All of us knelt in front of the crèche and prayed for relatives, benefactors, friends and enemies. Rory extended the recital: "God bless all Americans and make them good so if a bomb comes—*pfft!* they'll go right to Heaven."

The younger children were bedded down with visions of holsters dancing in at least one head and Joe, Russ, Glo, Jimmy and I finished the tree. It was twelve feet tall and we had placed it in the five-windowed bay. As I hung the last ornament Jimmy turned off the lamps and Russ plugged in the tree lights. Brilliance was multiplied by the window panes and flung into the night.

I took Jimmy's hand. "It's the most beautiful ever."

"You say that every year," he chided kissing me. "But this year I think you're right."

The ornaments seemed to dance liquidly in the shimmering rays from lights and silver.

Jimmy assigned everyone a closet or nooks and crannies in the cellar and we prospected for the packages that had been buried for weeks. Karen's were wrapped in blue paper, Rory's in red, Glo's in green and Marie's in white. When the last parcel had been added to the tottering heaps, we placed in front a most special present—the work of all the family save Karen, for it was for her. We had gotten her new crutches and although the wood was lovely we decided to make them feminine. In secrecy and stealth they had been painted and designed and initialled and varnished, and they were pretty and dainty and lady-like.

"Let's open our presents now," Gloria jumped up and began extracating parcels from the tops of things where they'd been safe from Rory. She had fixed a stocking for Jimmy and me. There were all kinds of treasures, lipstick, perfume, silver pen for Jimmy and delightfully silly things. Jimmy was down to the toe of his and pulled out a small flat package.

"It looks like three match books wrapped up," I observed.

Jimmy undid the wrapping and there were two tickets to a Broadway show and hotel reservations for a week-end in New York City. I was so happy that of course I wept. Not only because we hadn't had a week-end or a show in years, but because I knew how much loving and going-without had gone into this gift.

"Thank you, Gloria," Jimmy said huskily as he kissed her.

"Thank you—again," I hugged her. The "again" was for all the selfless, loving things she had done for all of us since she became our daughter at the age of fifteen. I watched her as she undid her gifts—her eyes, now blue, now green, her swift smile and deep dimples. She was slender, dainty, beautiful, good. "Thank you," I whispered to the Child in the manger. "But then, I have so much to be thankful for."

Russ and Joe had left and Gloria had gone to bed. Jimmy and I sat admiring the tree and our decorative efforts. It occurred to me that we probably used more boughs, pine cones and Christmas ceramics than anyone but Macy's.

This Christmas we had to count a veritable flood of blessings.

We had our house.

Russ had gotten home for Christmas.

No one was in the hospital.

Marie and Gloria, thanks to Dr. Grundy's treatment of their asthma, could now sleep in bed from May to October instead of upright in chairs so they could breathe.

We didn't owe one doctor's bill for the first time in twelve years. *"Te Deum laudamus"* I muttered, cringing at the memory of our financial burdens and marvelling that Jimmy had kept his sanity and his sweetness and his patience.

Karen, a book I had written about our family had been published and become a best seller.

Jimmy stretched and failed to conceal a wide yawn. "Time for bed, Sweetheart, your son will have us up before the stars have set."

"I'll be along shortly."

He kissed me. "Be sure it's shortly, you look exhausted."

The cold stillness of the night was warmed by the vibrant sweetness of church bells heralding the Hour of Birth. I thought of previous Christmases and the twelve difficult years that lay between—the years after we found out that Karen was born with cerebral palsy. Years when she couldn't sit, crawl or stand, and had very limited use of her hands. Years of searching for help, of hope and its annihilation; of near despair; of hope surging again and finally a line of action. In the last nine years Karen had averaged six hours of therapy a day of one kind or another. Wearing braces and using crutches she could now walk, albeit very slowly and with difficulty. She could use her hands moderately well and was advancing in reading, writing and arithmetic with a teacher who came to the house several times a week.

So many problems had been solved, so many heartaches eased.

But our life was like the summer's sea—its shimmering surface radiated warmth and brilliance, yet below the surface it was dark and cold and there were some fearful unknowns. We now faced unpredicted and seemingly unanswerable difficulties and the light of Karen's greatest victories was quenched by failure.

When first we had tried to enroll Karen in school, we had been told: "We cannot take her because she cannot walk." Now she was walking, and doing well in her studies with a home teacher sent by the public school. With but small uncertainty I again went to enroll her. Public, private, parochial—none denied her fine intelligence—but all rejected her. Their reasons were varied and in some instances a ludicrous deceit, for the truth was they wanted only children sounder of limb.

Attending regular school had been Karen's major motivation during these years of superhuman effort toward physical improvement. She had conquered—to fail. School represented a normal way of life in association with her peers, and sufficient teaching hours to appease the appetite of her intellect. She was consistently denied.

Her dark discouragement in the face of this defeat was heartbreaking but I had felt that more hours of home teaching would lighten it some. Supported by the report of her teacher, that Karen could profit greatly by additional instruction time, and that he had the time to give, I had appealed repeatedly to our Superintendent of Schools and our local Board of Education. There were in existence the legal statutes enabling them to grant my petition. The last time I had gone to the Board meeting to renew my request, one of the women members had asked: "Are you pleased with Karen's present teacher?"

"You know I am. I have so stated time and time again."

"You wouldn't want *more* time with a *less able* teacher, would you?"

It wasn't even a concealed threat.

We had thought nothing could dim the brightness of

our happiness when Karen had conquered so many of the difficulties with which she was born. We had not reckoned with the unknown. As a young child her hips had been x-rayed. The plates showed them to be perfectly normal. Now both were dislocated and there was good reason to believe that this could have been avoided if certain medical procedures had been followed.

Present problems were numerous. She endured being thirsty a good deal of the time for Dr. Temple Fay had limited her to nineteen fluid ounces a day. We found that this reduced her spasticity about thirty percent. In addition to this discomfort she had running pressure sores from the braces. Twice a week we took a fifty-mile drive for adjustments but it seemed that pressure could not be relieved on one spot without starting it on another. Since she wore braces all night as well as during the day, her sleep was constantly interrupted. Recently we had been applying tincture of benzoin to toughen the skin and this seemed to be helping. But sores were not all that plagued her days and nights. She had muscle spasms that were excruciating in their intensity. During the day I knew when one started because I could see the sweat break out on her forehead and her face grow pale. And yet, she never complained. A large statement—of a large truth.

I rose slowly and turned off the gas fire. Uppermost in my mind was a question that beat unceasingly against every waking hour—where do we go from here?

I went to extinguish the candles burning in the windows and beside the crèche. I addressed myself to the three central figures. "And lest I become obsessed by Karen's problems, it has been arranged that at this time Jimmy should develop a severe hearing loss, and Gloria should face the anguish of a problem that seems beyond resolution. She's so gay that no one suspects, and yet her heartache is constant." I extinguished one candle. In the remaining flicker of light, the Babe's eyes seemed to be closed in the sweet sleep of infancy. "Help them all," I pleaded, "and I might respectfully remind You, it is seven Christmases that we have been waiting for another child."

I snuffed out the last candle. "Fear not . ." had been the angels' greeting the first Christmas. In the darkness I couldn't see the figure. But I knew He was there.

ટે

chapter two

A year and a half before, when we were in Rye, Jimmy had brought me a present. "It's not my birthday, nor Mother's Day, nor any anniversary—or is it?"

"Nope," he replied succinctly and handed me Phyllis McGinley's *A Short Walk from the Station*. Never would I have dreamt that the grotesquely enchanting house on page fifteen would one day be ours. I read Phyllis' description of "Spruce Manor" and positively drooled. "Spruce Manor without children would be a paradox. The summer waters are full of them, gamboling like dolphins. The lanes are alive with them, the yards overflow with them. A nice medium Spruce Manor family runs to four or five, and we count proudly, but not with amazement, the many solid households running to six, seven, eight, nine, even twelve. ."

Larchmont, though only twenty miles from New York, had many of the virtues of a small town. Tradespeople were friendly and took a personal interest, whether we were buying a silver christening cup or a stopper for the old-fashioned sink. Jimmy had converted our coal stove to kerosene and Joe and Dom Vitulli who delivered the fuel, offered us the use of their outboard motor. "Red," who delivered for United Parcel, would wait to pass judgment on overalls and shirts ordered from Sears Roebuck. Mel, who drove the Good Humor truck, was so liked and admired by the kids that when the company transferred him, the youngsters got up a petition to have him returned. He was. Mel was important enough to rate a news items on the first page of the paper when he was taken ill. Mr. Kean, sexton of our church, built movable ramps to cover the steps for worshippers in wheel chairs. I didn't know whether nice people came to Larchmont, or Larchmont made people nice. We found neighbors were just that, in the fullest sense of the word. For a family facing a great tragedy, neighbors kept vigil in church all night.

While Jimmy and I were enjoying our week-end in New York there were any number of people on whom Gloria and Marie could call for a quart of milk or a ride to church.

I was putting the last few items in my overnight bag. Rory and Karen were out in the yard under my window. And Shanty, of course. He still didn't believe Karen was safe on her feet leaning on things that *moved*. When Karen fell, as she did frequently, she would drop one crutch so she could use that arm to break the fall. I knew he thought the crutches made her fall. When she felt herself going over, being a little fey, my daughter would yell: *"Tim-ber!"* crescendo. The dog never got the idea that this was a joke and he would race around her alternately barking insanely and licking her all over.

This morning I heard her *"Tim-ber!"* Subconsciously I waited for his consequent barking. Not a sound from the big red beast but a chorus of shouts from Karen and Rory. *"Catch him!"* *"Grab him!"* *"Stop thief!"* I ran to the window in time to see Shanty running down the hill with the offending crutch in his teeth, Rory in pursuit and Karen on the ground helpless with laughter.

"Shanty!" I yelled. *"Come here!"* He slowed, stopped and turned. "Come here!" I repeated. He looked up at me and gave every appearance of wrestling with his conscience. *"At once!"* I charged in stentorian tones. He lowered his head, placed the crutch on the ground and raced back up the hill to Karen. Obviously, if he couldn't take it far away, at least he didn't intend to bring back the menace.

"Go get it!" I ordered. He consoled Karen wetly, looked up at me, wagged his plume of a tail and stood his ground with ingratiating defiance. I knew when I was licked. "Rory, you get it—if I take time to discipline the dog I'll be late." I was torn between blessing and cussing his 'protection.'

Gloria went out to help Karen back up on her feet. "I wish I didn't fall so much," I heard Karen say to her.

"But you're improving all the time."

"I know——" Karen answered in a small voice.

"But it's so wonderful. Think of it this way—God made *us* walk, but God and *you* make you walk."

"I know," Karen said again, "but sometimes I wish God and I could make me run."

"I'm sure you do," replied Gloria matter-of-factly. "Let's feed the birds."

Our week-end in New York was marvelous and memorable. I made Jimmy order all my meals, I wouldn't even look at a menu. "No decisions for me for two whole days."

Sunday morning we went to St. Patrick's Cathedral. It was too warm to keep my coat on over my suit. We sat up front so that Jimmy would have no trouble hearing the speaker. When Mass was over we made our way slowly down the aisle in a press of people. Suddenly I tripped, grabbed Jimmy to keep from falling and looked down to see what entangled my feet. It was my suit skirt! There was I in the centre of gothic splendor in my white slip. With great élan (produced by shock) I stepped away from it. Jimmy flung my coat over my shoulders and I left him to retrieve. Finally we reached the back of the church and while Jimmy stood in front of me as a shield I wriggled into the skirt and examined it to see what had happened. The zipper had broken and the only way I could keep it on was by holding it until I found a safety pin. I knew that somewhere in this vast edifice was a dressing room. The church was almost empty and Jimmy took one side and I the other trying every door we came to. I was half-way around when I noticed a man following me. Each time I went to a door he would stop and wait and when I started to walk again he was right behind me. He didn't even pretend not to be following me. He kept his eyes glued on me and came a little closer. Any place else I would have known how to handle such a situation, but what does one do in a Cathedral! I quickened my steps and hurried toward the rear of the main altar. I glanced over my shoulder and saw my pursuer nod to his left. Another man came across from a side altar and blocked my path. I moved to dart into a pew when a strong hand seized the arm over which hung my overnight bag. "I'll take that please," said a courteous voice.

"You will not!" I grabbed at my bag with both hands and again my skirt settled about my feet. I looked wildly about me. Jimmy was nowhere in sight and the few remaining worshippers were acres away and deep in prayer.

The first man produced a badge.

The second man produced a badge.

"What is this?" I gasped.

Both had the grace to look uncertain. "It's like this lady —we've been on patrol here all morning. We got a tip that someone was going to plant a bomb.".

"A WHAT!"

"A bomb. And you've been acting mighty suspicious—so furtive."

"Oh—oh," I wailed and collapsed on the seat. I bent down, picked up my skirt and mutely offered it in evidence. "A pin," I squeaked, "I was looking for a pin," and went into paroxysms of laughter.

"A pin!" they repeated stupidly and in unison. They looked at the skirt, they gaped at me, they turned to each other, their faces curling with embarrassment like strips of bacon.

Jimmy charged up, spurred by my unseemly hilarity. "You tell him," I gasped. "He wouldn't believe. me."

We couldn't wait to get home to present this priceless vignette to the kids. We burst into the living room to find the children gathered around Karen who was weeping wildly. Marie flung herself into Jimmy's arms. "Shanty's gone," she sobbed.

"He can't be!" I ran over to Karen. She and Rory were hugging each other in grief and her braids were wet with his tears. I knelt and put my arms around the two tragic figures.

"I let him out this morning—" Gloria began, "about seven o'clock—you know he only stays a few minutes. We had breakfast and he wasn't back but I didn't think too much about it. But when we came home after Mass and he wasn't here I began to get worried. I organized the neighborhood kids into search parties, thinking he might have been hit by a car; I called the police. No word."

"Did you call the Humane Society?"

"Yes. When I told them what kind of a dog he was they said it was not uncommon for a field dog to be stolen. People take them for hunting."

"He must have been stolen—or killed—" Karen cried. "He never, never would leave me."

"I'm afraid I must agree with you, but we'll all pray very hard that God will bring him back safely."

The worst of that night was when we put Karen to bed and there was no big red 'angel' curled up beside her.

Jimmy and I took a flashlight and went out and beat the bushes, thinking perhaps he was injured and had been unable to crawl home. We walked the length and breadth of the Manor and through the Park. In the gray of early morning we finally gave up and went to bed. There wasn't much sleep; we kept thinking we heard Shanty whining or scratching at the door.

Monday and Tuesday came and went and no word. Karen had ceased weeping and grown frighteningly quiet. Wednesday we extended our advertising to papers in adjacent communities; called the police stations from Greenwich to Mount Vernon and the State Police. Everyone was sympathetic and no one had a lead.

Wednesday night Jimmy and I sat up late and decided that we must get a replacement for Shanty and as quickly as possible.

"We'll never be able to *replace* him," Jimmy said bitterly. Remember the day at Maryknoll when he chewed his way through a shatter-proof car window to get to Karen?"

"I wonder if the Bishop ever noticed the blood on his robe?"

"You know," said Jimmy, "we could always identify him by the scars on his tongue."

"I don't think he's going to be found." I felt the time had come to put hope aside.

We sat, pretending to read. In an hour Jimmy didn't turn a single page. We went to bed and lay sleepless. Finally I dozed and then awoke suddenly.

"Did you hear something?" I prodded Jimmy.

"No. It's wishful thinking."

"Maybe." I jumped out of bed and ran to the front door. As I reached it I thought I heard a whimper. I yanked open the door whispering—"please, God, please!"

Lying on the porch was Shanty.

I turned and yelled for Jimmy. The dog didn't move, but his eyes implored. We knelt beside him. His breathing was shallow and faint. Jimmy lifted him in his arms; I supported his lolling head and we carried him in and put him down on the rug in front of the hearth.: I saw a trail of blood across the floor. I put my face against him and cried and cried.

"Look at his feet!" said Jimmy in a horrified voice.

There not only were no nails but the pads were gone. The feet were wounds.

"What should we do?"

"I'll get a blanket and cover him and you call Walter Miller." Dr. Miller, our veterinarian, had seen us through many crises with our menagerie. It wouldn't be the first time I had gotten him out of bed in the middle of the night.

"Leave him alone," Walter told me. "Don't do anything to him or for him. Don't move him. See if you can get him to drink; you'll probably have to dip your finger and let him lick it—if he will. I'll be up in the morning—"

We sat with Shanty until the children waked. He didn't get a drop of water, he couldn't lick my finger. Still he was alive and that's all Karen could say over and over. *He's alive! He's alive!* She lay on the floor beside him, an arm lightly across his neck. She crooned—"You'll be all right, sweetheart, all right—you'll see."

Walter arrived and gave a most thorough examination. No one spoke until he was through. Finally he got up from the floor and said to Karen: "He *is* going to be all right."

"What happened—what's the matter with his feet?" Rory was almost shouting.

"I can only guess," said Walter. "His right shoulder is swollen and I can't tell how badly injured. As a matter of fact his whole right side is swollen and tender. My guess is that someone stole him—that he jumped from a moving

22.

ir. Looking at his feet, I would say that he travelled over
acadam roads from many, many miles away." He looked
own at Karen. "I'd bet he's been on the road for three or
our days. He must love you an awful lot."

"He does," said Karen simply.

"Bring him down to me for x rays; give him lots of love
and some milk with whisky. Let him be absolutely quiet
and I think he'll be all right in a week or two."

X rays of the shoulder were negative. Just a bad bruise.
Ten days later Shanty was back on the job, limpingly
alking Karen every walking moment and raising his usual
allabaloo when she fell. Karen's recovery from the event
ook a little longer. Every time he was out of her sight she
retted. She also got a glimpse of the future. "Daddy,"
he asked one night, "if I ask God for Shanty when I get to
eaven, will He give him to me?"

"If you want Shanty in Heaven, you will have him,"
answered Jimmy with exact theology.

I was distracted from Karen's problems by Rory. In the
mornings he complained of pains in his stomach; he had
o appetite and his color was pasty. By afternoon he would
e all right. I had taken him to Dr. Virginia Haggerty
(Larchmont was too far away for John Gundy) and she
ad found nothing. Another visit was indicated and this
 one she asked me to wait outside and she and Rory were
closeted in her office for a long time. He came out and she
called me in. I got up slowly, familiar tongues of ice licking
my heart—too often such a summons had meant—cerebral
palsy, tuberculosis, rheumatic fever, abnormality of the
esophagus, a hearing loss (temporary for Marie), pneumonia (14 times), the need for a pneumoencephalogram.
I sat beside the doctor's desk and went through the usual
routine of nonchalantly lighting a cigarette. (I don't think
is ever fooled a doctor but it helped to convince me.)

Dr. Haggerty came right to the point. "Rory's trouble
not caused by anything physical."

"I don't understand."

"A review with you and with him shows that this started
the beginning of school."

23.

"That's right. But he loves school."

"Yes, he does. I'm satisfied on that score."

"Then what does school have to do with it?"

"Everything. As you expected that Karen would st[a] school this year, so did he. After our talk this morning can tell you that he is very much disturbed because [s]chool will take his sister."

"We never discussed this in front of him."

"You don't have to. He a smart youngster. He figur[ed] it out for himself. Furthermore, each morning he drea[ds] going for two reasons: (1) Karen isn't able to go. (2) [He] feels guilty leaving her."

"What can we do?"

"He's reasoned things out on a pretty adult level so y[ou] must talk to him about all this on the same level. You c[an] do it. I don't look for an overnight change but I think a month or two most of the symptoms will have disa[p]peared."

Going home I had to chuckle when I thought of what had assented to that faraway day when I said: "I do." I w[as] saying yes to being wife, mother, physiotherapist, occup[a]tional therapist, nurse, teacher and now psychologist. knew I certainly wasn't equipped but one thing the pa[st] decade had taught me was that God does provide for parent's insufficiencies.

It was closer to three months before Rory's pains a[nd] pallor were gone and his morning appetite normal.

Karen was manifesting her discouragement over t[he] school situation by biting her nails. I had used every a[p]proach I could think of, from pride in her appearance coating her finger tips with foul substances *guaranteed* break the habit. Nothing worked.

Karen and I were home alone during most of the da[y] Gloria was working as an executive secretary in New Yo[rk] and Marie was attending Good Counsel Academy in Wh[ite] Plains. Rory should have been home about three but [he] had turned into a garbage hound and spent hours ea[ch] day searching for "treasures." When the pickings were sl[im] (no broken mirrors, old sneakers, handleless knives, o[ld] hats) he searched out his treasures on the beach—"so[ld] gold and solid silver rocks" which he shamelessly offered for sale to "poor old ladies who couldn't climb around in the sand."

It was a deceptively mild day and Karen and I were out in the yard hunting for crocuses. I was pretty depressed because I was facing up to my first total failure. When the Superintendent and the School Board gave a final refusal to an increase in home teaching hours for Karen I had sought to supplement. As a teacher I was an absolute bust but I persisted. The result was that I got both of us in a highly emotional state at each encounter.

In my work on the national association for cerebral palsy I had the good fortune—or the intervention of providence—to come to know Dr. Edgar A. Doll, doctor of education and doctor of psychology. At our first meeting I had been impressed by a touch of benign heresy: "Too many suffer from hardening of the categories. So much of the 'High Priest' dogma seems too costly, ritualistic and unproductive, but we have to be on guard for the 'trained' people. Our innocence is both shocking and threatening to the Brahmans."

I had written Ed Doll of my teaching problem and as I scratched away to find the tiniest spring sprout I was listening for the mail truck.

"Here's Jim," Karen called from the end of the driveway.

"Big pile today," Jim Brennan announced. "Must be thirty or forty letters from all over the world. Enough to keep you out of mischief for the rest of the day. Good thing you have a secretary in the family." He handed me the lot.

"Thank you." I dropped to the ground and flipped through the envelopes looking for the familiar, dearly undecipherable handwriting of Dr. Doll. Here it was. He had answered by return mail—bless him! The letter was lengthy and comforting. In essence he said that in doing therapy I had been able to make the transfer from mother-child relationship to teacher-pupil and, when the exercises were over, I had been successful in going back to mother-child. I should thank my stars for that; frequently this could not be done. Now in the teaching situation I was unable to make this transfer; it was not uncommon and no one was to blame and I shouldn't be upset. Let Gloria and Marie (not Jimmy) take over. For me to continue would be damaging to both Karen and me. My emotions were mixed as I put the letter carefully back in the envelope. My stuffy pride was affronted and yet I was greatly relieved. I think I had know all along that the girls could do a better job. I just hadn't wanted to admit it.

"Anything for me?" Karen chirped.

"Here's one." I took her crutches, unlocked the braces at the knees and sat her beside me. "Why look at the address!" I handed her the envelope. It read

KAREN
U.S.A.

"I wonder where it came from!" She tore open the envelope, settled herself against my side and read:

Somewhere in Korea

Dearest Miss Karen:

On behalf of myself, Cpl. Eddie Brothers and some of my buddies, we want to write you to say we got hold of *Time* magazine. In the spare moments we have here in Korea, we were reading it and as we looked through we came upon your picture in the protective hat your Daddy and sister Gloria, devised and we read all about you. Then we kind of took you as our pin-up girl. I have been asked to write and say that Robert Dunker, Ralph Baldwin, Albert Carter and myself want to ask you to keep your chin up and soon you will be strong. We are counting on you to keep up the good work and we know you will make the grade.

Right now we are in a place where we can't take pictures, but as soon as we can, we will send you one of the four of us. We hope this letter helps give you the spirit to go on for what is yours.

Always remember, we are all praying for you not to give up the fight. We would like you to write us and send us a picture of yourself. We are with the 187th Abn. Rct. and we are with a Tank Battalion.

We have named our tank after you—THE FIGHT-ING KAREN.

Well, as I said before, we wish you all the luck in the world. Say hello to all your family.

Good luck and God bless you,

from

YOUR FOUR LADS IN KOREA
EDDIE
ROBERT
RALPH
ALBERT

"Oh, Mom!" Karen said in a small voice, her eyes brimming over (as were mine). "Oh, Mom, it's so beautiful."

I couldn't speak.

"How could they? In so much danger and writing to encourage me! To tell *me* to keep my chin up—praying for *me*—they must be very brave. Let's answer it right this minute."

My voice was not quite steady. "I'll bring the typewriter to the kitchen table and I'll write and you write. I'll call the photographer who took that picture and ask him to make a print and mail it to the boys."

We worked in a silence broken only by the rat-tat-tat of the keys. When we had finished our letters Karen said: "Mom Pom, please hand me my crutches. I think I'll practice walking for a while and try not to fall at all. The boys are counting on me," she amended shyly.

As the days and weeks passed Karen's discouragement vanished. The courage and selflessness of four boys in Korea were contagious. She worked harder than she ever had before. It was slow and painful. Just when she seemed to despair of standing or sitting erect, with uncanny timing the boys wrote again.

Dearest Karen,

Today we are back off the line for a rest and we got our mail and there was your letter! You can't know how happy we were to hear from you. There is talk about us going back to Japan for a real rest.

Dear child, I have to tell you something I know will hurt you. Albert was killed four days ago and Ralph was sent back to Japan. He was wounded. I want you to know that I hate to tell you this, but I felt you would want to know.

Karen, naming our tank after you was our greatest idea and as soon as we can we will send you a picture of the two of us and the tank.

We, *all four of us,* hope you are keeping up the good work.

We are all four of us, from the South. Robert and I are from Burkhorn, Kentucky, and Ralph and Albert are from Lewisburg, Kentucky.

We will be glad to get your picture. You see, there is three miles difference from where we live to each other. We have been in Korea fourteen months and soon we will be going home.

Karen, Sweet, each company of tanks has its own emblem on its jacket. Your picture will be painted on ours.

To the four of us you are the greatest and sweetest thing we have. Someday, if the three of us that are left, come out of this alive, we will come to see you. So 'til then we want to say 'So long for now, keep up the good work'—

to a *brave* little girl,

Love

EDDIE, ROBERT, RALPH (ALBERT)

The next day at lunch I complimented Karen on her sitting posture. "Come to think of it, I haven't seen you slump all morning."

"I'm trying hard—for the boys. I'm trying to walk taller too."

"I noticed."

Karen continued working and writing. As a matter of fact, everyone in the family was now writing. We sent pictures of all of us, rabbits, cats, bird, Shanty, and of course a picture of the house.

Some days Karen fell only twice.

It was just as hard for Karen to make her hands and fingers work right as it was to make her legs and feet perform correctly. Learning to pick up a knife and fork or spoon, to use them gracefully and lay them down on dishes quietly, had been difficult and she had developed the habit of hold her fork during a good part of the meal. It was easier. Now, however, with no prompting from family, she began to work assiduously on fine table gestures. We were lavish with our praise. She retorted blithely: "The boys will have dinner with us when they come home. They must be proud of me."

One day a letter came addressed to me but inside—

CENSOR FOR KAREN IF YOU WISH

5th St. Field Hospital
U.S.S. Constellation
(Hospital Ship)

Dear Mrs. Killilea:

Today I lie here waiting shipment to a hospital in Japan.

I hate to tell you this, but Ralph died about eight days ago. Tell Karen in the way you think best.

I was wounded again—I caught a slug in the foot.

As for Robert—he went back to Japan for a rest on Monday. I was to leave that night and that afternoon I got hit. By this time, in a day or so I'll be in Japan and I'll write you from there.

I want you all to try and understand that what has happened is something of God's works.

Karen, Sweet, listen—We are fighting to preserve what is ours—the right to be free. To go and do and say what we want. If it were not for our country, I think someday people would be under One Ruler. You must remember, if it means giving our lives that the U.S.A.—and the world—may stay free, we are willing to give.

Big Marie—It is our hope that because we are over here now, Rory won't have to live in a fox hole.

Karen—remember how dear you are to us. How we count on you. We pray for you and all your family.

In answer to Rory's question: we've been trying to find a couple of sisters—but no luck.

So long for now. All our love to our SWEETHEART OF A GIRL

Of this hell in Korea, they said it was not a war—just a *Police Action!*

Marie had been doing well in her studies, but now her work was being impaired by her extra-curricular activities. Jimmy made rules that were rigid—no dating at home or abroad on any school night, curfew—11 p.m. He allowed a few exceptions, basketball games, the Stepinac High School plays. Marie didn't like the rules but she had the good grace to be pleasant about them while she protested: "But Daddy, *everybody* does!"

To which Daddy gave the level reply: "What *everybody* does has nothing to do with you."

Interestingly enough, the regulations deterred not Marie's male callers. Most week-ends our living room rug stayed rolled up and I remember one night after teaching the kids the Merry Widow Waltz, I offered to teach them the Charleston. "Oh, Mother!" expostulated Marie, "that's so old-fashioned!"

We disconnected the doorbells and removed the knockers, on the theory that we lived in an open house and it was just too time-consuming to answer the door. Let them walk in. We saw Joe almost every week-end and frequently during the week. We liked and enjoyed all the sprouts that came and for Johnny Forsman we had a special fondness.

During the summer months the parade of young visitors was endless. There were mixed attractions: a porch that accommodated thirty comfortably and sixty in a pinch, the beach across the street, a piano, a hi-fi and Karen's rapidly growing collection of records (over 200 albums), Jimmy Dengler, a friend who played the electric guitar and sang with magical skill, attractive daughters of ready wit (if I say so as who shouldn't), and Gloria's Italian cooking. The girls calculated that one memorable week-end we served over seventy meals to unexpected guests from Friday eve to Sunday night. The usual number was a little better than a dozen.

I know there were times when Jimmy would have liked some quiet and uninterrupted repose but he had a simple theory about kids: In the home there should be positive attractions as well as controls. It wasn't *our* house meaning his and mine, but our house, meaning that it really belonged to everybody in the family, and the living room should be used for just that purpose, again by everybody.

One week-end he went off fishing and returned late Sunday night bringing a friend. He might expect to find the guest room filled and maybe the couch in my office taken, but there was always the couch in the living room and the chaise on the porch. Only this night there wasn't a place whereon the friend could lie his weary head. Everything was already occupied. Wearily Jimmy blew up a rubber mattress and hospitably placed it on the floor of Rory's room. His friend inquired with tender solicitude: "Is it often like this?"

Jimmy looked around and answered somewhat vaguely: "I guess so."

"Letter from the boys," Jim Brennan sang out early one morning. Just look at the address on this one."

RUSH TO A SWEETHEART OF A GIRL

Sweet,

How are you? I'm feeling fine. I don't have to burn your letters any more. On the lines we have to; in case we are captured they might give away our secrecy as a unit fighting in Korea. You see the Chinese would really like to know how many regiments and how many divisions on the line.

Most times they brought us our mail when we were on the lines. I wish I could tell you what your letters meant. They gave us all something to look forward to. We read them aloud together. The other boys in the 57 Recoilless Rifle Squad, the guys in the platoon and we passed around the pictures. They all agreed that if you could fight so hard—they could too. You sure have built a lot of morale.

Rory asked me how many parachute jumps. Tell him 78. One behind enemy lines on October 20 at Sunshon. We went to get some of our guys off a train who were prisoners. We got about 360 out of 500.

God bless you. I ask Him every day to keep you safe for me 'til I get home.

Love always,
Eddie

Following the receipt of this letter, Karen asked for two full length mirrors. One between the living room and dining room and one in her room. "So I can watch myself and see if I'm walking and standing straight." Her posture difficulties stemmed in considerable measure from the fact that her adductor muscles pulled her legs into what is described as a "scissor gait." That is, when unbraced, the legs crossed. Jimmy and I wondered what should or could be done about this and by whom. In the meantime Karen spent hours trying to improve her posture.

One afternoon, I noticed Marie, standing off to one side, watching Karen. The smaller figure was shifting stance, swaying the body a few inches to the left, then some inches back. Karen's cheeks were flushed and her green eyes bright with the mental as well as the physical effort. Although Marie stood quietly, I sensed that she was working along with her sister. Marie was really beautiful. Her long hair, deeply dark, her skin tinted with olive, her face exquisitely moulded and soft with compassion. Abruptly she turned to leave the room. Her great dark eyes were filled with tears.

"You mustn't feel sorry for Karen," I put my arm around her shoulders.

"I don't feel sorry *for* her—I feel sorry *with* her."

That night at dinner, Karen held her hands palms down over the table. "Look everybody."

"Your nails!" Gloria exclaimed. "You've stopped biting them."

Jimmy went to the kitchen and returned with a bottle

of Chianti. He placed the bottle and glasses in front of Karen. "I was saving this for a special occasion. I didn't guess it would be as special as this!" He poured the wine and offered a toast: "To a young lady and her very pretty hands."

Rory offered: "I'll take my allowance and buy you a bottle of nail polish tomorrow."

Marie: "I'll give you your first manicure."

Karen thanked them both and suggested somewhat timidly, "if you don't mind Marie, I want to put the polish on myself. I want to be expert at it when the boys come home." She started to laugh and turned to me. "You can chalk it up to occupational therapy—'the practice of fine finger motions' " she mimicked.

"What color polish?" asked her practical brother.

Karen thought that over for quite a while. "Colorless," she finally announced.

"Don't you like the pink that Mommy wears?"

"Yes, very much."

"Then I'll get pink."

"I prefer colorless."

"Why, if you like pink?"

"Because," Karen spoke with deliberation, "my hands are spastic and pink polish would call attention to them."

"You're very smart." Even Rory was impressed.

We were having our after-dishes coffee. Rory had gone out to play and Gloria was wrapping the left-over fried chicken.

Jimmy observed: "That was good chicken. I'm just getting to the point where I can enjoy fried food again."

There was a burst of laughter from the kids as they caught his reference. It harked back to Rye. One night at dinner Jimmy had remarked crossly: "We've had nothing but fried food for three weeks. What's happened to baking and roasting?"

Karen had given me a scared glance. "Oh—oh."

"Don't you like fried food?" I countered.

"Not seven days a week."

"Oh, please let me keep him." Karen's voice was desperately pleading.

"Keep whom?" Jimmy was confused by the switch in topic and her passion.

"My mouse."

The mouse was out of the bag.

"What mouse? Have we been eating fried mouse?"

"Oh, Daddy, you're funny."

"What mouse?"

"In the oven." Karen explained eagerly if obscurely.

"What oven?"

"Our oven."

Jimmy addressed himself to Gloria and Marie, rather piteously I thought. "Do you know what she's talking about?"

They looked blank.

"It's our secret, Daddy," Karen's words tripped over each other. "Mommy's and mine."

My husband looked to me for enlightment.

"It's like this—" I began, feeling a little foolish.

Karen took over. "One day we opened the oven and there he was—this dear, sweet, little gray mouse. Just sitting there, on his hind legs, eating half of a baked potato. Of course the oven was off. He was hungry and he wasn't fat. But he is now!" she caroled. "The first day we watched him eat, and then he curled up over the pilot where it is nice and warm and went to sleep. I asked Mommy if he could stay just a little while and she said 'yes,' but I don't think she wanted to," she interpolated honestly. "Daddy, his name is Fred and he isn't at all afraid of us. Take me to the kitchen and I'll show you."

Jimmy looked at me as though he doubted the wisdom of our alliance.

I said: "Why don't we all go out and meet Fred and decide what would be best for him."

Karen, perched on Jimmy's knee, had opened the oven door with the flourish of one exhibiting an original Picasso. Freddie was sleeping blissfully, curled in a tiny mound on top of the pilot.

Silenty, Marie and Gloria ogled the mouse and then me.

"Let's not wake him," Jimmy whispered, and gently

34.

closed the oven door. He sat down with Karen on his lap. "You know, Sweetheart, that any creature needs lots of fresh air and sunshine if it's going to be healthy and strong."

Karen opened her mouth to say something but Jimmy hurried on: "Now dear, out in the back yard he would have plenty of room to run and play. In the oven he's very restricted—"

This was too much for me and I fled to the dining room where Glo and Marie were trying to stifle their laughter.

After family prayers Karen said: "You know Daddy has explained very clearly that it would be selfish to keep Fred indoors. Besides," she laughed, "Daddy says the whole family could get ulcers from so much fried food—so the decision is made."

Later, Gloria asked me sweetly: "Have you been working too hard?"

"Don't be snide."

"I think some explanation is called for," Jimmy stated, reasonably enough.

I defended myself: "Karen has a tutor for her school work and that's good. But that's no substitute for the fun and varied interests of school. Even when the kids are here there's so much talk about things in which Karen has no part that frequently in the midst of company she's lonely. This was a diversion. Mad—I agree, but therein lay its worth. Besides, it gave her a secret to share with the other children that under no circumstances should be imparted to an adult. That had some virtue too."

My audience nodded understandingly.

"I'm glad he's gone. Tomorrow I'll roast you a leg of lamb; but I'm glad he was here. You must all realize that my role with Karen is always one of driving, prodding, encouraging: 'Push, Karen; pull; stretch; relax; straighten; try a little harder—' It made good sense for me to slip into the role of conspirator in an irresponsible, ridiculous enterprise."

"Very good sense," said Jimmy with conviction.

When weeks went by and Karen did not get a letter from Korea she was frantic with worry and disappointment. I caught Jim Brennan sneaking in and out so he wouldn't have to face her.

But one morning we heard him before we saw him. "Letter from the boys!" he yelled as he came up the driveway. Karen and I were polishing silver. Our hands were covered with black goo. "Read it," she commanded.

Jim read:

"Hi beautiful!"

I am in the hospital and am O.K. I think I got all your letters. I pass them around to my buddies and the nurses and the doctors. The Japanese internes read them too. I've showed them all your picture and they think you're beautiful too.

Karen, I want you to remember the things that have happened are because God let them be. We don't know why but He does.

And now, darling of my life, *I am coming home.* .

"Oh, Mom," Karen's question exploded: "What shall I wear?"

"You can't be much more feminine than that," Jim laughed. "Do you want to hear the rest of the letter?"

They are giving me treatments and therapy now too. I am having to learn to walk again, so let's work together.

My love for always and always
EDDIE

Karen, spurred on by Eddie's homecoming, worked too hard and the muscle spasms grew so intense that I had to declare a moratorium on all work and therapy for several days. Her nails grew strong and long and she learned to file them, sometimes quite crookedly, but she persisted in refusing all assistance. "What those boys have done for my girl," Jimmy's voice was hushed. "How I bless them!"

One morning at dawn I was awakened by the shrill ringing of the telephone. We were always getting calls for the railroad station, our numbers were similar, and most ungraciously I mumbled: "Yes?"

A pleasant female voice said: "I have a call for Miss Karen Killilea from Beppu, Japan."

"Jimmy, Jimmy!" I shouted on a wildly rising note. "Jimmy—quick—Japan—" I thrust the phone at him.

"Who—what—what's wrong?" He grabbed the instrument and listened. He tossed the phone back at me and ran from the room. I kept mumbling into the mouthpiece "yes—yes—yes—in a minute."

He came running back with Karen in his arms. I handed her the phone and with more control than I knew I possessed I said to the half-awake child: "Karen—it's Eddie—he's calling from Japan." I put the phone in her hands. She stared at me, clenching it tightly and listened unmoving. Then a gasp: *"Eddie! Eddie! Is it really you?"*

I bent closer but I couldn't catch what he was saying.

Karen was nodding her head. "Yes—yes—YES!" She waited. "Good-bye. I love you too." She hugged the phone to her. As though in a trance she whispered: "He's coming home! He's really coming home!"

We made a calendar and kept it on the kitchen table. Every morning with a shiver of anticipation Karen crossed off another day. The paper got pretty gritty as the weeks went by and picked up a nice patina of peanut butter and jam. We were sanely and sinfully extravagant and bought Karen a gorgeous green and white striped organdy dress with wide green velvet sash and matching ribbon for her braids.

I was struggling to make a palatable fish dinner when the phone rang. Karen answered. *"It's Eddie!"* she shouted. "Where are you? How are you? When? *Sunday! One o'clock!"* This on E above high C. *"Hurry! Hurry!"*

Karen didn't sleep much that night, nor the next. She didn't eat much either. Sunday morning we went to an early Mass. A few parishioners gave our arrival the studied attention usually reserved for brides. We had a beat-up Austin, originally a dashing red, now faded to a nauseating pink. The Austin was one of the first really small cars and when Jimmy had parked I could understand that it must have been fascinating to watch this small vehicle disgorge man and wife, four children, wheel chair (which we used for church, museums, shopping and long hauls) and Irish Setter. In front of church was the only place where Shanty would stay in the car without Karen. I heard one enraptured spectator exclaim as we piled out: "Just like the car at the circus!"

By eleven o'clock, we had had breakfast, tidied the house and pretended to read the headlines. The following long two hours we spent cutting and arranging flowers, grooming the dog and checking one clock against another to see if they'd stopped. By a quarter to one Karen was standing at the open door of her room. She didn't have to wait the last four minutes for suddenly Eddie was there striding up the path.

She lifted her face. He took the final few strides, bent and took her in his arms.

chapter three

In the sprawling many-chimneyed house next to us lived Charles King, a tall, elderly patrician gentleman renowned for his inventions which included the pneumatic hammer and the V8 motor. He had built and operated the first automobile in Detroit. He had a housekeeper, Shirley Shelley, a large, strikingly handsome woman, kindly and full of fun. He also had a parrot named Mr. Hopkins, a bird of wicked wit and large vocabulary whose most renowned invocation was: "Let's get F.D.R. the hell out of the White House!" Our introduction to Mr. King took place one night when he knocked on our door and, pointing to our house, lit up like a Christmas tree, he had inquired if we had stock in Consolidated Edison.

On a mild purple evening we were sitting on the porch watching the gulls dive for dinner. I saw Mr. King ambling about his lawn and called to him to join us. He accepted a glass of wine and announced calmly: "Mrs. Shelley just fell down stairs and broke her leg."

There was a concerted gasp and questions exploded:

"What hospital is she in?"

"Simple or compound fracture?"

"Was she in great pain?"

"Did she yell much?" This from Rory.

Mr. King looked a little bewildered by the barrage and stated calmly: "She's home. She's quite all right. I fixed it." He sipped his wine.

There was a wide silence as we sat stunned.

"How?" inquired our son reasonably enough.

Mr. King gave his full attention to Rory. "I have every conceivable kind of tool. I just studied the break, went to work and in half an hour it was as good as new."

"Will you have some more wine?" Jimmy's hand trembled as he refilled Mr. King's glass. I privately wondered if our guest hadn't had enough.

"Can she *walk* on it?" I could see Rory in the throes of a new hero worship.

"Of course!" Mr. King was a little miffed.

The rest of us stared fixedly out to sea not daring to look at each other.

"Ah—" Mr. King rose and walked to the porch railing. "Here she comes now." He waved and Mrs. Shelley came across the lawn. She walked gracefully and there was no hint of pain in her face. She did ascend the stairs somewhat slowly and Rory, with consummate bad manners, stared fascinated at her legs. With horrible certainty I knew he was going to ask her to lift her skirt and show him her leg. I threw a verbal block and asked inanely: "Isn't it a lovely evening?"

Before she could reply Mr. King smiled at her and said: "I was just telling them how I fixed your leg."

She nodded. "You wouldn't believe what my boss can do with tools."

"Is that so—" Jimmy muttered and drained his glass.

"That's a real gift," I contributed brightly in a choked voice and stole a glance at my spouse. His face was purpling in alarming fashion.

Mrs. Shelley fielded my glance. "I guess you didn' know—" her voice broke on a low laugh as she saw u brace ourselves to keep control in the face of the nex revelation, "—that my leg was amputated some years ag and I have an artificial limb."

The expressions that raced across our faces must hav been ludicrous for she threw her head back and laughe uproariously. Our own amusement, held so rigidly in check erupted in a torrent of mirth.

Minutes later, Mrs. Shelley wiped her eyes and said "I was going to play along with your interpretation of th story—but you were all suffering so. What wonderful con trol you had."

Rory had not joined in the hilarity. He said: *"Gee Whiz!* and a light faded from his eyes.

The following afternoon Karen and I were out in th yard. I was giving her a putting lesson. Willard Mullir sports cartoonist for the *New York World Telegram an Sun,* had suggested that Jimmy get an extra pair of crutches attach a putter to one and let Karen have some sport. Sh was getting pretty good at sinking the ball in a coffee ti set in the ground. It was enormously gratifying and ther was therapeutic value also, for when she swung the 'putte she had to balance on just one crutch (the while Shant circled her apprehensively, making soft protesting noise deep in his throat). It was a small venture but one in whic she could compete with the nonhandicapped kids on *thei* level. That made it triply important.

I was retrieving a wide shot when the man who read the meter came across the lawn. His face was ashen. "A you ill?"

He shook his head.

"You look awful. Should you be working?"

"Not on this job," he answered with feeling and collapse on the bench.

I watched him helplessly.

"Fourteen years on the job and I never had an experienc like this." He ran his hands through his hair. "I'm re: shook-up."

"What happened?"

He stood up, crooked his finger and moved some distance from Karen. I followed. With his eyes riveted to the toes of his shoes he said: "I wouldn't want the young lady to hear anything like this."

"Like what?" I asked impatiently.

He didn't look up. "I just came from next door—you know Mr. King's got a housekeeper—"

I guessed that Mr. King had told him about the broken leg, but why couldn't Karen hear that?

"That *woman!*" He kicked the ground in great agitation. "That woman calls to me—to *me!* 'Come on in Sweetheart, I've been waiting for you.' I left fast I can tell you and I'm not going back."

I was shocked. "Surely you misunderstood!"

"Not on your life!" Without once looking at me he stamped into the house.

Mrs. Shelley came through a break in the hedge. I wondered if she'd heard. "Has the meter man been here?"

"He's here now."

"That's funny. I saw him coming toward the house and went to open the door and he'd vanished. Ask him to come back when he's through here, will you?"

"Surely." I hesitated. "But he's a little under the weather."

Karen said, "Mom, would you get my ball. I overshot. Watch me putt, Mrs. Shelley."

Mrs. Shelley was rightfully impressed. "I must leave now, it's time for Mr. King's drive. Karen, I wish you'd come over and meet Mr. Hopkins, he's a most unusual pet. He calls Mr. King 'Charlie' and issues some fine orders like: 'Charlie! get the rum!' " And when he hears me in an adjoining room he calls: 'Come on in, Sweetheart, I've been waiting for you.' He's amazing. Sounds human. Well, so long, keep practicing." With a cheery wave and a grin she left us.

Karen continued to practice; I continued to retrieve and Shanty continued to mouth uncertainties. After a while the meter man came out of the house still looking 'shook-up.' I offered him a can of beer which he accepted greedily. "Sit down," I told him, "I'm about to restore your faith in human nature."

He perched uncertainly on the bench and eyed me suspiciously. Barely keeping my composure I explained about Mr. Hopkins. He was first incredulous and then abysmally sheepish. "I'd best go back—" he hesitated, then downed the last of the beer. He planted the can on the ground and announced challengingly: "But she's gonna have to *show* me that bird!"

Weather permitting, Karen and Jimmy had a putting competition each night after dinner. She improved so that we took some pictures and sent them to the instigator, Mr. Mullin, with a thank-you note. Not long after we opened the *Telegram* one night and there on the sports page was his cartoon, depicting Patty Berg, Babe Didrikson and Karen Killilea! He had printed under his drawing of Karen "and you should see Karen putt with a blade fastened to her crutch. Best wishes—Willard Mullin."

"Wow!" exclaimed Jimmy ."You're certainly traveling in distinguished company!"

Karen was dumbfounded, then with justifiable pride: "Everyone who sees it will know I'm getting good!"

"Good—you're *great!*" Rory's enthusiasm for Karen's victories was always extravagant.

"I could use a few lessons," suggested Gloria.

"So could I," Marie said.

"Delighted, I'm sure. How about you, Mom Pom?" Karen offered graciously.

"Delighted—I'm sure," I mimicked gently.

In the evening Jimmy and I took Shanty to the beach. An old moon rose late, blushing at its tardiness. The dog swam a while, attacked some floating seaweed and routed a few ducks from their slumbers in the marsh grass. "He's elegant even when he romps," Jimmy observed, his voice warm with affection.

"I wish he were younger. I can't imagine Karen's life without him."

"Nor can I."

We walked slowly across the sand. "You're very quiet tonight," my husband said with his non-masculine perception. "Something bothering you?"

"Yes. It's strange how big little things can be." Jimmy waited for me to go on. "When I was getting Karen ready for her bath, she looked at her shoes as I took them out of the braces and said with such wistfulness, 'I wish I could have dainty shoes like other girls instead of these heavy brown, lace-up things.'"

"That's easy," Jimmy said quickly, "let's buy a pretty pair of regular shoes, send them to the brace man and have him adapt them to fit the braces."

"Of course! I should have thought of that long ago." I was greatly cheered. "Black patent leather pumps. What a thrill!"

Jimmy laughed. "I hope this is the biggest problem we ever have to face. Order them tomorrow but keep it a surprise until they're fixed and ready to be worn."

Shanty came bounding back to us, took a strategic position and shook vigorously, splattering both of us with cold salt water. "I hope he approves of the shoes," Jimmy chuckled. "His worrying disapproval can be very trying."

We walked on to Pirate's Cove. The budding trees, the rocks and water were laved by gold spilled by the moon.

"They're starting early for stripers." Jimmy pointed to three dark, rectangular blobs about fifty yards off shore. The whir of the cast line and the occasional words of the fishermen came clearly across the water. "Remember the first one you caught?" he asked me.

"Does one ever forget one's first striped bass? I think it was the more exciting because it was only two hundred yards from our back door."

Jimmy laughed and reminded me: "You said with a great affectation of calm, 'I may be caught on a rock,' then you yelled 'Ship your oars and grab the net.' Landing that fellow was quite a battle. I thought you were going to have a heart attack."

"So did I," and felt a slight flutter of the remembered thrill.

We climbed down the rocks and sat on a ledge about twenty feet above the water. A strong wind sprang up from the northeast and the waves embraced the shore with a velvet roar that curved to sudden quiet. The sailboats, tethered at their moorings, darted and danced.

"Warm enough?" Jimmy asked.

"Quite. In his prayers tonight Rory said: 'Please God take Karen's spasms away for at least two or three weeks.' Then he added: 'maybe even longer?' "

Jimmy made no comment and we sat in silence but it was a silence loud with a question we had been facing for months—a question that was never out of our thoughts while we talked, while we worked, while we tried to read and tried to sleep. I felt that when we had left the house tonight it was because we both realized that we were going to arrive at a decision.

Jimmy lit his pipe using me as a shield from the wind. Bending over the bowl he raised his eyes to mine. They were very blue and very anxious. He came directly to the question: "Shall we have Dr. Moore operate on Karen?"

I moved closer to him and lit my cigarette from the glowing tobacco. "I think we should. Dr. Fay thinks we should, and what is more important, Karen wants to go ahead with it."

He put his arm across my shoulders. "After her last three hospital experiences that surprises me."

I shivered a little and he took off his coat and put it around me. "And what do you think?"

"I think Karen's decision is based on three factors: One, she adores Dr. Fay and he's in favor of going ahead; two, the way Dr. Moore handled our visit—including Karen in the total discussion so she has a full understanding of what's involved; three, she's pretty discouraged at the very limited improvement for all the time and effort she's exerting."

"I think the last reason is sufficient." How often had I heard this note of pain in Jimmy's voice. His pipe, forgotten, had gone out. He relit it and went on. "She almost broke my heart the other day. After practicing walking in the driveway for over an hour she said 'You know Daddy, I don't *walk*, I have stilted progression.' 'Mouse' (Mrs. Schnirring to you) came across the street from her house and Karen said to her most matter-of-factly that she was thinking of having a bilateral tenotomy of the adductors.

44.

Mouse, who is never caught off balance, was momentarily silent then commented: 'It sounds like something you'd have on Sunday.' "

I stood up. "Let's start back before you get cold." We clambered back up the rocks and took the path home. "How do you feel about it darling?"

"I think Karen is right. You should have heard her explaining to Mouse, 'I have a scissor gait because my adductors are too tight and that makes my legs cross. There is also internal rotation. This operation would loosen the muscles and I'd have a 'spread' between my legs. Doesn't that make sense?' Mouse agreed it did and left abruptly and with suspiciously moist eyes. I would say Karen has made a well-reasoned decision. What a kid!" He spoke with soft pride. "What a great little girl!" He put his arm around me. "Thank you for her—for all of them."

We paced the path around the harbor. I thought aloud, "There are some encouraging 'maybes.' " I ticked them off on my fingers. *"Maybe* she'll walk better; *maybe* she'll have better use of her hands; *maybe* she'll even be able to propel her own wheel chair." I paused and then remembered. "Just think how vehemently and how long I opposed getting Karen a wheel chair. *Mea culpa!"*

"Charting any new course one is apt to go astray. I think we must recognize this and know that it can and probably will happen again. I opposed it too—remember?"

I smiled up at him. "I remember that, long before I, you saw it as a step toward experience and independence. For months I felt it was giving in—almost a defeat."

"You were afraid she'd substitute it for walking—O ye of little faith!"

"The doors that chair has opened. The museums, the zoo, the basketball and hockey games with Russ at Madison Square Garden!"

Jimmy spoke hesitantly: "To get back to surgery. We must consider the things against it: the pain, immobility in casts for a very long time, the hospital siege, the long absence from home, the starting to walk all over again." He paused and knocked his pipe out against the trunk of a tree. "And even after the casts are removed they will have to be put on every night and she'll have to try to sleep in them for God only knows how long."

It was typical of Jimmy that he never mentioned the staggering expenses involved. "We recognize all of this and so does Karen."

"Well, have we decided?"

"I guess we have. All three of us."

We stopped and leaned against the fence at the beach. "I cabled Dr. Fay in Norway that Dr. Moore could schedule us for two weeks from now but that we hadn't definitely decided." I gave a little laugh. "He must have known what our decision would be for he cabled back that same afternoon—'Wait until I get home in May (that's only three weeks) I want to be with my girl.'"

"What a friend he has been to us! Now, what are we going to do about running the house while you're away?"

"When I discussed the possibility of surgery with the kids, Gloria wanted to quit work and stay home. Marie would have none of it. She pointed out, quite reasonably, that when Gloria was eleven, she managed to run a house and go to school. She says she's perfectly capable and she and Rory make a good team. I think we should let her do it. It will be good for her. Gloria does so much we have to be careful that the others are not deprived of their opportunities for responsibility."

"I'll come down week-ends. I can be in Philadelphia just about four hours after I leave the office."

"I've made some inquiries and there's a house right across the street from the hospital where I can rent a room. Far from elegant, not even a private bath, but clean as a whistle and very inexpensive. There are a couple of restaurants right up Broad Street."

"You're not going to like that no bath set-up."

"It will be all right."

"What instructions will you have for Pop?"

"You might see if you can get Rory to take off his pajamas before he dresses for school. I've been trying for weeks. His reasoning: 'It saves time, so I'm being efficient.'"

Jimmy chuckled. "He told me that when he grows up

he wants to be a priest who flies an airplane and collects garbage! Quite a concentration of ambitions."

"He's also going 'to marry Gloria on top of the George Washington Bridge if Russ doesn't come back.'"

"He got a fine imagination. The other day he described a sailboat as looking like a feather in flight, blown along by the wind."

"That's really quite lovely."

We started across the street to the house. Jimmy said: "Before we take off for Philadelphia we'd warn Marie that she just might run into trouble with the police."

I stopped and stared at him. "The *police!*"

He grinned at me. "The other morning on the bus a number of men were discussing a team that was a neighborhood menace. It seems there's a large gray cat and a big red dog—"

"*Oh no!* Shanty and Misty Morning! What did you say?"

"I said nothing, just buried myself in the paper and listened. It developed that your two pets canvass the neighborhood. That the cat can take the lid off any garbage pail, the dog knocks the pail over and they both have a feast."

"Oh Lord! And I still have a suspended sentence hanging over my head from Judge Cahill in night court last year when Shanty courted that collie hussy through the doctor's lily pond."

"Don't worry. You'll be in another state and I don't think they'd go so far as to extradite."

"I've got something really big to worry about. I'm going to miss a lot of national cerebral palsy association meetings and it's a critical time in the life of the organization."

"What must be—must be."

"I wish I were three people."

"I don't. One is quite enough."

I stopped on the top step. "And just what do you mean by that?"

He kissed me for reply. "Will you write Dr. Moore tomorrow?"

"I shall."

"We have to keep in mind, all three of us, that we mustn't

47.

hope for too much. The greater the need the greater the temptation to too much hope. Let's help Karen to think solely in terms of relief from the scissor gait. That alone would warrant going ahead. If the other possibilities develop —well, that's so much icing on the cake."

Two weeks later Karen invited me to see the Father's Day present she was preparing for Jimmy. Up to now Karen had been printing. Just to complicate her difficulties, she had an eye problem and was left-handed. "Watch, Mom Pom, watch carefully!" She picked up a pen, clamped her teeth over her lower lip and started to *write*. "Dearest darlingest Daddy—"

I grabbed her and hugged her. "It's wonderful and your script is quite pretty. How long has this been going on?"

"I've been practising in secret for weeks. It does look nice doesn't it?" She surveyed the paper critically. "I thought I ought to get the final one finished before surgery, even if it is a month to Father's Day. I may not be able to write for a while afterward, because I won't be sitting up."

"This will be the best present any Father ever had. Daddy will be so surprised, and so proud!"

"That's what I thought." replied my daughter serenely.

Red drove up in his United Parcel truck. "Package for Karen," he called as he came through the door.

"Your shoes!" I exclaimed when I saw the box, forgetting it was a surprise and I hadn't intended to give them to her until the family was all together.

"What shoes?" Karen asked excitedly.

"Your young-lady shoes."

"Really! Red, open the box. Mom, call Shirley and Mouse."

Red stripped off the paper and put the box in Karen's lap. "Hurry, I want to see them too."

She lifted the lid and gazed in awe at the gleaming pumps inside. "They're *beautiful!*"

Red admired them extravagantly and left.

"Oh, Mom, thank you. Thank you so much. You don't know how much I've wanted pretty pumps. Can I have them put on now?"

"Right this minute." I began to unlace the heavy brown shoes.

Shirley and Mouse arrived together. Quickly I substituted the pumps for the orthopedic shoes, handed Karen her crutches, locked the braces at the knees, and put her up on her feet in front of the mirror. She looked at her reflection and was enraptured.

"Aren't they exquisite?" She asked her audience. She took a step and then another. She stopped. Her face crumpled. She bowed her head to hide the gushing tears. "They won't stay on. I need laced high shoes."

Mouse fled the room. It was more than she could bear. Shirley said with consummate compassion: "It's a damn shame."

I almost said: "Try again," but I realized immediately the steel plate, required by the brace in the sole of the shoe, made the sole inflexible. Karen's arched foot would come out of all low shoes because the soles could not be bent. Wordless, I picked her up, carried her to the bed and removed the shiny pumps. I wiped her tears.

"Did Daddy and the kids know about them?" she asked after a little.

"Yes."

"Don't tell them, Mommy, they'd feel so bad."

"I won't." I couldn't say more. I fitted the heavy brown shoes back in the braces. "My heart aches with you."

"I know." She patted my cheek.

Shirley said: "Well, at least both your feet are yours." And picking up a crutch she rapped the foot on the artificial limb.

"That's a comforting sound," and Karen managed a small smile.

We all went out to the kitchen. The room was empty. "I wonder where Mouse is?" Karen looked around hopefully.

"Here I am," Mouse called as she came through the screen door. She was cradling something in her arms. "Sit down Karen, I have something for you."

I took Karen's crutches, unlocked her knees and helped her into a chair.

Mouse sidled over, hiding her burden, then turned and placed in Karen's lap a snow-white kitten. Shanty came over, nudged the tiny morsel, then washed him thoroughly.

I didn't say—"What I *don't* need is another pet." We had five cats, two of them prolific queens and they had given us sixty-eight kittens in fourteen months.

Mouse read my expression. "You've always wanted one."

"I have?"

"It's one of our Siamese."

"Oh Mouse, I love you!" Karen lifted the kitten to her cheek. "What shall we name him?"

"My name is really Alice Mary," Mouse said suggestively. "Or—lots of people call me A.M."

"Then we shall call you A.M. from now on." There was a small sparkle in Karen's eyes. "But what shall we call the kitten?"

"Why not wait until the family is all together and we'll have one of our caucuses?"

"Good idea." Karen bent lovingly over the tiny form. "How can he be white if he's Siamese?"

"They don't begin to get their 'points' (their coloring) until they're older. He's what is called a seal point."

"He looks like a Disney cat—angled, not round." Karen held him up studying him. He cried an objection and she returned him to her lap.

"I must go start dinner," A.M. bent and kissed Karen. "I know you'll be very happy together."

I walked across the lawn with her. "I thought you'd sold all your kittens."

She was embarrassed. "We had, but I'll think of something to tell the man who had bought this one. I think I'll tell him the truth." She brightened at this inspired solution.

"You're an angel."

"Nuts," she flung over her shoulder as she left me.

The family was enchanted by Karen's acquisition; well, the kids were; Jimmy gave a convincing performance but he didn't fool me. A dog, six cats, and a bird were a little much.

Karen managed to conceal any trace of her bitter experience. Throughout dinner we discussed names. "It seems we've been engaged on this naming project for as long as I can remember," said Jimmy. "How many have we named this year?"

"Sixty-eight," answered Marie before I could stop her.

"*I've got it!*" Gloria timed her exclamation perfectly. "We've named so many, why don't we just call this one 'Etcetera'!"

"Great!"

"Clever!"

"Perfect!"

"Distinctive!"

Approbation called in loud voices. But from the end of the table I heard an incredulous whisper from Jimmy. "*Sixty-eight?!*"

"Cetty could be a nice call name," said Karen, "but I think I'll stick to Etcetera. It has a precise sound and he's a precise kitten."

When everyone was in bed, I wrapped newspaper around the pumps in their box, tied it securely and put them in the bottom of the garbage can.

Rory was coughing when he came down to breakfast the next morning. He had no fever but I decided to keep him home from school because there was a high wind. We passed a profitable afternoon plastering a bathroom. The next day he went off to school and on his return announced: "Sister said she was surprised that you kept me out of school to plaster."

"Did you explain about the wind and the cough?"

"I didn't think of it."

"That's just dandy." I glanced at him, looking for some clue that this was a sample of his perverted wit. His cheeks were flushed so I put my hand on his forehead. "You have a fever—off to bed. How do you feel?"

"Funny."

"Funny how?"

"Just funny. I must be sick. I'm not hungry."

"Go get undressed and I'll be up in a minute."

"I'll go up with you," Marie said. She was back directly. "He's got spots—looks like measles." I called Dr. Haggerty who came and confirmed the diagnosis. It was only a mild case and Rory made the most of having trays served him in bed. Saturday afternoon Gloria was reading to him. One character in the story said to another: "What a pity Tom had to die!"

"That's silly," interrupted our son. "We all come from Heaven and the only way we can get back is to die. Adults don't make sense."

When this conversation was reported to us that evening, Jimmy repeated a quote of Father McSorley's: "A child knows what a philosopher knows only after he has resolved his philosophical difficulties."

"Until *we* obscure his vision with thoughtless talk and writing," I amended.

Sunday afternoon we were all painting the garage, all except Rory who was directing operations from his bed at the window. From my perch atop the ladder I could see the breakwater, the jade of the marsh grass against silver rocks and the water glinting as the sunbeams shot through it. I could feel the spring, hear it, smell it; the fragrance of moist earth enriched by winter's snow. I heard the glad cry of a hundred seagulls as they sported between sea and sky. A half-dozen of them were engaged in a beautiful and exciting game. Diving, they would seize a clam from the warm mud, fly rapidly upward and then, when a satisfactory altitude had been reached, drop the white shell, watch it fall, then swoop down and catch it before it hit the rocks. The young birds, unsure of their skill, would move after the disc when it had dropped only ten or fifteen feet. The older, experienced birds would wait until the shell had fallen a hundred feet or so and then plummet to snatch it just a few feet above the breakwater. The spectator birds were loud in derisive cries no matter how excellent the performance.

"Telephone!" called Rory from the window.

I descended and went to answer it. It was Jim Meighan, he who had taken the place of my father who had died when I was eleven. "Where are you?" I asked.

"At the Lambs'" He referred to the theatrical club where he lived.

"Are you coming up?"

"I may have to, to win an argument."

"What kind of an argument? With whom?"

"With Pat O'Brien. He says he met you and Karen out West at a cerebral palsy benefit and that you gave him a copy of your book and autographed it."

"He must be crazy. I've never met him. Karen and I were not out West; as a matter of fact you know we would never let Karen make a public appearance—too easy to get prideful."

"That's just what I said, Here—I'll put him on."

"Hello, Mrs. Killilea," said the rich Irish voice. "It's so nice to talk to you again."

"It's nice to talk to you, Mr. O'Brien. I've been a fan of yours for years—but not 'again.' I've never met you nor spoken to you."

"Isn't that your daughter's picture on the jacket of *Karen* with the braids and what looks like a jockey's cap?"

"Of course it is."

"I told Jim I did a benefit. They presented to me a little girl with pigtails and wearing the same hat, and they said: 'This is Karen.' Then they brought *you* over and you autographed a copy of *Karen* for me."

"I'm sorry, Mr. O'Brien, you're mistaken. I wasn't there. Karen wasn't there."

There was a silence then Jim's voice again: "Are you going to be home for a while?"

"Yes. Why?"

"The only way I am going to convince this thick Mick is to bring him up and let him meet you."

"Come along. I enjoy you most when you're steamed up about something."

"Good-bye." I went out to the garage and reported the strange business to Jimmy. "What goes on?" I asked him.

"It seems fairly obvious that some group passed off two other people as you and Karen."

We were just cleaning our brushes when a cab pulled up. Jim got out followed by a stranger with a dearly familiar face. Both silent, they strode up to us.

"Have you met *her* before?" Jim challenged, pointing to me.

53.

I wiped my hand on my dungarees and extended it. "How do you do, Mr. O'Brien." I introduced my family, leaving Karen until last.

He stared.

From the window came a shout: *"It's Pat O'Brien!"*

Mr. O'Brien nodded absently in the direction of the group, then stared again at Karen and at me. "I never saw either of you before in my life. The whole thing is incredible. They told me—" He shook his head. "It's conceivable that there is another girl, wearing plaits the same way Karen wears hers, and the same kind of a hat, and having the same name—but—they told me the woman was *you.*"

"I told you so." Jim Meighan was grimly victorious.

"How about a drink?" asked Jimmy to relieve the awkward situation.

"The whole thing is incredible," muttered our guest, as he followed us to the porch.

"Well, here you are," I said with transparent gaiety. "It's a delight for all of us, so let's forget the other."

We sat in an atmosphere of decidedly uncomfortable restraint.

"What movie are you working in now?" Jimmy asked.

"I'm making a circus picture." Mr. O'Brien answered briefly and fell silent.

Jimmy struggled to keep the conversation alive. "Were any of your family in show business, Mr. O'Brien?"

"Everybody calls me Pat, Jim. Yes, in a manner of speaking. I had an uncle with the circus. He and his wife trained the first high-school horses."

Jimmy was passing a glass of ginger ale to Jim. "Now that's curious," he said over his shoulder, "because my uncle and aunt trained the *first* high-school horses."

"How could that be?" asked our visitor a trifle nettled. Then challengingly: "What was your uncle's name?"

Jimmy was helping Karen into a chair. "Marty Hines," he answered.

There was a moment of silence, then Pat shouted: "Hi, Cousin!"

Jimmy almost dropped Karen. "How's that?"

54.

"*My* uncle was Marty Hines.

Rory was screaming. "Hey—can't I come down? Just to shake hands with Pat O'Brien?"

Jimmy just stood there gaping at Pat.

Rory yelled again: "Hey! Can't I—"

Jimmy recovered somewhat and called back: "Sure son, come down and meet your cousin or uncle or whatever," and broke into a roar of laughter.

Pat jumped and and thumped him on the back. "How bout *that!* How *about* that!" He swung around to us. "What do you know? Isn't this the darnedest thing. Talk bout coincidence." He said to the girls: "Give your Uncle Pat a kiss." Before Glo and Marie reached him, he bent and put his arm around Karen. "What a privilege to have a bonnie lass like you in the family."

Rory ran out on the porch and Pat seized him and swung him around. "How does it feel to discover a new uncle?"

"I thought Daddy was kidding."

"Not a bit of it."

"Gee—it's great." Rory stepped back and looked up at the big man in awe. "*Eeka-Freeka!* Wait till I tell the kids." He moved toward the porch steps.

"No you don't. Not now. You're sick remember? But if you will sit quietly I'll let you stay with Uncle Pat for a while. But you must be quiet. O.K.?"

"Yes, ma'am." He settled himself docilely on the couch, his eyes glued to Pat's face.

I turned to Jim Meighan who had said nothing since the Great Revelation. He hadn't even moved. "What are you thinking?"

"I'll be damned."

I never heard Jim say this before; and I never heard him say it again.

Marie turned to Pat and with a most engaging sweetness said: "Uncle Pat, I've loved you for years."

"Thank you, my dear," he gave her a courtly bow. He sat in the chair beside Karen and picked up her hand and held it.

"Have you ever been to Ireland?" Gloria asked. "I missed being born there by two weeks."

55.

"Many times. I could tell you were Irish the minute
saw you."

"I have relatives in Belfast," Gloria told him.

"I love Belfast. I used to stay at a theatrical boardir
house there, run by a darlin' woman. Let's see—what w
her name—"

"Lindsay?" Gloria asked.

"Yes, that's right. Lindsay." Then Pat did a double tal
"How did you know?"

Gloria started to laugh and for a few minutes could
stop. "She—" again she dissolved in mirth. "She—was r
great-aunt!"

Pat was stupefied. "It's too much. It's just too muc
If someone handed me a script containing a series of c
incidences such as we've had here this afternoon, I'd tu
it down. Nobody would believe it."

ह∾

chapter four

It was a soft Spring evening. Tomorrow we were leavi
for Philadelphia and Temple University Hospital.

Jimmy and I were driving down Park Avenue on o
way home from church. As we approached the turn in
our street we could see it was blocked off. Cars were park
in all directions and people were hurrying down the stre
toward the water. Jimmy spotted the red car of the Fi
Chief. He pulled up on somebody's lawn, jammed on t
brakes and we both jumped out and raced for our hous
All the fire engines were there and the hook and ladd
had their extension up to the third story. Lit by searchligh
men shining in their rubber coats were going about the
business with hurried calm. Dauntless boys darted p:
restraining arms, slithered through a forest of legs and lea
over huge hoses spread around the ground like so ma
dormant boa constrictors.

In front of our house, in the middle of the street stood our family. Gloria, ashen, was supporting Karen, Shanty quivering against her. Marie, close beside them and equally pale, had one arm around Rory and the other arm aloft holding the bird cage. Rory's eyes were wide and dark with fright, and he was desperately trying to hang on to two struggling cats. A.M. and Shirley, like guardian angels, hovered around vainly trying to shepherd the other four cats. I retrieved Ash Wednesday, Marie's white Persian, from under the wheel of a truck, and thought my friends looked pretty calm considering that our dream house might well vanish.

"Thank God you're safe." Jimmy tried to embrace all his children at once.

"Of course they're safe," said A.M. with the asperity of relief.

He asked Gloria: "Where did the fire start?"

She looked at him, shook her head with confusion and replied: "I guess it didn't."

Shirley was cupping her mouth with her hands, trying to make herself heard above the hubbub. *"It's a practice,"* she shouted moving between us, "the regular Monday drill."

It took some seconds for us to absorb this piece of intelligence. Jimmy gasped like a trout on the bank.

Rory had recovered. *"Isn't it exciting?"*

Marie rudely told him to "Shut up," and sat down right in the street.

The din began to subside. Karen looked down at Shanty and said: "How about that, boy—they're celebrating my departure." She threw back her head and laughed with just a small note of hysteria.

"Everything's fine," said the Chief, coming up to Jimmy. "The water pressure is splendid!" he added enthusiastically.

"I'm so glad," replied Jimmy dryly, "and thank you so much."

"That's O.K." The Chief beamed and moved to direct retreat operations.

We filed up the steps, across the porch and into the living room. Marie put the bird cage on the piano; the various livestock released, ran around the room and Jimmy demanded, reasonably enough and of no one particular "Why the hell didn't someone tell us?"

"Never thought of it," said Shirley.

"Thought you knew," said A.M.

"I suggest," said the still-quaking mistress of the house, "that as an act of Christian kindness, we pledge ourselves to inform any incumbent of this excellent practice. If someone had a weak heart, we might save a life."

"You're dramatic," observed Rory appreciatively.

"Good thing for you we have strong hearts."

"Sure is, and when I think of how old you are," marvelled our son.

"Were you terribly frightened?" I looked at my brood whose color and eyes were returning to normal.

"We were too busy," Gloria answered, and Marie assented.

"I wanted to take the dress you got me for Eddie's home coming," Karen said, "but Glo said there wasn't time."

"All's well that ends well," said Jimmy with forgivable lack of originality.

We followed A.M. and Shirley out to the porch, thanking them effusively.

"One day soon, you'll tell this story with glee," A.M. said as she left.

I jeered at her departing back.

"I'm glad it happened," my husband told me.

"You're crazy," I replied with wifely affection.

"No, I'm not. Can you think of anything better calculated to distract Karen from a natural dread of what lies ahead?"

"No I can't. You're not crazy, you're sweet and perceptive."

When we rose next morning, a pearl fog hung over the still water. Gradually it receded, unveiling the reflections of rocks, summer house and trees, like so many Japanese prints. Crows hawked. Ducks squawked.

"This is the hardest place to leave," I said to Jimmy as we loaded the car.

"That's all the luggage." He stowed the last suitcase.

Back in the kitchen we all sat around the big maple

table and I gave last-minute instructions to supplement the pages I had typed the night before. (The care and feeding of animals took a page and that was pretty silly since the children had been doing it for years.) This was my favorite room: wainscoting yellow, doors and cabinets red; the Welch cupboard with its burden of pewter, old china and books; the little black desk; the captain's chairs; the windows overlooking the sea, curtained in bright fabric of Indian Head. My eyes wandered over the Pennsylvania Dutch patterned paper above the wainscoting on which hung trivets and a large collection of photographs. It was a real 'living' room where endless poker games were played and equally endless discussions were held. In the summer it was stilly cool, like a well, shaded by maple, birch and cedar. In the fall, winter and spring, it was flooded with sunshine from dawn to sunset. In the winter it was kept snug and warm by the great stove we blackened and polished. Beside a wood carving hung a small sign, donated by a frequent visitor: "If you can keep your head in all this confusion, you just don't understand the situation."

I held back a sigh and rose. "Curtain time."

Shanty beside Karen, placed his head in her lap.

"You'd think he knew," said Jimmy.

"He does," replied Karen and stroked the satin ears. "Don't worry, fellow, I'll be home soon."

The children had last-minute instructions for Karen.

"Maybe you'll get a chance to help people who are sick," Gloria said kissing her.

"Find me a handsome intern," Marie requested brightly.

"Get your casts autographed!" Rory flung himself on her.

"Good-bye! God bless you!"

"God bless you!"

We had picked May as the perfect month for hospitalization—not too warm but warm enough to keep windows open. Before we reached Newark, Jimmy removed his coat as the temperature climbed into the eighties. "This heat can't last," he said as he rolled up his sleeves.

Temple University Hospital was a huge and faded old edifice on Broad Street. It was different from any of the other hospitals in our experience in three respects: it was shabbier; there was a marvelous warmth and humaneness; the medical care was uniformly far superior.

Karen's room was on the fifth floor with a view of roof tops and a few punctuating chimneys. When we unpacked her suitcase we found at the very bottom, the children had hidden brightly wrapped presents. From Gloria, two exceedingly feminine bed jackets; from Marie, toilet water and bath powder; from Rory, two pairs of wide satin ribbins to hold the loops of Karen's braids—one pink, one blue; from Joe there was a book of Francis Thompson's poems.

On the first day Karen was pricked, probed and prodded. Dr. Moore came with another doctor in the evening. "You look fetching," he admired, sitting beside the bed. "This is Dr. John Lachman, my associate," he introduced the tall, handsome man with him. "Tomorrow you can spend your time getting acquainted and the anaesthesiologist, Dr. Bob Lachman, will be up to meet you. The next day we'll get to our little business. Dr. Fay will be here, of course. Now, do you have any questions?"

"One—" Karen blurted "—Do I have to have ether?"

"No dear. Dr. Fay told me you had a pretty bad experience with ether. Dr. Lachman wouldn't use it in any event. You talk to him about the anaesthesia tomorrow, but I think he'll be using sodium pentothal."

Karen gave a great sigh of relief. "Thank Heaven!"

The doctors stayed for half an hour, and it was an informative visit for them and a pleasant visit for us. As they were leaving, Dr. Moore stopped at the door. "My daughter Suzy is just down the hall. Rheumatic fever. You two must get to know each other."

"Tomorrow," Karen promised.

Jimmy had taken the next four days off. Our room, across the street, was immaculate, if hot. It was on the top floor of the house and there was no air chamber above it. We didn't get much sleep. After six o'clock Mass, we had breakfast at the Automat and were in Karen's room when they brought her breakfast tray. She had ordered a soft-boiled egg and soft it was. "Loose!" Karen exclaimed when I

60.

cracked it. The one thing Karen couldn't eat was a loose egg, so I put it aside.

"I want it," she told me as I spread some jam on toast.

"What do you mean you want it? You know you're unable to swallow a loose egg."

"Please—this morning, I want it."

"O.K." Jimmy and I exchanged a questioning shrug.

While she was eating, he picked up a magazine and pretended to read. I got busy filing my nails. From time to time we stole surreptitious glances at our daughter who was obviously struggling with the slippery mess.

"Want to tell us about it?" Jimmy asked without looking up.

Karen captured the last evasive spoonful and quickly bit into the toast. "I remembered what Gloria said—about helping people who are sick." She took a drink of milk. "There's a lady across the hall who had a serious operation and she can't stop vomiting. I asked the nurse about her. They've used the Levine tube and everything but the vomiting doesn't stop, and now she's on critical. So I prayed for her during the night and when I saw that egg, I thought I could make a little sacrifice—you know, kind of back up my prayer, and help her."

Karen, out of her vast hospital experience, made her judgments: "The graduate nurses, student nurses, aides— all wonderful. Doctors, residents, interns—all wonderful. There's a young resident who looks like a college sophomore—"

"I hope you didn't tell him that," I said.

"Of course not. His name is Walter Margy. We got talking about my family and I told him we had a menagerie. I told him all about Shanty and he said he'd like to meet him. Dr. Margy has a cat and the day after surgery . ." she dropped her voice to a conspiratorial whisper, "He is going to bring his cat to see me. He said I can have him on my bed!"

Jimmy said: "He sounds like a doctor who knows that many things can play a part in healing."

From down the hall came the sweet notes of an har-

61.

monica and a pleasant voice singing. Karen turned to Jimmy. "Daddy, let's go see who's playing and who's singing."

"I'd better inquire if it's all right." Jimmy left the room. He was back shortly, grinning. "The answer is short and simple, 'Of course,' and the head nurse seemed surprised that I should ask."

They went off down the corridor and I tightened the bed and tidied the room. They returned an hour later to report that the music came from the room at the end of the hall where one boy named Danny was waiting for back surgery and Fred, who played the harmonica, was recuperating. They had met another nice young man, Johnny Vinci, who had had skull surgery. "He's going to bring his tray in and have dinner with me," Karen told me. "Mommy, you never met lovelier people—and you know what—(you mustn't repeat this), one of the boys said that most of the patients on this floor are Dr. Moore's, and they call it 'death row.' "

I gasped and looked quickly at Jimmy who was smiling.

Karen explained: "It's because so many patients come to Dr. Moore when nobody else could help them. 'Death row' " she repeated, and went into gales of laughter.

I mustered what I hoped was a convincing chuckle.

Johnny Vinci not only had dinner with Karen but stayed the evening. He was a gentle young man, very sweet with Karen and most offhand about his difficulties. It was obvious to us that both patients felt there were many things worthier of discussion than their own infirmities. Dr. Bob Lachman came and discussed with Karen the procedures he would follow on the morrow. She lost her heart to him. When he left she commented: "Anyone would feel safe with him."

At eight o'clock, a pixyish student nurse, with the enchanting name of Molly Twitchell, tactfully suggested that we could all profit by a good night's sleep. "Karen knows I'm here if she wants anything," she said as she flitted out.

The room was hot and before I left I thought I'd save some nurse a step or two and went to get a pitcher of ice water. When I came back Karen was happily holding hands with Dr. Fay. Rarely have I been so glad to see anyone. "He made it!" she caroled as I came through the door. "I knew he would!"

"So did we!" I resisted the temptation to throw my arms around him.

We had some small talk about his trip to Norway and then he said: "I saw Dr. Moore and we're all set for seven o'clock tomorrow morning. I made inquiries and there's a Mass at that time. I might suggest that you come over here early and when we go upstairs you two go to church and work with us."

"Good idea," said Jimmy, "that will give us an unbeatable team."

Dr. Fay took Karen's hands. "And now I think this pretty young lady should get out of her finery and get some sleep." Dr. Fay turned to us. "See you in the morning." And with a cheery wave he left us.

We knelt beside Karen's bed and said our night prayers. The only inkling Karen gave of apprehension was when she asked God to make her a "good sport."

We settled her for the night and left.

Evening brought no relief from the heat and as we wandered up and down Broad Street Jimmy said: "I hope it's cooler tomorrow."

"So do I." I wasn't seeing the traffic, or the people or the lights. I was really in a room on the fifth floor—I was watching the small frame under the sheet; it was dim, there was only the night light. "Please don't let her be afraid and please help her sleep," I prayed.

"I hope we've done the right thing." Jimmy's voice was choked. "I only hope it's worth it."

It was eighty-five degrees when we rose at six the next morning. "God help the doctors," Jimmy said as we went to Karen's room. They had given her some medication and she was drowsy. We kissed her and she gave a small smile. "I forgot to ask Dr. Margy if his cat was a tom or a queen," she said sleepily in an effort to distract us.

"It's a queen," said one of the nurses who was getting her ready for the operating room.

Karen held out her hand to us. "Don't worry."

Dr. Fay joined us at the bedside. A second nurse unclasped the chain that held Karen's religious medal around her neck. "I'm sorry—but you can't wear this into surgery," she told her patient kindly.

Karen winced.

Dr. Fay quickly took the chain from the nurse and slipped the medal off. He tucked the medal into one of Karen's braids, put the white surgical cap on her head and pushed the hair securely underneath. Her smile told him how much this meant.

The stretcher was brought into the room and in a minute Karen was being rolled down the corridor, Dr. Fay at her side, Jimmy and I following. It was trundled into the elevator and we stood staring at the closed door until the whirring ceased. As we turned away we found Johnny Vinci right behind us. He had followed the stretcher too.

By nine o'clock the thermometer read ninety-one degrees. Karen's room was stifling. The operating room must have been unbearable. I don't know how many hours Karen was upstairs, for I marked the time in endless minutes composed of endless seconds. We didn't read; we didn't talk; we tried to pray. After a while we paced the corridor, fingers intertwined, never getting too far from the elevator door. It stopped frequently during our vigil and every time the door clicked we hurried to it. We were less than a foot away when it clicked, opened, and Dr. Fay stepped out.

"She'll be down in about half an hour. The operating room was crowded," he told us as we walked down the corridor to Karen's room.

"It couldn't be. Dr. Moore never lets anyone in when he's operating." I motioned him to a chair.

Dr. Fay's eyes twinkled. "It was full of angels and of saints. Many, many people must have been praying. I don't think she lost a dozen drops of blood. Dr. Moore is truly a great surgeon."

"And everything is all right?" Jimmy offered Dr. Fay a cigarette which he declined.

"Perfect." Dr. Fay assured him. "I am so glad you decided to go ahead with this operation."

Jimmy walked to the window. Without turning he asked:

"How much improvement do you think we can hope for?" The rigidity of his body expressed the tension with which he awaited the answer.

Dr. Fay's voice was gently matter-of-fact. "We'll just have to wait and see."

Jimmy turned to face him. "You know if it weren't for you, this wouldn't have been done. We're very grateful—for this—for all you've done for Karen."

"I've never known anyone more worth helping," Dr. Fay said warmly. He looked at his watch. "I must leave, I'm three hours behind schedule."

When he was out of earshot I laughed. "Three hours behind schedule! That's about par for the course. I remember the times when our dear doctor invited me for his morning office hours; then we went the rounds in several hospitals, then a clinic or two. 'How about a bite of lunch?' I would ask feebly about 3:00 p.m. Dr. Fay would take out his pocket watch, stare at it unseeingly and reply: 'The day's just begun.' We never even stopped for a cup of coffee before 4:00."

"I think he's unaware of such things as time, hunger or fatigue. I guess that's the difference between being dedicated and consecrated."

We went back to the elevator. Once again it whirred, it clicked, the door slid back, and they wheeled Karen out. We walked on either side of the stretcher back to her room, anxiously watching color and respiration. Quickly and deftly she was transferred to her bed. Standing at the head, waiting, was Johnny Vinci. He didn't glance at us but bent over the quiet form, took the limp hand and placed in the palm a package of orange lifesavers. Then he gently closed the lax fingers and murmured: "They'll taste good in a little while."

Jimmy stood gray and still. His mouth drew down in pain as he studied the mounds and ridges of cumbersome, inflexible plaster. His eyes glazed with anguish as Karen began to react from the anaesthesia and moan with pain. It was heartbreaking to watch the return to spasticity as the medication wore off, like cold flames licking the muscles stiff again.

65.

Dr. Bob Lachman was in and out of the room at frequent intervals, assuring us that she was fine. Late in the afternoon she was completely 'recovered' from the anaesthesia. The pain was severe, but God answered her prayer and she was a good sport. Her only complaint, which she voiced with great feeling, was over the vile taste of chloryl hydrate, a pain killer.

Hour after hour Jimmy stood suffering and silent and sweating. Johnny stayed too, though the temperature of the room was almost one hundred degrees. About eight in the evening, Johnny's doctor sent him to bed. Johnny bent and kissed Karen's wet brow.

She smiled and whispered: "Thank you, Johnny dear."

Jimmy and I left the hospital about eleven. The heat had fairly melted the surface of Broad Street and there were planks across the road on which we had to walk. "As if she didn't have enough to contend with," Jimmy groaned, "without this infernal heat!" We took cool showers and sat up the rest of the night. It was too hot to lie on a mattress.

Karen's recuperation was without incident, but the pain coupled with the continuing, hideous heat and immobility, made a special hell. The thermometers had to be refrigerated; then, if they stood on the trays any time at all, had to be shaken down before they were given to the patients.

Two days later, Jimmy went back to New York. I got to the hospital before 7:00 a.m. and stayed until 11:00 p.m. Karen was soon back on a regular diet and still eating loose eggs. On the tenth day of this egg intake, I reported to Karen that the woman across the hall was off 'critical' and she could order a hard boiled egg.

"How many days did I have loose ones?"

I shuddered: "Ten!"

"Then I think I'll eat them ten days in thanksgiving," replied my daughter.

Twice each day, cards or letters came from the Frieses, our children, Uncle Leo (Monsignor Madden, uncle by virtue of love rather than kin). From Johnny, Joe, Russ, A.M., Shirley. Boxes and boxes of presents arrived and the room began to look like the Ark with stuffed creatures from a tiny soft mouse to a three-foot lion. There were masses of flowers and enough toilet water, fragrant soaps and bath powders to stock a drugstore.

"Letters from *everyone!*" Karen exclaimed. Ed Doll had written a chatty epistle about his ranch and ended: "Remember, my dear, that: 'our hardest job is not to attain our ideal best, but to learn how to bear our handicaps graciously; to accept our imperfections with poise and dignity and yet continue to strive for improvement; to admire and respect the abilities of others without feeling sorry for one's self; and to meet the world with something to offer rather than to seek concessions.' I am enclosing a gem from the pen of daughter Kathy, Grade 6."

HOW DOGS BECOME MUTTS

"When a dog is about 6 months or a year old it begins to what we call 'mate'. After the dog mates it begins to have pups. If the mother is a Cocker Spaniel and the father is a Red Setter then the pups, if any (puppies) become mutts. . .

If the mother dog is a mutt when she was born and the father dog was a mutt when he was born then of course the puppies are mutts because the mother and father are the same breed. This is just like the Hunting Dog Family.

Mutts are not expensive like other dogs. . ."

Laughter may be good therapy but it is hell on stitches and this little piece brought joyful misery to many as it was passed up and down the fifth floor.

Hospitals were old hat to me. In the last fifteen years, I had spent over 600 days in their sterile halls. Figuring that out whiled away an afternoon. This was no record I was sure, but an impressive score. Karen was right in her evaluation of this hospital; here we found what we finally defined as a collective "educated heart." When Dr. Margy brought his cat for frequent visits with Karen, no starched soul so much as raised an eyebrow.

The heat continued a torment. Inside the heavy casts it must have been all but unbearable. The perspiration kept Karen's body drenched and itching unmercifully. You can't scratch inside a cast. I had found that grapefruit juice quenched her thirst better than anything else. Nobody, but nobody, can drink Philadelphia water. I kept a large jar of the juice in the floor icebox.

One night just before leaving I went to get Karen a drink. I took her glass, filled it from the jar in the icebox and started back to her room. Halfway there, a small thought that had been nudging my consciousness finally broke through. There was a label on that jar. Well, I had a label on mine. Yes, but wasn't there some thing different about that label? I stopped and thought—the printing was in ink on adhesive tape. Well, so was mine. But there seemed to be more printing than I had used for designation. I stood undecided then wearily dragged myself back up the corridor to the refrigerator. I opened the door and looked at the jar from which I had poured: Adhesive tape. Printed in ink. The notation *was* longer. It read: "Fluid from Mrs. Drownbeck's thoracic cavity!"

We were getting a little desperate for laughs. This episode was like a breath of cool air. Karen wept with merriment and the consequent discomfort. I was reminded of a poem and recited the last six lines:

> Which then of all thy creatures knows not pain?
> Yet none save we thy children have been blessed
> With mirth; let me my heritage regain
> In laughter's joyous strength—I can only jest
> At my own self, and for a little while,
> And ask no blessing but the right to smile.

Karen, though worn by heat, immobility and pain, was eager to get out of her room and resume some social life. Danny, still waiting not too patiently for his surgery, appointed himself teen-age guardian angel, chauffeur and— woe is me! mother. He'd have Karen moved off her bed and onto a stretcher and then, with a cavalier wave of the hand dismiss me, and off they'd go. Susie Moore became Karen's particular love. She was pretty, gay, gentle and sweet. Karen and Danny didn't limit themselves to their own floor but toured, usually ending up in pediatrics. In the evening he'd take her out on the roof, hoping to find a cooling breeze, and fuss if I didn't provide a light coverlet —and the temperature still in the high eighties.

I put off calling home as late as I could so the telephone booth would be a little less like a Turkish bath. Marie's latest report on Rory lightened Karen's spirits considerably: "Last night we were listening to Tschaikowsky and he said: "Close your eyes, Marie, and when you listen you can see mice tumbling in the snow.' "

"Nice imagery," I commented, "anything else?"

"Yes—the other night before dinner, I had to send him back three times to wash *clean*. That dear son of yours then told me that I had 'dirty eyes!' "

I laughed. "Anything else?"

"Yes. We miss you terribly and Daddy misses you most of all. Hurry home."

ॐ

chapter five

While Danny and Karen, or Johnny and Karen, were off on their safaris to other floors in the hospital, I sat in the oven-like room and tried to answer some of the letters that were pouring in from the readers of *Karen*.

This afternoon the heat had lessened a little (a cool ninety degrees), but I was very tired and just couldn't concentrate. I sat staring out of the window, my thoughts blowing aimlessly as dandelion down. Gloria came to mind; Gloria, who was suffering as much as Karen, but in a far different way.

Like Jimmy, she had started to work when she was twelve, to support herself and to help support her family. It was at this time that she first came to our house as a baby-sitter. She took whatever jobs she could get, after school, evenings, week-ends and vacations. The going rate was twenty cents an hour. She cleaned houses as a 'mother's helper,' worked in the Five and Ten, made frozen custards and sold hot dogs at the Playland Amusement Park, worked in the Village library. While taking a secretarial course in high school she had come to help me as we struggled to launch a national association for cerebral palsy. At fourteen she took dictation, typed speedily and filed. When school started, she came afternoons to help Rose Hurley, the dark-skinned angel who was 'mother' to my children when I had to be away on C.P. affairs. In three years we had all come to respect Gloria and to love her dearly.

The summer she was fifteen, with the dissolution of her own family, she became our third daughter.

The year she graduated from High School, she went to work for a firm of attorneys. She was most efficient but she had been on the job only five months when her sense of humor almost lost her the position. One of the attorneys was a judge, graduate of a well-known university and law school. One day on her lunch hour, Gloria picked up a match folder on the outside of which was printed "Are you the one who didn't finish high school?" Inside, in small print, it told how one could study at home and secure a diploma. A representative would call, outline the course, and all would be kept CONFIDENTIAL. NO ONE WOULD KNOW. On the black flap there was a space to fill in Name . . . Address . . . of the applicant. Fired by I know not what unholy inspiration, Gloria filled in the Judge's name and office address.

A fortnight passed and late one afternoon, a very polite gentleman came to the office and asked to see the Judge.

"Is he expecting you?" Gloria asked.

"Yes, but he didn't know when I'd be here."

Gloria thought that a little odd. "I'm his secretary, would you like to give me your name and the nature of your business?"

"I can't. It's private."

"Well, I'm his private secretary," Gloria replied crisply.

"Sorry," he declined. "Is he busy now?"

"Yes, he's at a closing."

"I'll wait."

When the closing was over, she ushered him into the

Judge's office. Shortly the indignant voice of her employer penetrated to the outer room. "Of course, I have a high school diploma. I'm a lawyer."

The visitor's voice answered knowingly: "There are ways . . . we understand . ."

"What do you mean—you understand—there are ways? Those are my diplomas hanging on that wall," the Judge shouted.

"I said—there are ways—" repeated the caller insinuatingly.

"I don't know why you came here—but get out."

"You sent us your name. Don't you want a high-school diploma? I told you we keep everything confidential."

Gloria had been listening, fascinated. Suddenly dawn came up like thunder. "Holy smoke!" She felt she should skip out of the office until the meeting was over, but couldn't bring herself to miss any of the animated exchange.

The Judge bellowed like a bull: *"I never sent my name to anyone. I'm a high school graduate, a college graduate, a law school graduate, a practicing attorney and A JUDGE!"*

"We've done this for judges before—all very confidential."

"GET OUT!" Her boss flung open the door; he was red-faced and trembling. "GET OUT!"

In the face of such wrath the man retreated. As he passed Gloria's desk he muttered: "Wonder what made him change his mind?"

"Did you hear that?" The Judge looked on the verge of apoplexy.

"I'm sure they heard you in all the offices in the building," Gloria answered with angelic sweetness. She was innocence itself: "What was that all about?"

"It was about—" the Judge sputtered, then threw up his hands, marched back into his office and slammed the door. The diplomas on the wall danced under the impact.

The summer that Gloria was eighteen, she met Russ. For a while he was just one of a parade of young men who pursued this blond beauty. As Fall approached he was at our house more and more frequently. He would drive up the hills in his Triumph, the envy of every kid on the block.

With the talent, special to engineers, he had rigged some kind of gimmick so that he could play records in the car. As he approached the house we would hear the racing "William Tell Overture," and when he left, there would be wafted back up Hill Street the strains of "Let Me Call You Sweetheart," to the delight of most of the neighbors and the annoyance of a few.

We had evenings of endless discussion and as often as not, we would get around to religion. There were never any arguments, but Russ was calmly and unflinchingly anti-Catholic. Gloria was not always so calm as he; a recent convert to Catholicism, she was eager to share her happiness with others. Jimmy and I had not known that for two years she had been taking instruction in our religion. Always we had been very much on guard to say nothing that might be taken as 'encouragement,' fearful that she might be prompted to consider the Church by some false sense of gratitude or conformity. It was, therefore, a happy shock when she had said to Jimmy one Easter Saturday morning: "I hope your blue suit is pressed. You're going to need it this afternoon."

"I don't need my blue suit to put in grass seed and that's what I plan to do this afternoon."

"You'll have to change your plans. I'll need you at church and I want my godfather to be well dressed."

Rory's comment to Gloria after the Baptism was: "Aren't you a little old for this?"

The deeper Gloria went into the study of theology the more she wanted to discuss it. Russ, who was now coming to the house several nights a week, was drawn into these discussions but his attitude remained one of kindly tolerance. We had given Gloria a copy of Frank Sheed's *Theology and Sanity* which she offered to Russ. He refused laughingly with a shrug: "I'm just not interested."

"I think you would be," Glo encouraged. "The more you know about God the more you love Him, and the more you love Him, the more you want to know about Him."

Good-humoredly Russ asked her: "And do you think any amount of study would persuade me to want a picture like that?" He pointed to a painting hanging above the fireplace. "That's supposed to depict Christ! He simpers and looks like a refugee from a Greek Chorus holding an overripe tomato in his hand."

Gloria was gathering for an explosion.

Jimmy spoke quickly and lightly. "It has often occurred to me," he hurried on not giving Gloria a chance to break in, "that a proof of the divinity of the Church is the bad religious art that it has survived for so long."

"Hideous," Russ concurred, smiling at Jimmy. Then turning to Gloria he said seriously: "You know, I wish I could go along with what you believe, but I can't and I'm certain I never shall."

Unable to think of any intelligent distraction I asked inanely: "How about some coffee?" I went to the kitchen and Jimmy followed me.

"How about this Russ business?" he asked pacing from the coal stove to the door and back. "Glo doesn't seem really interested in anyone else."

I measured the water into the percolator. "She isn't. Neither is he."

"How do you know?"

"I just know."

"Oh!" He put his arm around me. "Russ is as good as bread, but—" He was reluctant to articulate the difficulties that were beginning to take shape.

"He is as good as bread," I repeated, "I've rarely been so sure of anything."

Jimmy sighed. "She's only twenty. I guess we'll just have to wait and see."

"And pray." I was far more concerned than I wanted him to know.

By the end of the following year, Gloria was seeing Russ exclusively. Loath as he was to intrude, Jimmy had asked her: "Don't you think it would be a good idea to go out with someone else once in a while?"

"I don't enjoy being with anyone else," Gloria answered simply.

Jimmy was finding his role extremely distasteful. He

plunged with the idea of getting the discussion over as quickly as possible. "And does he love you as much as you love him?"

"He does." She faced him. "Jimmy, if it's O.K. with you and Marie, I'd like to go away and make my yearly Retreat. I feel I need a spiritual inventory."

"Of course. When would you like to go?"

"I was thinking of leaving Thursday night and coming home Sunday. I have a lot of thinking to do."

"It seems a good idea. We'll meet you Sunday at the Harmon station. Just call and let us know what time."

Gloria went to him and lightly kissed the top of his head. "Thank you—for everything."

At noon on Sunday, she called home: "Ask Little Marie if she'd mind baby-sitting. I'd like you and Jimmy and Russ to meet me. My train gets in at six."

"We'll be there."

It was a soft April evening. Beyond the railroad tracks the broad surface of the Hudson River was alternately, blue, green and silver, varying with the strong currents. Around us belligerent locomotives grunted great bursts of steam and sound. Far up the track we could see an eye of light, which seemed not to be moving at all, then quickly was upon us. With a great dissonance of metallic melodies, the train halted.

We scanned the alighting passengers who wore similar expressions of solitary endeavor. "It's sure been bleak with Gloria away," said Jimmy to no one in particular.

"It sure has," agreed Russ with feeling. "There she is!"

She was coming toward us, her dainty figure trim in a gray suit, a wisp of a lavendar hat set saucily on her head. She was not hurrying as I might have expected. We went to meet her. She threw her arms around Jimmy, then me, then Russ. She clung to Russ for several seconds, then backed away. She looked around the now deserted platform and spoke in an even voice: "Russ, I have something to say and it would be easiest to say it here and now."

"Jimmy and I will walk on ahead."

She shook her head. "Please stay." She turned to look up at Russ. "I went away to think and pray. I thought

74.

about how difficult it is to make a go of marriage even when people are of one mind about the important things." She gave a small sigh. "You and I, my dear, do not think alike about—what is to me—the most important, religion." Her voice stayed controlled and calm. "To you, the Rosary and much of Catholic liturgy is sheer superstition. You would object, and rightly so, from your point of view, to hanging that hideous painting of Christ in *our* living room. And there's so much else . . ." her voice grew smaller. ". . the rearing of children in a religion which would be alien to their father . ." She turned slightly and looked across the water. Russ took a step toward her. She halted him with a small motion of her hand and looked up into his face. "There's more, much more."

We waited.

"And so, my dearest, we would have two strikes against us to start; and because I love you so much, I am not going to marry you and I won't be able to see you any more."

Caryll Hauslander wrote: "To the Christian, suffering is not a problem to be explored by the human mind but a mystery to be experienced by the human heart." Russ's absence left an enormous gap in all our lives. Gloria was not alone in her suffering. Karen felt the separation keenly for it was Russ who took her places *without* the family, and that's important to anyone. Russ who brought her an orchid when she achieved some enormously difficult task—like buttoning a button. Russ who was big and sweet and thoughtful and gentle and shamelessly spoiled her. "I miss him more every day," she yearned. But young as she was, she had the wisdom to say nothing of this to Gloria.

Two years later we went to Russ's wedding—all of us. Not then, nor ever, did Gloria give any hint of her pain. I whispered to God that day: "Karen *we* can help; but only *You* can help Glo." Then for both our girls my heart cried: "Ah! Must Thou char the wood 'ere Thou canst limn with it?"

Gloria had invitations from young men, and most attractive ones, for almost every night of the week. She accepted only occasionally. Jimmy tried to encourage her to a wider social life outside our home. "I'm happy as I am," she told him gently.

"What can we do?" he asked me with deep concern.

"Nothing. She's a woman—and a woman who knows her own mind."

"She sure does," agreed Jimmy unhappily. "Oh, she's always attentive, respective and sweet—but adamant!"

Russ kept in touch with Jimmy and me. He was at Sandia Base doing top secret work on the atom bomb. His letters spoke of his work in general terms, the climate, the austere beauty of his surroundings, hunting, but to his personal life he made no reference.

Thanksgiving night we were having a songfest in the living room when the telephone rang. I went to the kitchen to answer it. It was Russ. "I'm on leave," he told me.

"Wonderful! When will we see you?"

"I think it best if I don't come to the house," he said, "but I was wondering if you and Jimmy could have dinner with me tomorrow night?"

"Are you alone?" I asked sensing some strange tension in his voice.

There was a pause. "Yes, I am." Another pause. "How about Larden's Restaurant—say, seven?"

"We'll be there. I'm so anxious to see you."

"Don't say you're meeting me until we've had a chance to talk. O.K.?"

"As you wish." I was both curious and anxious. "Till tomorrow then—"

"Good-bye."

I put down the receiver and stared thoughtfully out the window. A tumbling oak leaf spread-eagled itself against the pane and peered in.

The children were delighted, if surprised, when I announced that Daddy was taking Mommy out to dinner. Russ was waiting at the restaurant when we arrived. He lifted me off my feet in a bear hug and wrung Jimmy's hand until he winced. He was full of questions and we were sipping our demi-tasse before they were all answered. Quite out of character, I left most of the answers to Jimmy while I tried to discover in what way Russ was different from the young man of two years ago. It was not physical although he was leaner and harder, but rather an intangible tranquility, a quality of suffering, of waiting without impatience. My speculations were interrupted by Jimmy who asked Russ: "Shall I tell you the latest Rory story?"

"By all means." He smiled in anticipation. "What's my pal been up to now?"

"The other day," Jimmy related, "a lady came up to Rory and me outside Futterman's stationery store. She said she had heard Marie lecture and had read her book and thought she was wonderful. Your pal digested this praise and before I could speak my appreciation, he said, "Yes—*but can my sister Gloria cook!*"

Russ laughed delightedly. "There's a male who knows what's really important."

"You're so sweet!" I acknowledged with charming acidity.

He grinned at me. "It's nothing. How's Shanty?"

"Just as overprotective as ever. He's got some white hairs on his muzzle and in his old age he thinks he's a Dalmatian. The Shore Club catches fire at pretty regular intervals and the minute the engines turn up the street he's off."

Russ stared at the steady flame of the candle. "I miss them all," he said gently.

"Tell us about yourself," Jimmy prompted. "Your letters have been very interesting but not very informative."

Russ looked squarely at us. "I want you to know, that's why I asked you to meet me tonight. I applied for an annulment of my marriage and it was granted on the grounds of non-consummation. Like you, I believe in marriage and I would not get a divorce although my lawyer urged it vehemently because it would have been much simpler. How could I ask for a divorce when I was convinced that no marriage had taken place?"

"You couldn't." I agreed.

"Was securing the nullity a long, drawn-out affair?" Jimmy asked.

"Surprisingly, no. I certainly expected the Court to want sworn medical testimony but they took our word."

"Surely," I said, "they called in witnesses who had known

77.

you prior to your marriage, and friends and acquaintances who had known you during your marriage?"

"The Court called no one."

We sat quietly waiting for him to go on.

He continued: "After it was over, I began to do some reading about Catholicism. The result was that I have been going for instruction to the Chaplain for some months. And—" He leaned forward and his voice was vibrant, "Father says that I will be sufficiently prepared to be baptized on Christmas Eve."

We sat in stunned silence, then Jimmy quoted: "More things are wrought by prayer—"

Russ finished: "—than this world dreams of."

I could find no words. I placed my hand on his. What a strangely ironic situation! Gloria had refused to marry Russ because of a profound need that her husband and the father of her children should share the faith that was so deeply her life.

Hesitantly Jimmy spoke: "Forgive me, Russ, if I seem to intrude on anything so personal, but there's something I feel I must say."

Russ nodded for him to continue.

Jimmy spoke with great deliberation. "The Church won't recognize your civil annulment. No one can say at this time whether you can get a declaration of nullity or a dissolution of your marriage from the Church Court. However, I am sure you can get a hearing in the Church Court whether you become a Catholic or not; but bear in mind that the Church is not easily satisfied as to the validity of a claim of non-consummation, and any investigation they would make would be very, very thorough and involve scores of witnesses. The Church Court must secure proof of the facts you allege." Jimmy continued, his voice pitched low. I just want to be sure that you realize all of this before you are baptized—and if you apply for a declaration of nullity, and if you are refused, as a Catholic you can never marry."

"I realize fully," Russ said calmly.

Some time later, on the Feast of St. Jude (patron of hopeless cases!) Russ petitioned for a church nullity. Weeks, months dragged by and Russ wrote from his base that there was not a word of encouragement. Quite the contrary. So far they had not even been able to locate his former wife to take her testimony.

Months stretched into years as the thorough investigation of the Church continued, and the faith of us all was tested. We began to perceive what may well have been a part of God's plan in Karen; her example to all of us had been a generous acceptance without bitterness or despair; of constant disappointment; of ever widening removal from an ordinary way of living; of achievements reached only under great difficulties; of maturity.

So it was now with Gloria and Russ. I think it may be truly said that Karen's unconscious example was the greatest gift—with love—from Karen.

 є❧

chapter six

In Karen's room, the giant of heat continued to beat against the hospital walls, bored through the window glass and trod upon me with heavy feet. I went down to the plaster room to cool off and stayed half an hour. When I returned I found the room in a hubbub. Frank Burke, a friend of twenty years standing, was directing operations. "What goes on?" I surveyed the scene quizzically.

"I have the afternoon off and I'm taking you both for a drive. I thought that by now you might have cabin fever."

I looked at him to see if he'd lost his wits. "And just how do you propose to take this rigid, supine young lady for a *drive?*"

Frank was blithe. "It's all arranged."

I stood apart while the stretcher was rolled beside Karen's bed and she was deftly transferred, whisked down the hall, on and off the elevator, and trundled to the Emergency entrance. There Frank had a rented station wagon with a

79.

mattress and pillow in the back and Karen was gently 'loaded.'

"We're off!" Frank called gaily as I climbed in beside him.

"Hooray!" Karen shouted from the back.

Frank drove easily and skillfully. "You drive as though I were a basket of eggs," Karen laughed.

"Far, far more precious," her chauffeur replied with what was for him unaccustomed solemnity.

How beautiful the hills of Pennsylvania! How sweetly cool and fragrant the woods! With what healing gentleness the fresh breeze caressed us! It was blissful. I looked at the minister in sport shirt and told him: "After much thought, I can say that this is the best present anyone ever gave me."

"What's the second best?" he asked, turning down a narrow winding road.

Karen laughed from the back. "A bath!"

"A bath?"

"A bath," I repeated. I explained about my room in the boardinghouse with no bath and only a shower in a communal bathroom. "We have friends living outside Philadelphia, the Hoehls. Russ and Jimmy grew up together and Eileen was my nurse when Little Marie was born. Three times they have driven in to fetch me late in the evening, driven me back to their house, fed me, and then let me soak a whole hour in a cool tub! That was bliss too."

"They must be pretty nice people."

Karen said enthusiastically. "Just about the nicest in the world."

We drove under arches of trees and beside tumultuous brooks whose spray sweetened and cooled the air. I watched the color creep back into Karen's cheeks and saw the harsh angles of tension fade leaving her face soft and childish. Around 6:00 p.m., Frank stopped at a lovely restaurant. He had telephoned ahead of time and a lavish dinner was served to us in the car. Karen ate ravenously.

In a dusk of long blue shadows we headed back to Philadelphia. The heat enfolded us with moist arms as we re-entered the city. Our gratitude to Frank was so deep we couldn't speak it. In silence we kissed him good-night.

Dr. Moore had said that if we could find a way to transport Karen, we could take her home in her casts. She would return at the end of June to have them removed. Frank had shown us how to transport Karen (the cost of a private ambulance was prohibitive). Margaret and Jack Chambers had a station wagon which they would joyfully lend us.

The day of departure while I was packing, Jimmy and Karen went for their last visit to Pediatrics. The kids loved to see Jimmy come for he had taught them that they could talk right "into my heart." He would take the little ones on his lap; they would whisper against his heart and he would answer. Only the very wise seven-year olds knew about the tiny hearing aid box that rested on his chest. With grace they kept their counsel.

I was just closing the last suitcase when there was a half-laugh, half-cry from Karen. I spun around. Bending to kiss her was Eddie Brothers. "This is the first leave I could get."

"You're here!" She hugged him close. "Look at my casts!" She displayed the lengths of plaster, waist-high, covered with endearing and laudatory messages—"To the littlest angel on the 5th floor." She raced on: "You know what Eddie, I was stitched with Allegheny Steel!"

It was the only reference that Karen ever made to her surgery.

We were home.

"I'd forgotten how beautiful Spring is," Karen rhapsodized as we rolled her across the lawn. Flat on her back she was looking up to our elm as it towered sixty feet above her, and spread its heavy branches an equal distance in width. The entire tree was entwined, festooned and garlanded with wisteria. Only patches of sky could be seen through thousands of great purple clusters and a veritable cascade of perfume poured from opulent blossoms.

Karen had an impressive escort as she was trundled to her room. Joe, Johnny Forsman, Michael Milward, Uncle Leo, A.M., and Shirley and their kids, Rose and John Hurley, a horde of Learys, and Glo and Marie and Rory who hovered over her as though she had come back in porclain rather than plaster. Shanty, after prolonged hysteria, was walking sedately beside the stretcher at just the right pace so Karen's hand could rest on his head. Ash Wednesday and Yum-Yum were conducting a joint tree-climbing lesson for nine of their kittens, Etcetera rode on Karen's chest, and her canary, Mr. McBride (named for Mary Margaret who had given him to Karen), heralded the procession with a variety of trills and sustained notes from a bursting throat.

"There's so much to come home to," Karen laughed unquenchably.

There was a fair breeze and looking to the sound we could see sun-lit whitecaps that tumbled like up-ended children somersaulting, chased each other around the rocks and collided with gleeful shouts.

"Just smell the salt!" Karen inhaled deeply and rapturously. "Quite a change from ethered halls!" She threw her arms wide. "It's cool!" She stroked Etcetera. "Look at his points!" she exclaimed. "He looks like *café au lait.*" Cetty was creamy and tan and his face was like a black satin mask. He nipped Karen's chin. "See how he kisses?" she invited.

Her room was a riot of blooms. There were flowers on tables, window sills, desk, bookcase. Jonquils, tulips, hyacinths, lilies-of-the-valley, carnations, roses.

Karen gasped at the profligacy of these gifts.

Gloria remarked appreciatively: "It looks like a gangster's wake!"

"Holy smoke!" Karen pointed to the foot of her bed where there was a television set.

Gloria untied a card and handed it to her. She read aloud: "From Margaret and Jack Chambers who want you to be able to visit other lands while you are in bed. With all our love." Karen kissed the card. "It's too much. It's just too much."

The Welcoming Committee had the good sense to leave so Karen could take a rest. After I'd settled her I wandered upstairs and down, in and out of the rooms, seeing them as if for the first time. I rediscovered their size, that none were square and each a different shape. I went from window to window overlooking the harbor. I wandered some more and noticed that Marie had washed the tiny tiles and polished the copper frames of the fireplaces.

Jimmy was standing at the foot of the stairs as I came down. "I think you love this house like a fifth child," he said reading my thoughts.

"I hope I never have to leave it, 'til I leave feet first," I said with more feeling than I intended. "Your children have done some job. It shines, it glitters, it glistens. I'd say they'd done too much."

I peeked in at Karen and found her asleep. I went out to the porch where the children were waiting with frosted glasses for iced tea. "You look like hell," Gloria told me with more emotion than tact.

"You're skinny and gray," my son observed with harsh concern.

Marie fussed over me as though I were the patient. Glo went inside and returned a few minutes later. She spoke to Jimmy. "It's going to be too heavy a load for her," she glanced at me, "to carry alone. I just called my boss and resigned."

All my protestations were in vain. Gloria was adamant. "Besides," she hurled her final argument, "you need a secretary. There are over *four thousand* letters to be answered and more pour in every day."

I leaned back in my chair and closed my eyes. "It will be wonderful," I surrendered.

"You're an angel," Marie said to Gloria.

"She really is," Rory spoke enthusiastically.

"She really is," echoed Jimmy.

Gloria said: "Knowing about casts isn't the same thing as seeing someone you love strapped inside them."

I spoke without opening my eyes. "I was glad Karen was looking upward when you saw her. You all looked stricken."

"Well, I was," said Marie. "She looks so light and they look so weighty."

"How long will she have to keep them on?" asked Rory with a shudder.

"Until sometime in June. Then she'll have to wear them at night for about a year," Jimmy answered.

"Poor kid!" Rory's voice throbbed with compassion.

Marie cleared her throat and asked hesitantly: "Can you tell yet what Karen will be able to *do?*"

Jimmy shook his head. "We'll just have to wait and see."

Marie came over and sat beside me. "I think you should know what your good Baptist friends, Rose and John Hurley, did for Karen." She took my hand. "Rose came down the day of surgery and when I got home from school she had the washing and ironing all done. She got our dinner and stayed the evening, knowing we'd be missing you and Daddy." Marie's dark eyes were wide. "She and John not only prayed, Mommy, they *fasted!* For *two days* they took nothing but water. I tried to get Rose to take a cup of tea, at least, but she said that when they asked God for something so big, they felt they should make some small sacrifice. 'God fasted when He prayed,' she told me. They made me ashamed of doing so little."

I squeezed her hand. "You did a great deal and did it well. We couldn't have managed without you. You gave up dates and reading time and all recreation. At your age that's probably a most difficult fast."

Jimmy grinned. "Most difficult."

While Rory was talking to Karen, Marie gave me a whispered report on her brother. "You couldn't know what a big help Rory was. He kept the porch clean, worked on the rugs and helped polish furniture. He kept his room very nicely but I do think you should speak to him about the magazines on the floor under the bed." She glanced at Rory to be sure he couldn't hear her. "I think it's good that he has such an interest in bugs but maybe you'd ask him not to put them in my cosmetic box. Now that you're home maybe you can also help him find a substitute for the word 'stink.' This sounds as though I'm complaining. I'm not. He was very good and very helpful and told me last night that I'd been 'a good substitute mother.'"

"I'll speak to him about the 'stink' and the bugs, but we don't want to discourage a budding biologist."

"Make it loud and clear," urged Marie. "It seems to me

that we tell children so much that, as a defense mechanism, they acquire a partial deafness."

"I've had the same thought myself."

C.P. Board Meetings, trips, the care of Karen, and dealing with the mail, all were possible because I had Gloria to help me. True, we stretched some days to sixteen or seventeen hours, but we managed well.

Jimmy and I had made strict rules concerning Karen and our book. (1) She should be deflected from reading it herself until she was quite a bit older. (2) We would screen all mail and keep from her those letters filled with praise, justified as it was. (3) She would not see T.V. shows nor hear radio programs on which I appeared, since she was the topic interviewers wanted to discuss. (4) Despite good arguments to the contrary (it would do so much for the cause) she would make no public appearances. These decisions were questioned by many and severely criticized by some, but any other course would have been not only foolish but dangerous. We had had wide experience in the deleterious effects of publicity on adults who, we would have thought, would be unaffected. How much more hazardous then for a child, and a child with a handicap.

We did give Karen a present sent her by a Mr. and Mrs. Baldwin in Louisiana. Mr. Baldwin had fashioned for Karen an altar from the 'knees' of cypress trees. It was beautifully shaped and the wood was burnished until it gleamed like red gold; it fit perfectly on the top of her bookcase. A deep and enduring friendship was thus begun which has grown precious to all over the years.

Karen's incarceration was lightened by a visit from Uncle Pat. Glo rigged up the loud-speaker right outside Karen's room and as Pat's cab drew up he was greeted by the blaring of "The Wearing of The Green." He was delighted (a napping neighbor wasn't). It was while we were all sitting with Karen that evening that she discovered a totally unexpected result of her surgery. Shanty was panting on the bed beside her, his head on the pillow next to hers, one foreleg across her chest. "I love you darlin'," she told him, "but you make me too hot. Down."

He rolled his eyes and thumped his tail persuasively.

"You're making Karen too hot. On the floor," said Jimmy firmly and snapped his fingers.

Karen put her thumb against her third finger in imitation and we heard a soft crack. She looked at her hand as though it belonged to someone else. She repeated the gesture and sure enough—she could snap her fingers. "I've waited twelve years to do that," she said snapping over and over. "Isn't surgery wonderful!"

Rory cheered: "I'll bet your operation cost a million dollars . ." (To our eight-year-old, anything of value ran into millions). "I'd say it was worth it."

Shanty, his bruised feelings manifest by the droop of ears and tail, stalked out. He returned shortly wreaking a large revenge. Diabolically he embraced us all and leapt on Karen's bed. The party broke up with shouts and screams for he had been rolling in fish long dead, and had brought home not only the stench but also a considerable piscene residue. Pat left a little later, he *said* he had an early morning appointment. Rory delayed him somewhat by presenting him with a hundred strips of paper. With mortifying candor our son requested: "Will you please autograph these Uncle Pat and then I can sell them to the kids for a dime a piece."

Our telephone rang from early morning until late at night. Like so many of the letters, these calls were appeals for help from desperate, frightened and sometimes despairing relatives of children with cerebral palsy. It was heart wracking to hear from a mother that her five-year-old daughter, who was an athetoid (uncontrollable body movements) had been given the "water treatment" at a state hospital—to quiet her down; from a mother whose husband, a musician in Detroit, had despaired and killed their child; from a doctor who had been friendly with the family next door for twelve years and did not know they had a child with cerebral palsy—they "hid" it.

We did what we could. One reason I made trips was that I would not recommend a clinic or a treatment center unless I had visited it myself within a year, or had assurance of standards from someone like Dr. Doll. We sent out lists of literature related to all aspects of the condition and were particularly grateful for the writings of Dr. Doll. His book, *Measurements of Social Competence,* was of inestimable value to parents, physicians of whatever related specialty, therapists, teachers, social workers. His Vineland Social Maturity Scale was to many a most important guide. For those working in the field on the community level, we would copy quotes from Dr. Doll's speeches: "Our philosophy is getting through the dignity and worth of every child and his right to remaining in circulation among his fellows and peers. How to work this out with justice to teacher, class and special child takes some doing." And: "The I.Q. test is a measure of *performance,* not *potential.*" There were requests for me to come and set up organizations and treatment centers from as far away as South Africa. This last from Harry Kessler, who really didn't need any help and went on to do a remarkable job both from the standpoint of medical assistance and education.

To many we sent, in the same package, *My Way of Life, Dennis the Menace,* and Father McSorley's *Hope, the Forgotten Virtue,* on the theory that courage is a fusion of faith and humor. The expenses involved in these undertakings came out of Jimmy's salary and my royalties.

A letter addressed to Karen typified the reaction of readers not personally concerned with cerebral palsy. It came from a young woman named Barbara in Columbus, Ohio.

Dear Karen,

I just finished reading the story that your mother wrote about how hard you've been working to learn how to do things. I've looked at your picture so much that I feel as if I know you—probably because I'd like so very much to know a girl like you.

You have courage, Karen, and that is a wonderful thing. They give people medals for having the courage to face death. The people who have the courage to face life usually get success instead of medals. When courage comes wrapped in gaiety, it's something bigger, so much bigger that, instead of just getting, the people who have it *give*.

It's like a daisy in the field. It can't stay the same forever. It's a bud, then it's a flower, and then it goes beyond that and becomes a little packet of seeds. The next time you go by, there's a patch of daisies, and after years go by, a whole field of daisies is growing where only one had the courage to grow before.

I want to thank you for the seed you've given me, Karen. There isn't anything much wrong with my body, but my disposition sort of needs a brace—and a lot of exercise too, I guess.

And if little Karen can work so hard, I certainly ought to be able to stand on two good legs and face the world.

What you have done for yourself isn't just for yourself; it's for all of us. By fighting and slaying your own personal dragons, you give us all courage, not just to fight dragons, but first to face them.

So God bless you Karen! And, thank you so much.

This letter we saved and gave to Karen one dark day when hope was teetering on the scale of the 'known' and the 'unknown'. We thanked God then, and now, for all the Barbaras of the educated hearts.

Karen still treasures a clipping sent her by a Methodist minister. "Why has God made me like this?" asked a cripple querulously. "My dear," said her friend: "God has not made you, God is making you."

We were racing into summer and it would soon be time for Karen to return to Temple University Hospital to have the casts removed. Before we left I wanted to get a little more furniture; our rooms were beautiful but rather empty. Money was very tight and I discovered, not antique, but second-hand stores, the Salvation Army shops and the attics of friends, to whom Victorian furniture was passé but too good to throw out. We couldn't afford curtains or drapes for fifty-nine windows, so Gloria went to New York and fetched, in relays, sixty pounds of fish net and amber and colorless glass floaters. All this decorating activity provided a helpful diversion for Karen. Much of the furniture we had to sand down and repaint, and she spent hours with Joe poring over the book of Peter Hunt designs, selecting appropriate motifs. It was a proud family that figured out we had painted, furnished and decorated the guest room for a total of $31. . . . Marie commented: "How much people miss who can hire a decorator and painter and buy whatever they want."

Karen had a host of visitors but the most important was Russ, home on a brief leave. The report on his case was that the church lawyers were lining up witnesses but had not yet been able to locate his wife, as her testimony was vital, the whole picture was pretty discouraging. Gloria saw him only at home or double-dating with us.

Russ was with us the night before Karen was to go back to hospital. She explained to him that Dr. Moore was going to remove the casts but that he would not have her attempt steps for a week or so. She would then have to forget previous patterns and learn to walk all over again. She would start in a walker, practise diligently, and in a month should be proficient enough to come home. She spoke of returning to the hospital in terms of renewing friendships, but when she was alone with him, Karen confided to Russ: "There are times when I get a 'prick' of doubt about this whole business."

To keep this last evening as much on the up-beat as possible, Jimmy suggested that I tell the joke about the Quaker and the cow which we had heard from John McCarthy.

Inspired by necessity I told the story funnily enough, but when I came to deliver the punch line—I forgot it. It was just gone. All gone. What did the Quaker say to the cow? I was taking an unmerciful ribbing and finally went to the phone to dial John's number. After several rings a sleepy voice answered.

"I hope you weren't asleep," I said, knowing full well that he had been, "but what *did* the Quaker say to the cow?"

"Huh?" grunted through the receiver.

"You know, the joke you told us. What did the Quaker say to the cow?"

"Who is this?" The voice was now awake.

"Marie Killilea."

"And who am I?"

"Oh, come on, John, just give me the punch line and go back to sleep."

"John who?"

Of a sudden the now wide awake voice sounded strange. "Isn't this John McCarthy?"

"No!" There was a bang in my ear and I sat looking foolishly at the receiver. This little *faux pas* brightened the evening far more than the joke would have.

I was very sound asleep when the phone rang. I glanced at the clock. 3:00 a.m. "Yes—" I answered groggily.

"Say," said the voice of my faulty dialing, "I can't sleep. What *did* the Quaker say to the cow?"

Philadelphia was still an oven.

Since many of the patients on the fifth floor were in for a long stay, Karen's return had something of the air of an alumni meeting. A number of new patients were visiting Karen from time to time and from one of the doctors we learned the reason: "I send my patients in to see her the night before surgery," he told Jimmy and me. "That youngster has so much faith it's contagious. I know my cases are better surgical risks after they've spent some time with her."

With ear-splitting whine, Karen's casts were sawed horizontally in half. This had to be done ever so skillfully to avoid cracking or breaking. For a year to come they would be put on at night, sort of like a sandwich with Karen's legs the filling. Her comment on this procedure: "Doctor dear, that noise puts fuzz on my teeth."

Next she was measured for new braces, this time by an artist, a German gentleman named Greiner.

Karen, now able to sit, spent long hours with Suzie Moore, Danny, Johnny, and Freddie and his harmonica. Doctors Moore, Lachman, Margy and Fay came to see her every day. But in spite of her increased mobility, this time of waiting to see what she could do when she got up on her feet was trying in the extreme. Some of the hours were spent in therapy; there were always letters, cards and books, but Karen found it hard to concentrate. Her mind was almost exclusively occupied with wondering. So was mine.

At long last The Day arrived—and it was hot, in the nineties. Dr. Moore came, bearing the new braces and crutches. The latter, he quickly explained, were just so Karen could practice standing. After being supine for so long, she would not attempt steps for at least a week. He repeated that she would have to learn to walk all over again; that she would walk differently. He hoped that in a month she would be walking well enough to go home.

When the braces were laced snugly but comfortably, we placed the crutches under her arms and with considerable trepidation stood her on her feet. We stayed close to her, supporting her at the waist, as she wavered erect for several minutes. "That's enough for today," Dr. Moore told her and lifted her back on the bed. "That was fine," he encouraged, "I'll be back this evening and you can practise again."

I picked up *The Collected Works of Francis Thompson* and began reading "The Making of Viola" . . . .

> Baby smiled, mother wailed
> Earthward while the sweetling sailed;
> Mother smiled, baby wailed,
> When to earth came Viola. .

"Mom Pom, I'd like to get back on my feet."

I hesitated, but only for a moment. I put the crutches under her arms and slid her off the bed and on her feet. I lifted her over to the door so that she might catch any small breeze too shy to come in. I stood behind her, supporting her. Under my hands I could feel her steadying herself. She moved the crutches experimentally. She was perspiring so heavily that I had to wipe her eyes. I was perspiring freely myself, as much from nervousness as from heat, for I remembered well the weakness of my own legs after only a few weeks in bed, and I'd been able to sit up and move my legs as I pleased.

I put my wet handkerchief in a pocket only slightly less damp and Karen moved her left crutch ahead of her body—and *moved her right foot!* I placed my hands on her shoulders.

"Let's go . . ." She moved the other crutch and shrugged off my hands. I didn't know what to do. Discourage such enterprise? Instill fear? On the other hand if she fell it might take months to rebuild confidence. I moved to put my hands back on her shoulders—then dropped them to my sides. It was one of those split-second decisions that parents make that alter the course of many things. Karen took a third step which brought her just outside the door.

"I'm going to walk down the hall and see Susie."

Susie's room was forty feet away. It was visiting hour and there was considerable traffic. Not the best circumstances under which to solo. By some special grace I checked the involuntary "Oh *no!*" that rose to my lips; instead: "That should do Susie a lot of good." I said no more but silently addressed myself to all the angels and saints that Karen would be protected from probable disaster as a result of my folly.

Many of the visitors knew Karen and they stopped in gawking amazement when they saw her erect. Karen was concentrating too intensely to notice anyone or anything. As I walked beside her I saw the nurses leave their station and fly to us on tip-toe. The patients who were able, came out of their rooms and many of the others demanded wheel chairs so they could watch this wonder. Word got around the hospital that something miraculous was happening on the fifth floor, and friends, patients, nurses, residents, interns and visiting doctors came from other floors.

Karen kept walking.

Danny and Fred had come out of their room when they heard the hubbub. When Fred realized what was happening he darted back into his room and came out with his harmonica. He started to play—"The Battle Hymn of the Republic." Some voices joined, timidly at first, then more strongly— "Mine eyes have seen the glory of the coming of the Lord . . . Glory, glory, Hallelujah! . . . *as we go marching on.*"

Women wept; men wept;—and Karen kept walking.

She walked to Susie's room.

Someone had called Dr. Moore in a hospital on the other side of Philadelphia and as Karen got to Susie's bed, he came charging into the room. I couldn't hear what he said but I watched him kneel in front of Karen, gather her in his arms and hold her close against him. The imperturable doctor had tears in his eyes.

Head against his cheek, her face radiant with gratitude and joy, Karen murmured— "Thank you, thank you!. *You* did this for me!"

ॐ

chapter seven

Verily, Independence Day! We agreed it was eminently suitable that Karen came home on the Fourth of July and six weeks ahead of schedule. Her previous homecoming was as nothing compared to the jubilation of this occasion.

During our absence, Marie and Gloria had acquired an English bell, used during air raids. Its voice was shatteringly loud and raucous; it had to be, to recall their wandering brother from his hunting for buried pirate's treasure, and prospecting for solid silver and solid gold rocks in the far reaches of the cove.

As the crow flies (and we have flocks of them) the Larchmont Yacht Club was a bare quarter-mile away. Following the coastline northwest, with its deep cuts and humped points of rocks, the Club was a mile from us to our left. To our right was the Shore Club and both of these establishments put on a Fourth of July fireworks display that was extravagantly beautiful.

As soon as it was dark, Jimmy and Marie and Rory went

out to the end of the breakwater, some two hundred and fifty yards from the house, from which point they could get a panoramic view. After the excitement and exhaustion of the trip home, it would have been too much for Karen to be pushed through heavy sand and jounced across the rocks, so Joe and Gloria and Shanty and I sat with her on the porch.

The displays, (which Rory insisted: "Would be all for you Karen, if people only knew how brave you are"—) started promptly at 9:00 p.m. We, from our position on the porch, saw more than we bargained for. A stiff breeze had come up, enough to warrant small craft warnings, and a host of smoldering, colorful rocket flakes were blown inland. There was quite a fall over the roof of Mr. King's house, and this, Jimmy was watching from the tip of the breakwater.

Without thinking I picked up the air raid bell from its place on the floor. "Could they hear it so far out on the breakwater?" I asked Glo.

"I imagine so."

"Let's test it. I'll ring it and when they come in we'll ask them." I stood at the railing and swung the bell madly for several seconds. Simultaneously there was the long, eerie wail of a fire siren, the roar of the trucks as they tore past our house to King's, and Shanty's wild, insensate barking.

"Holy smoke!" said Glo, intending no pun, "Mr. King must think his roof has caught fire—but you can see it's all right."

Looking toward King's I saw, in the pale glow of the street light, a figure racing across the grass on the far side of the beach fence. It did not veer to reach a gate but in a gigantic bound cleared the fence and tore toward the porch.

"It's Daddy—" yelled Karen above the dog's earsplitting yowls.

Jimmy charged up the street and took the steps three at a time. "Move!" he shouted, then saw the engines were at King's. He collapsed on a chair and in the light of the kerosene lamp, his face was ashen.

"Poor darling, you thought it was here." My voice was warm with wifely compassion. "What a fright those engines gave you."

"*Engines be damned!*" He was still gasping for breath and the words issued explosively. "*You!*" As his gasping decreased, the timbre of his voice became positively fierce. "*You and your damned bell!*"

"You heard it?" I was pleased.

"Heard it! I took it as a *fire summons*. Shut up!" He shouted at Shanty who was still in full cry.

"Oh, Daddy," Karen unwisely intervened on behalf of her dog.

"Don't 'Oh Daddy' me," he glared at us in turn. "I could see you all burned to death before I reached you.

Shanty and Karen subsided.

"I'm sorry. I'm sick about giving you such a fright." I was really worried, he looked like death.

He stood up. "You'll be a lot sicker when you see my good pants." He turned his back and there was a large, gaping hole in the seat.

"Oh—NO!" He was right—I was sicker. "The material's *gone*—not just torn—but gone!"

"You will find it," he hissed with impressive vocal control, "on the fence. The one I went over to get home in time to rescue you."

"But you looked like a gazelle—"

"Well, I feel like a damn fool."

Karen unwisely contributed: "You've said 'damn' three times."

"Oh, hell!" He backed into the house and slammed the door.

Marie and Rory came up the steps. "I'm sure glad we're not on fire. King's is all right too. We checked," Marie told us.

"Yeah!" agreed Rory and I thought I detected a note of disappointment. He lit a sparkler. "Think of it Karen, the fire department sent you off, and welcomed you home."

"Where's Daddy?" Marie asked.

Joe, who had wisely kept silent through the fracas, answered honestly: "He's inside; cooling off."

"Some run!" Rory's eyes gleamed with pride at his father's athletic prowess.

"I wouldn't refer to it for a while," I suggested. "Daddy was a little upset."

As a special coming-home treat, Rory was allowed to sleep in Karen's room that night. The last item on the retirement agenda was Karen's imprisonment in plaster. I doubt that packing a Rembrandt for shipment was ever more painstakingly executed than this entombment in casts. The girls and Rory watched fascinated, as the lower shells were placed in position on the bed and Karen's legs laid therein. A number of spots had to be padded with cotton and the top shell then put in place. There could not be the slightest deviation of position as they were exactly the contour of the legs. Jimmy then took wide strips of adhesive tape and while I held the casts slightly elevated above the bed, he strapped them shut. It was tricky, for in raising and holding and strapping, we mustn't shift the position of the paster so much as a centimeter, or the fit would be wrong and considerable discomfort would ensue.

"This will take a bit of practice," Jimmy said as we started all over again for the sixth time.

"And patience," amended Karen, watching her perspiring father.

"That he has aplenty," said Marie, unwinding some more tape.

Glo held the scissors and Rory fetched some more cotton. Jimmy laughed. "I didn't realize this job would require a team!"

"And what a team!" I looked at the faces of my children; there was no smallest trace of fretfulness, nothing but interest and loving compassion. "This is a good thing for them," I thought, "to learn the joy of service so early in life." I was reminded of Dr. Menninger's definition of a well-adjusted person— "One who has learned that it is better to give than to receive."

"You're very well-adjusted," I murmured to my brood.

Jimmy looked up. "What did you say?"

"Nothing."

An hour and a half later Karen was ready for sleep; rigid, flat on her back. Rory hopped into the adjoining bed. He propped himself up on his elbow and surveyed his sister. "She can't turn over!"

Gently I put him down. "That's right."

"I turn all the time in bed. I'm not comfortable staying in one position."

"You'd get used to it," Karen reassured him.

"Yeah?" He was not convinced. Neither was I.

Long after their light was out they talked and, as we had so often done when they shared the same room in Rye, we sat on the floor outside the door and listened.

Rory tried to direct Karen into a clinical discussion of her hospital stay. She recited tales of fellow patients, but of her own experiences she said only that Philadelphia water was foul.

We heard the springs give as Rory left his bed and sat on hers. "If you get too hot in those darn things let me know and I'll get you some very, very cold water."

"I'll be fine, but you're sweet."

"I'm not." Indignantly. "Men aren't sweet."

"Oh yes they are," Karen soothed him. "Daddy's sweet —he's always thinking of other people first." There was a silence. "For instance—you know he likes chocolate-covered jellies but if there's one in a box he always gives it to Mother because she likes them. And remember how he got up every two hours at night to feed those orphaned baby wrens? Now do you see what I mean?"

"Uh huh." Another silence. With the facile irrelevance of the young, Rory announced: "I got into trouble when you were away."

Karen's voice was anxious. "What did you do?"

"I didn't do anything wrong. Gloria found me in the park smoking. She wouldn't let me talk at first—she just dragged me home and punished me."

"But you knew you shouldn't."

"I did not. Mummy said never light a match and I didn't. I had Tim light the match. She *never* told me not to smoke."

A poorly suppressed giggle from Karen.

"It wasn't funny. I stayed in my room a whole afternoon before Gloria listened and saw she was unfair."

"I'm sure she was sorry."

"Yes. She apologized and was so sorry she baked me

97.

some brownies so it wasn't bad after all."

"Poor Shanty," Karen said next, "he's miserable because he can't sleep on my bed."

"He can sleep on mine," Rory offered generously. We heard him get back into his own bed. "Come on Shanty," he invited, then a few seconds later, "He's with me but watching you. You can touch him if you reach your arm out all the way."

"My darlin' " Karen purred drowsily.

"Now he's happy."

Dr. Fay had told us that he wanted Karen to see an eye specialist, a Dr. Guibor in Chicago. Under the circumstances we were not looking forward to such a trip. Then we had a letter from Dr. Fay in which he said that Dr. Guibor was going to be in the East and had arranged to borrow an office from a friend in New York and would see Karen there. It was love at first sight. He ordered a number of procedures, no surgery, and we were to start off with eye exercises to strengthen weak muscles. When she heard this Marie exploded. "For the love of Pete! she does three hours of exercises a day now. *Can't she have glasses?*"

Jimmy laughed. "She'll have glasses in a month or so— but the exercises must continue for a while."

"Nuts!" ejaculated Marie with more feeling than elegance.

Shanty's constant attendance on Karen was more of a comfort than ever. We felt it important that she go out alone but we had to know if she fell for she couldn't get up without help. We didn't need to stay glued to a window as Shanty had a special bark to announce this calamity. When he gave voice to deep-throated dismay, I could also detect a stern note of disapproval of the whole dangerous business and of me in particular. But his joy at having Karen back on her feet was unmistakable. Jimmy said: "Shanty's tail is an apostrophe and he walks as though he were clapping hands."

As a result of the leg 'spread' which Karen now had, and the elimination of internal rotation, there was an activity open to her of which we had long despaired. She could straddle a horse! True, her balance was precarious but ride she did. We took all the children to Bob Gussenhoven's stable where he gave Karen special lessons. At the end of the month when I came to settle the bill there was none for Karen. "It's a joy," said Bob, "and please don't mention it again."

The kids came back from the ring one day and were in the yard waiting to dismount. Karen sat happily inhaling the stable smells. "What perfume!" She breathed in rapturously. A woman who had been down at the ring watching, came up to Karen and with more heart than wisdom said: "I notice you have to work to keep your balance."

"Yes, I do," agreed Karen cheerily.

Most tactlessly the lady drove on: "Aren't you afraid?"

"Sure," answered my daughter with a smile.

The woman stared then blurted, "Then why do you ride?"

Karen looked puzzled. "What's that got to do with it?"

Slowly the questioner's eyes travelled over the bright little face, then she reached up, laid her hand for a moment on Karen's knee, and turned away.

I think it was this brief encounter that finally ignited a spark. Since we had bought our house we had been searching for a name for it. The children had made many suitable suggestions, like MORTGAGE MART, but none was exactly right. That night at dinner I suggested the Latin for—"lift up your hearts"; there was immediate and unanimous approval, so our house became *Sursum Corda*.

For our wedding anniversary, the children had a sign made and we hung it on a birch tree at the end of the driveway. A week or so later I was out hanging up the wash. To two women walking down the street I was invisible behind the hedge. I couldn't see them either, but I could hear them. They stopped beneath the sign and one lady said to the other: "Oh, the Killileas have moved. I wonder what the Cordas will be like."

Inspired by her success at riding, Karen expressed a wish to learn to play the piano. We turned to a friend of ours, Dominick Tranzillo, talented composer and organist as well as pianist, and asked him to teach her. He agreed with alacrity. Karen was excited and complained of the length of the days prior to the first lesson. It never occurred to me that there could be some insurmountable obstacle to execution. The day Dominick came for the first instruction I went off to market leaving them alone on the theory that any lesson progresses better if mama is not hanging over the shoulder of teacher and pupil. When I came home I could hear Karen singing a Gregorian Credo in the living room. I went in and asked quickly, too quickly: "How did the piano lesson go?"

Karen looked from Dominick to me and her mouth trembled.

Dom said: "Karen has a very sweet voice, quite true, and we decided to switch from piano to singing." He put his arm around her shoulders. "She has a funny little quirk of her fingers and we've been laughing at the way they misbehave."

Karen smiled tremulously. "They're really funny. I'm disappointed but I have to laugh. I'm so double-jointed that all my knuckles cave in when I put any pressure on the keys. But I love singing . ." she hurried on, "and Dominick is going to teach me Gregorian chant and Gilbert and Sullivan."

"What a combination! I'm sure Piux X would find that an interesting blend. How about some iced coffee?" There was a familiar heaviness in my chest.

Karen looked at Dom. He gave her a little hug. "Not right now, thank you. Karen and I are going to sing some more. We're not yet ready for an audience," he dismissed me gently.

I was glad to go. I wondered—will she ever become inured to disappointment? I thought about this as I started dinner. Yes, I guess she could, but only if she ceased to aspire. We'll take the disappointment—thank you—to give up aspirations would be far costlier.

A.M. came in for a cup of coffee. "My own coffee tastes like sheep dip," she said as she poured herself a cup. "I've had an idea," she said lighting one cigarette from another. "Karen does a lot of practice-walking but she doesn't have a real goal, for when she gets to a house she can't go up the steps alone. I've been thinking of how she could walk with a productive purpose."

I sat down opposite her. "So have we—and we haven't come up with a thing."

"See what you think of this. A lawn mower is heavy. Now your lawn isn't flat enough, but if Karen came to my house, she could use the mower for support—no crutches —walk behind it, and cut grass as she walked. A purpose—" she reiterated.

"That's a great idea. We'll try it tomorrow."

From my bedroom window I watched as Karen tried this new approach. So did a lot of people who passed A.M.'s on the way to the beach. Karen had no trouble keeping her balance and though she walked very slowly she was able to push the machine and leave a satisfying wake of mown grass. A couple of hours later they came home and they were both tickled. Walking without crutches and doing something productive.

A.M. stayed for lunch and she and Karen spent a good part of the afternoon congratulating each other. About 5:00 p.m. I left them to go to Futterman's store for some carbon paper. I took my place beside two women standing at the counter. The first woman addressed her companion: "Do you know people named Schnirring? They live on the corner of Park Avenue across from the beach?"

"I don't think so," the second answered.

The first woman leaned closer to her friend. "I don't think you'd want to," she said in a stage whisper. "Wait 'til I tell you . ." she paused to make sure she had her partner's full attention. "This morning on the way to the beach, I passed Schnirring's house and—" she hesitated impressivley, "she had a *crippled child* cutting her grass!" She slapped her hands to her temples, "Imagine!"

"*No!*" gasped her companion.

"*Yes!*" with happy malice. "Isn't that *awful!*"

My laughter bubbled, then burst. They hadn't taken any notice of me before, but now they turned and watched me with amazed excitement. I finally controlled my sobbing hilarity, wiped my streaming eyes, introduced myself as the cripple's mother and went on to explain what a truly wonderful idea the grass cutting had been.

101.

As I talked, the speaker looked to the right of me, to the left of me, and over my head. A deep flush suffused her neck and face and she clasped and unclasped the catch on her handbag. I began to feel sorry for her. I tendered some comfort, "We all misjudge when we don't understand—and so often we can't understand. Please don't be upset." I then negated by giggling whatever solace I might have offered.

She gulped and fled, her companion walking hesitantly in her wake.

As soon as I got home, and with the best dramatic effects, I portrayed the scene for A.M. and Karen. They hooted with glee. Between gasps A.M. exclaimed: "It's rich—too rich! I can't wait to tell Bill, and the kids, and my bowling team. Oh, oh!" and she danced out of the kitchen.

"Your name will be mud," Karen called after her.

"And my grass will be cut. See you tomorrow." Her laugh bounced back to us.

ॐ

chapter eight

It was late August. On a summer day that never really came awake, I took a pad and pen out to the rocks to write a report to Dr. Moore, copy to Ed Doll, a report that was to vary little in the year to follow. I couldn't find enough quiet to do the necessary thinking at home.

Since the publication of *Karen*, the phone calls from anxious and/or frantic people had increased to thirty or forty a day. Many came to the house, uninvited, unannounced. It had become a serious problem and everyone's nerves were on edge. There was no such thing any more as an uninterrupted meal, uninterrupted therapy, uninterrupted anything. No possibility of working or resting quietly on the porch for a few minutes or trying to maintain a semblance of the order necessary to family living. In addition, the letters continued to pour in, now from abroad as well, since the book had been published in many foreign countries. A large percentage of the correspondence was congratulatory but the balance was from frightened, desperate families. Jimmy, Gloria and I shaved our hours of sleep down to five, but even this curtailment did not give us enough time. There were compensations: hundreds of letters from young men and women who said that after they had read *Karen* they had decided to go into the field of cerebral palsy, but they too wanted advice—what doctor should they study under? what states had the best programs? What scholarships were available? what colleges and universities had the best courses? All the letters had one thing in common—what was Karen doing now?

There were times when we felt that the weight of others' accumulated grief was insupportable, and we would put out a little more effort to be of assistance. Things had come to a point where, when we did go to bed, neither Jimmy nor I were sleeping. Too many shadows of too many problems hung above us. Desperately we turned to Father McSorley for advice. Father, a Paulist, had been guiding not only Jimmy and me, but our children for several years. He knew us inside out (as only a spiritual director can) and had a complete understanding of all the facets of our lives.

Jimmy and I recited the many, many situations with which we seemed unable to cope. Father listened attentively, asking only an occasional question. His serene attitude was in itself healing. Father had the face of a medieval scholar, and a great scholar he was; but it was his perfect priestliness that drew people to him from all over the world. In a XIV century manuscript I had read lines that depicted the full measure of his 'fatherhood'—"He abideth patiently, he forgiveth easily, he understandeth mercifully, he forgetteth utterly." We knew his compound of effectiveness—faith, love and humor, and the oft repeated phrase: "To those who love God, all things work together for good."

When Jimmy and I had finished our story, we sat back enormously relieved.

"It's very simple," Father said, a hint of smile in his voice, "you can't overload the lifeboat!"

Jimmy and I looked at each other. Jimmy interpreted first, "If you do, *everybody* drowns—right?"

"Right," Father answered quietly, looking intently at both of us. "Your *immediate* family, (for in a real sense all people are family) has priority. They need *both* parents and need them sound in *mind, body* and *spirit*. When they are assured of this daily, then and, then only, do you have the right to extend yourselves and you must always keep within these bounds. So it would seem that you have no choice but to learn to be tough—to say 'no.' In your circumstances, there will be many times when you should do nothing."

I leaned toward him and spoke urgently. "How can we? We know what they're going through—how desperate they are! They'll knock; they'll hammer doors down if need be to get help, *just the way we did!*"

Father's voice answered me quietly. "From what you and Jimmy have told me of the upheaval in your lives, and your children's, and realistically considering that it is going to get worse, I don't see that you have any choice."

Following his advice was terribly hard and was taking longer than it should, so, coward that I was, I fled to the rocks leaving Gloria, Marie and Joe to answer the phone and to deal with those who knocked at the door.

My rock jutted far out in the water and I sat within the cincture of a sequinned sea. Gulls coasted above me or hung motionless, suspended between sky and water. Flocks of sails gathered and dispersed, unhurriedly. The soft air was salty. I drew my eyes and my mind back to the job at hand. Unbidden, there came to my mind the picture of Karen when she was born, an infinitesimal mite 1 lb. 12 ozs., 9 inches long, but exquisitely formed. I thought of the nine months she had had to stay in hospital before she could come home to us. My thoughts leapt ahead five weeks from now; school would be opening, but not for her. There would be the trauma of another defeat. Then I saw her astride her horse, pigtails glinting on her shoulders, eyes laughing, and her pert face ashine with a gaiety distilled by suffering. I saw her walking painfully, but properly. I said to the heedless birds: "In thirteen years we've come a long, long way."

I took up my pen and began to write:

"Pain in the rump, I think gluteous maximus. Walking slowly but well. For three weeks pain and spasms increasing rapidly—day and night. Braces fit perfectly! NO PRESSURE ANY PLACE. God bless Mr. Greiner! Since surgery, Karen can propel her own wheel chair!

NIGHT REPORT

Sleep not before 11:00 p.m., sometimes 2:00 or 3:00 a.m., then interrupted several times; wakes crying, sometimes screaming. Have not removed casts until four days ago, again last night. Child soaked bed with sweat.

DAY REPORT

After talking to you we cut down on her walking efforts. She is carrying full therapy prescription. Severe pain in coccyx. Keeping brace locked only on left knee. She falls if lock slips open. When we unlock knee we get painful contractions. Pain in rump, sitting, standing, or walking. Describes pain 'like a knife.' Reports at times a noise 'like a click' when it happens.

Speaks the most beautiful words: *"Don't help me!"* This to drying herself, using deodorant, putting cap back on toothpaste which is a pretty fine finger motion."

I put down my pen and stared at the seaweed so gracefully undulating just below the surface of the water. The kind that Karen liked to pop. I prayed. I formulated no words nor even thoughts, just put myself in the presence of God, totally dependent.

As I was walking home across the sand, there came to me, as gentle as the brush of a summer's breeze—"I don't know what the future holds—but I do know God holds the future."

I came into the kitchen with unusual verve. "More bounce to the ounce," observed Gloria who was explaining to Joe the mysteries of concocting a cheese cake.

"A little, but oh so big an inspiration has given me a marvellous lift." I told her the thought that had come to me.

"That will help me too." She emptied the bowl into a pan. "I just had a letter from Russ. They have located his wife but two other key witnesses have died." She put the pan in the oven.

Wordlessly, Joe cleared the table of cooking utensils.

I bent over and kissed the back of her neck, and left the room without comment. What was there to say?

I was typing my report to Dr. Moore when Glo brought me a list of calls for the afternoon. The last on the list was Mother Mary Dolores from Good Counsel and would I please call her back. "I want to get this report to the post office, I'll call her when I get back. I'll bet she wants some information for a family who has a youngster with cerebral palsy."

When I reached Mother Mary Dolores she said she wished to talk to Jimmy and me on a personal matter and could we find the time to come over for a visit sometime Saturday afternoon.

"I knew it," I said to Glo when I hung up.

Karen went with us and Mother invited her to join us on the porch. We settled ourselves comfortably in old-fashioned wicker rockers, looking across wide lawns to an orchard and a garden.

There was some desultory conversation and I marvelled as I watched Mother Mary Dolores that anyone so dainty could be so queenly. Here was a woman—tranquil, reserved, yet one felt instantly a great humaneness. Her voice was low pitched and musical. "I became acquainted with Karen through our mutual friend, Maureen McKernan."

I spoke with unrestrained enthusiasm. "I cannot tell you, Mother, how helpful Maureen and the Macy newspapers were in launching our organization for cerebral palsy."

"You know she teaches journalism here?"

"You're fortunate. Many consider her the top woman journalist in the country."

Mother looked from me to Jimmy to Karen. "I asked you to come today so that I could tell you that we should like to have Karen come here to school."

A concerted gasp—

Silence.

A bee droned languidly by. A tiny breeze made faint tracings in the grass, found its way to the porch and softly stirred Mother's veil.

"Why?" I blurted, the word propulsed by years of denial.

Mother was smiling at Karen who sat, leaning slightly forward, breathing quickly, her lips parted, her cheeks flushed, her eyes glowing with incredulity and joy. "Because I think we can do a great deal for Karen—and—I'm sure Karen can do a great deal for us."

A simple statement. Less than two dozen words that would transform a life.

I whispered to myself, "Mother Mary Dolores, R.D.C., Religious of Divine Compassion indeed!"

Then we all started babbling at once—about opening date, uniforms, books, location of classroom, teacher. Marie and Karen could come together in the taxi pool. Mother was smilingly composed. We were frenetic. Our gratitude, like unleashed torrents cascaded about her.

Once off campus, we shouted and sang and quite exceeded the speed limit racing home with the great news.

We burst into the house, still shouting, and when the children grasped the import of our ravings, pandemonium broke loose.

The kids made out a list of friends who should receive telegrams heralding the glad tidings. "Western Union is a poor substitute for a horse, a rider and a clarion call!" Marie said.

Father McSorley's and Dr. Doll's went first. Dr. Fay's and Dr. Moore's followed.

Karen spent the next three days on the telephone. "Rejoice! Rejoice!"

107.

Our telegram to Dr. Moore had crossed his reply to my report. He sent a list of instructions and concluded: SHE'S WORKING TOO HARD. *SLOW HER DOWN*. Two hours later we received from him a responsive telegram. It was succinct: "HOORAY!"

Slowly the days crawled toward the First Day of School, but there was one item on our agenda that would make at least three days fly by—the first in preparation, the second in participation, the third in recuperation.

Every year, over the Labor Day week-end there is a real county fair at Goshen, Connecticut, and although we had a family policy of not travelling in a car on holiday week-ends, we made this the single exception. Jimmy knew the way to Goshen on back and dirt roads where there was little traffic. It would seem that we were all frustrated farmers at heart, for the sight of a spacious barn and a sturdy silo would evoke far more rapturous exclamations than the finest skyscraper in all of New York City.

It was a warm, soft September morning, the air heavy with the sweetness of salt, when we left Larchmont shortly after sunrise. Driving through New England villages we attracted more than a few prolonged stares. They were not hard to interpret for our packed station wagon and the passengers bore more than a slight resemblance to the Joad family. We might be city-folk, but *we* knew how to "dress" for a country fair. Bare-legged of course, the children in dungarees (with only a few paint stains), gingham shirts and old sweaters. Daddy in chinos and Mommy in a very old, very faded cotton print skirt and a mocha-colored blouse that had once been brown. There was an incongruous dash of elegance in Karen's smart, protective, yellow linen, Cavanagh cap.

Our piled baggage overflowed the tailgate. There were hampers with cold chicken, sandwiches, cucumbers, tomatoes, pickles, bananas, apples, oranges, plain crackers, cookies, several thermoses of hot coffee and several more of cold milk and fruit juice. There were blankets and pillows for the late ride home, a battered suitcase of extra sweaters and jackets, raincoats, rubbers and overshoes, facial tissue, two ponchos and two sets of foul-weather gear borrowed from the sailing bag, Karen's wheel chair, crutches, two collapsible chairs. And Shanty. That great red brute had long ago learned that he had to adapt himself to the most trying driving conditions if he was to accompany Karen, and he could slither in and around packings and find purchase in an unbelievably small space. Counting Shanty there were eight of us including a friend of Marie's, Sheila Kelly. Joe couldn't go. He was working.

We hadn't driven far into the Connecticut hills when great black, humped clouds began racing across the sky like buffalo over the plains. In an hour they gathered into an impenetrable herd—and then the rains came. We drove the remaining forty miles through a steady downpour and only as we entered Goshen did the skies lighten and the downpour slacken. But we were prepared. We sloshed round the fair grounds, ankle deep in mud wearing our galoshes. The only real problem was pushing the wheel chair. Jimmy tilted it back on the rear wheels, grasped the handles tightly, lowered his head like an angry bull and charged. It was hard work, his feet kept slipping, but he bore on, missing no tent, no exhibit. The rewards were great: The children were present at the birth of a calf to a beautiful Jersey; the hogs were splendid; the roosters exotic; the oxen weight-pulling contest more exciting than any competition at Belmont; the cabbages like jade green mounds of procelain; the preserved fruits and vegetables masterpieces of color and symmetry. At noon we sat in a tent filled with spicy fragrances and had a delectable dinner served by the American Legion. In the adjacent tent a band played with gusto.

The rain continued.

We spent a wonderfully ambrosial hour with lambs and sheep. When we left them the going was slower than ever. Jimmy, forced to pause for breath, glanced over his shoulder. *"Look!"* Not ten feet behind us, the tent canvas, insupportably weary from the thousands of pounds of water it had been holding, gave up the struggle and slowly caved in.

The wind increased to gale force.

We were all tired just from pulling our feet out of the

mud. Slowly we made our way to the stands where, huddled under ponchos and top-siders, in solitary enjoyment we watched the teams of Percherons and Clydesdales and the parade of the bulls. The last massive creature was just plodding out of the ring when over the loudspeaker came a sepulchral voice: "We have a report—as yet unsubstantiated—that this storm is the beginning of a hurricane. *We urge you to clear the Fair Grounds!*"

Nobody needed any urging. Certainly not us. With incredible swiftness, the tents were struck and there ensued an exodus the like of which I never again expect to witness —an outpouring of people and animals, a debacle of churning mud, bellowing cattle, cackling fowl, squealing pigs, barking dogs, yelling herdsmen, profane exhibitors, shouting spectators. We steered a wide course away from the melee and by a circuitous route came at length and at last to the haven of the car.

We loaded in record time and started for home. We were all shivering more from excitement than chill. The children hugged themselves and burrowed under blankets. We turned on the car radio and heard that this was the fringe of the hurricane moving rapidly east away from us, and the forecast for the rest of the day was intermittent rain.

We hadn't been driving long when Jimmy turned off the road and followed a dirt track some half mile through tobacco fields to a huge tobacco barn. He stopped the car and ordered us all out. Shanty was ecstatic and ran circles around Karen as Jimmy wheeled her in. We brought in our hampers, our suitcase and a baseball and bat. We stripped off sodden shirts and sweaters and pulled on dry ones. While I spread the blanket and put out the sumptuous repast, the kids and Jimmy played baseball, Karen umpiring from her wheel chair. The high-ceiling barn was about three hundred feet long and sixty feet wide. Shouts slapped the walls and bounced upward to vibrate above us.

"Dinner is served!"

Between mouthfuls and gulps of scalding coffee—

110.

"Does rain whet the appetite?"

"Bad pun."

"I like puns with coffee."

"I don't like them any time."

"You're a snob."

"I wish I could have brought that calf home with me."

Mother: "There was the most beautiful rooster—" I sighed.

"You and your roosters."

"How many have you now?"

"Thirty-one, but they're not alive."

Father: "Good thing."

"Isn't this exciting?"

"I feel like a pioneer. Pass me the olives."

"I liked the black sheep best."

"Why can't we have one? It would keep the grass cut?"

"What grass?"

"We have more than enough livestock."

"Enough for whom?"

"For me," said Jimmy and I in duet and with feeling.

We stretched out on our backs and luxuriated in the rest, the dryness and the warmth. The barn was dimly quiet. I could see Jimmy's eyelids drooping. "Come on," I got up, though reluctantly, "we have over seventy miles to drive and we must be alert!"

"Yeah." Jimmy rolled over on his side.

"Rouse your father, children." They were a little too enthusiastic and grumbling, Jimmy got to his feet. At forty, one doesn't have quite the resilience one had at thirty, and he had waded and pushed through miles of mud.

The loading was well organized and in twenty minutes we were ready to start. "Just a moment." I grabbed my purse and ran back into the barn. I took out a pad and pencil and write: "Dear Host, we wish to thank you for the haven you afforded us and for the happy two hours we spent in your lovely barn." I signed it and stuck it on a nail where it would surely be seen. I looked around once more to be sure we had left our refuge as elegantly ordered as we had found it.

Jimmy, I thought, needed rest, so I drove. I kept to back roads and we saw very few cars. We wound up hill and down dale. The highway was very narrow, and the twisting road was unfamiliar so I drove most attentively. In the back, the kids were singing with more volume than finesse. Ahead, the black macadam snaked up a steep hill to a hairpin turn. As I approached the bottom of the hill I saw a car speeding toward me, around the turn and on the wrong side of the white line. I slowed down to give him plenty of time to get back in the northbound lane. A second —two seconds—and I realized that he was going to continue speeding directly at us. With this realization my driving became automatic; my reflexes took over. To left and right were fences—no place to drive off the road. The car raced toward us—dead ahead. I accelerated, but not too much or I'd have jumped the fence; swerved sharply into the guard rail on the right to avoid a head-on collision. As we hit, the car crashed into us, ricocheted across the road into the fence on the other side. The noise was deafening—then silence. Total. Paralyzing.

How long I sat stunned I don't know, but I was brought back to awareness by Karen's voice piping from rear: "What a time I picked to take off my protective hat!"

Jimmy had his arms around me. "Darling, darling, are you all right?"

"Yes. Are you?"

"Yes." He turned to the children. They sat pale and still. "Don't shake your head. Answer yes or no. Does anybody hurt any place?"

A chorus of feeble "no's"—and Karen amended: "Shanty is O.K. too."

"You see to them." He jumped out and across the road to the other car.

"*Don't move,*" I told the kids, "until I've checked you." Carefully, thoroughly, I went over each: "Do you hurt anywhere?" "Can you move your fingers—your toes?" "Any headache?" "Any dizziness?" "Any nausea?" "Any discomfort in your neck?—your back"

"No, no, no, no, no, no," from each in turn and Rory added reassuringly: "No blood."

The windows on the left had been thoroughly smashed but I found not a scratch on the children. Marie was on the right side of the car. When I was sure she was all right, I rolled down her window and told her to lean forward and inhale deeply for the car was stuffy and hot. She did so. Immediately she turned ashen, her respiration became rapid and shallow and she trembled violently. She was in shock. I grabbed a blanket and wrapped it around her. I was feeling queer myself and I put my head out the window for a gulp of air. No wonder she had gone into shock! From this position one couldn't see the guard rail, it was under the car, and we seemed to be hanging over the drop below. Behind me, cringing in her seat, Sheila kept asking like a broken record: "Would anyone like an aspirin?"

Shanty barked and I became aware of voices and forms outside the car. A young man pulled open the front door and climbed in. "I can't believe you weren't all killed!"

"How about the men in the other car?" I asked him.

"Unharmed—and very drunk. Anyone here hurt?"

"I have one young lady in shock."

"We live in that house up there," he pointed to a grotesque Victorian monstrosity athwart a steep and barren hill. It looked like the set of a Hitchcock movie. "I better take the children up to my wife. My friend," he inclined his head briefly over his shoulder, "lives in the same house. We'll take the dog too."

I hesitated. Strangers, and, now so dark, I couldn't even see their faces.

He interpreted my reluctance. "I think it wise to get them out of the car as fast as we can. There are no street lights, no flares, and chances are another car will come along and plow into this one. You might not be so lucky a second time." He started backing out of the car. "It's still raining hard and the visibility is nil."

That decided me. I climbed out between the two young men. The first man said: "This is Frank and I'm Bob Herbst."

I explained about Karen.

"No problem," said Bob, "I'll carry her."

"I'll shepherd the others," said Frank. "How about the dog?"

"He'll follow Karen."

Bob leaned through the door, slid Karen over, lifted her out and took her in his arms. "I'm not fragile," she told him putting an arm around his neck. "I never break."

Shanty circled Bob, sniffing questioningly.

"It's O.K. fellow," Karen said to him, "come on."

Apparently satisfied, the dog offered no objection to the porter, took his place at Bob's side and paced along with him.

Frank summoned the others and turned to me. "We called the Troopers when we heard the crash. You'd best wait for them, they shouldn't be long." They trudged off, Glo with her arm around Marie who walked waveringly, shivering and shaking inside her blanket.

I saw Rory reach up and take Frank's hand.

"Bless these Samaritans," I whispered as I leaned against a post waiting for the police. People had gathered round and a man said to me: "Boy, are you lucky!"

I wiped the rain from my face. "It was a miracle!"

"You don't know how much of a miracle. There used to be an old wooden fence here." He pulled his collar higher around his neck. "It was rotted through. They put in this new one *this week!*"

Two State Police cars arrived. One man went across the road to the other car. Another set up flares and a third seemed busy with a tape measure. The fourth came over to me. "I'll call my husband," I said to him.

"We'll question you separately." He was kind but firm. He took out a notebook and a pen. "Who was driving the car?"

"I was." I had trouble speaking so he could hear me. Talking seemed to require more air than I could get into my lungs.

He looked at me closely. "You don't look so good. You'd better sit down—we'll go to my car." He took my arm and I found I needed his support to walk. My legs were like mush and and slow to respond.

We got into the rear seat and I leaned my head against

114.

its back. I felt so tired.

"How many passengers in the car?"

I didn't answer right away. I had to count and I had trouble counting. Finally I said: "Eight—counting the dog."

"Who are they and what are their names?"

"My husband, four children, and a friend." The words came slowly.

"Their names?" he prompted.

"My husband . . . Jimmy." A long minute passed. "Jimmy . . . and . . ." I repeated: "Jimmy . . ." But it was no use. I couldn't remember their names.

He glanced at me with puzzled solicitude.

"I can't remember."

"We'll come back to that. Was it raining?"

I closed my eyes and tried to force my mind back, but it just wouldn't go. "I don't know."

"Were your windshield wipers on?"

I tried pushing my mind again. "I don't remember."

"How dark was it?"

"I don't remember."

"Were your lights on?"

I struggled so hard for recollection I broke out in a sweat. "I can't remember." My voice trembled.

He turned sideways so he was looking directly at me. He asked softly and with no hint of impatience: "Suppose you tell me just what you can remember. Don't push now. Relax, and see what comes to you."

"May I have a cigarette?"

He gave me one and lit it.

"I remember a voice . . ." I began uncertainly. I felt a hand on my arm and turned to the door. Jimmy was there.

"A voice—" the trooper encouraged.

"I remember—" I felt relieved and pleased to recall something. "I heard a voice praying. It was loud and clear."

My uniformed companion gave me a very strange look, slowly closed his notebook and put it in his pocket.

Jimmy spoke. "It was you, honey."

"Me?" But this was too big a problem to wrestle with.

To Jimmy my questioner said: "You may as well take

her along." To me he said: "Don't worry lady, I've seen this sort of thing happen before."

"Thank you. You've been kind."

So far as the accident went, I was to know two years of blankness. When memory did return, it took time, and came back in bits and pieces.

ॐ

chapter nine

On the wall of Karen's room, we hung a three foot square calendar on which, with great ceremony, we daily crossed off the blocks before the start of school. We had only two days left.

It was early morning and she and I were doing therapy. As always I was working with my eyes closed. This way I could "feel deep." As I held her legs and moved them to get maximum abduction, I remarked: "You seem warm."

She didn't answer me.

We were half done when she said in a small voice: "Mom Pom, I feel very sick."

I was arrested by the adjective, so unlike Karen to say 'very' sick. I opened my eyes and looked at her carefully. She certainly didn't look right and her cheeks were bright beyond the effort of therapy. "I'm going to take your temp." I fetched the thermometer, handed it to her and sat down to wait. For the last two days she had been coughing a bit and now that I thought about it, she hadn't been eating well. But Karen was never sick so I hadn't paid much attention to either symptom.

She handed me the thermometer; I read one hundred and two degrees. I shook it down. "How long have you been feeling punk?"

"A couple of days."

"Why didn't you tell me?"

116.

"I can't be sick. It's only two days to the beginning of school."

I took her hand, "Do you hurt anywhere?"

"Yes. Here." She put her hand on her chest.

I went to the phone. "We'll see what Dr. Virginia has to say."

When the doctor had my report she said: "I'll be down as soon as I can get there."

She came in about an hour and her examination was lengthy and thorough. I walked out to the kitchen with her. "Well?"

"She has pneumonia."

"Damn and double damn!" ejaculated Gloria who was standing by.

Marie and Rory came into the room. "What's the matter?" I told them.

Marie exploded: "She can't have. School starts the day after tomorrow!"

Rory kicked the wall and bolted from the room.

The doctor went to the phone and called in a prescription. When she had finished she said: "It's a shame." She picked up her bag. "You know what to do. How many times has Marie had pneumonia?"

"Thirteen or fourteen."

She nodded. "You are experienced." She went back into Karen's room. We couldn't hear what she was saying but her voice was soft and matter-of-fact. I smiled at the girls: "When Dr. Virginia gets through talking, Karen will be more cheerful."

Karen was very ill that night. She seemed to breathe more easily when her shoulders were elevated, so we ensconced her under blankets in a club chair in the living room, and Glo and I made up beds on the floor. Karen vomited frequently and we were busy rushing basins and clean sheets and blankets. At 2:00 a.m. the washing machine emitted a great groan, a whine of agony, and gave up the ghost. Glo and I had to laugh. This was the third time it had died during an emergency. We took turns the rest of the night washing bed linen and towels in bathtubs.

Karen was unable to retain any of the antibiotic so her

temperature continued to climb. The doctor came early in the morning and used a suppository to control the vomiting. An hour later, she was able to keep down the first capsule, and by nightfall the fever had decreased. We had an anxious three days before Karen was out of the woods, and the big question then was how quickly she'd recuperate. She kept hounding the doctor and on the tenth day Dr. Haggerty said: "I'm sure you'll be ready to start school September 28."

The night of the 27th, great preparations were made. Glo said: "How thrilling to make lunches for *three!*" We sharpened pencils, filled pens, and packed them with pristine pads, in a shiny new book bag. We set our alarms for 5:45 a.m. (as if we'd need an alarm) for Karen would have to have her casts removed, an hour of therapy, braces put on before she could get dressed, and have her hair brushed and braided. The cab would come at 8:00. The students were not yet wearing their uniforms so we had bought Karen a red and white candy-striped dress with a white linen Peter Pan collar, and Joe had brought wide red ribbons for her hair. Jimmy polished her shoes until they glowed like old mahogany.

"This is going to be a painful separation for Shanty," Jimmy said as the great dog took his place on Karen's bed for the night. (It had taken Shanty just a few experiments to figure out how to stretch lengthily on the bed so he wouldn't touch the casts.)

NOTES FROM MOTHER'S DIARY
ON KAREN'S FIRST DAY AT SCHOOL

Monday, Sept. 28

Temp. 63°
Humidity 15%
Sun brilliant
Marsh grass shiny
Water dazzling
Gulls loquacious

Called Jimmy to come down and waken Karen with me. Kids heard us and came down too. Rory ran ahead of us into her room. Karen was already awake. Rory danced over and grabbed her, hugged and kissed her and hugged her some more. Shanty lolloped around getting in everybody's way.

Decided to skip therapy. Afraid of too much fatigue the first day on top of too much excitement.

Karen sang while we took her casts off; sang while she washed; sang while we put her braces on. She asked: "What am I having for breakfast?"

"Oatmeal, orange juice, toast, milk, eggs."
"Wonderful! Just wonderful!"
This was her breakfast menu four days a week.

While she pretended to eat she talked, talked, talked. Put small amount in mouth, slight chew, swallow, talk.

Marie looked lovely in corn-colored blouse, dark green skirt. Never said a word but kept her eyes on Karen throughout breakfast.

Karen had paper bag with lunch in front of her. I said: "Where will you carry your dime for milk?"
She answered: "Scotch tape it to the bag."
"Did you say your morning prayers?"
"The minute I woke up and I started with a thanksgiving."

Taxi horn. She put on her cap. White linen for this outfit.

Rory carried her crutches and I wheeled her to the cab. With the new timetable I had not allowed the time necessary for her to walk out. And horror of horrors: she had to leave without brushing her teeth. Move schedule ahead 15 minutes tomorrow.

Shanty made himself very small and tried to wriggle through car door after her. Fortunately no time for farewells to him or cats or kittens. Karen instructed: "Give Shanty a lot of attention and love while I'm gone. He's going to be excruciatingly lonely."

Glo said: "He's not the only one," and looked forsaken.

119.

Rory said: "The cats will cheer him up."

We took turns leaning through the cab window kissing Karen good-bye. Rory took two turns. "Be good, honey; have fun; hurry home."

Marie laughed. "He's going to make us late."

"Good-bye! Good-bye! Good-bye. . . ."

Jimmy tore off for his bus, a half hour behind schedule. Gloria. Rory and I raced around to the front of the house and stood on the wall waving as the car went by. Karen didn't even look up at the house until we yelled. After all, she was on her way.

Rory pranced around until I sternly reminded him that if he didn't get a move on he was going to be late for school. He pranced up the street. A few minutes later he came back; he'd forgotten his lunch. He left. He returned. He'd forgotten his milk money.

I bet this is one day he'll come home from school on time.

Jimmy called at 9:15. Made much small talk. Glo and I felt a little less lonely. He said we should keep busy. That's not hard.

2:00 p.m. Shanty still lying at end of driveway, watching for car that took Karen away. Wouldn't leave even to get his dinner.

How quiet is the house!

How full is my heart!

⁊∾

chapter ten

Russ had finished his years in the Air Force and was coming home. He wrote that he would like us to look around for a house for him; he stipulated *not* close to Larchmont, he didn't think it wise to live within droppin'-in distance of Gloria.

Gloria agreed.

He asked further, if we would please find him a place where he could keep goats—he hastened to explain . . . all too easy for a bachelor to stay in town, on the town. Therefore he would have female goats, breed them, and he would have to come home every evening to milk them. If possible, he would like a place where he could do some hunting on his own land; a fireplace was a must, and he would be ever so pleased if there was an artesian well—! He'd like a barn, so he wouldn't have to build one, so keep that in mind too. Try for at least three acres. Of course, the price range was restricted! He guessed that was all and he was confident that our search would result in just what he wanted. Oh, yes, one more thing, he'd like to be near a lake for fishing.

He was a lot more confident than we, who had house-hunted for seven years before finding just what we wanted —and with no goats to consider. But it was a challenge and each member of the family welcomed it as such.

Week-end after week-end we set out on our hunting expedition. We centered our search on upper Westchester County working east from the Hudson River. It was delightful to have a legitimate excuse to leave chores of house and maintenance, and spend hours driving across the hills, through pine forests, around lakes placidly reflecting cottony clouds, running through deep valleys, exploring dirt roads. We picnicked beside streams full from abundant summer rains that sounded Rory said: "like an orchestra tuning up." We consumed gallons of fresh-pressed cider and put in a winter's supply of bright, hard McIntosh apples.

It was a Fall day of extraordinary clarity and beauty—a day of metals and jewels. The trunks of beech, aspen, and birch were silver and platinum spears; hardwoods flamed like rubies or glowed with the subdued lustre of garnets. There were tiered trays of topaz, gold, copper and brass, and emerald pines against a sapphire sky.

We had looked at three houses miles apart and were of

two minds whether to call it quits or to drive some distance to see the last house on the list. We decided to press on.

Some ten miles later we circled a lake and found the road to the house. It snaked sharply up and down heavily wooded hills, chasmed by steep walls with frequent outcroppings of granite; it plunged tortuously into a ravine, and followed a stream which raced between banks of pine and cedar. We passed only an occasional house, faultlessly colonial, redolent of the history of Yorktown.

We rounded a turn and Jimmy cried: *"Look!* There's Russell's house!"

It, too, was colonial, red with white trim. Set some distance from the road, it nestled at the foot of a tree-burdened hill. Before it and beside it were elm, maple, and oak, several hundred years old, that stood in a carpet of tumbled leaves, brilliant and varied as an Oriental rug.

"Look!" yelled Rory, *"A barn!"* It was small, neat, straight, and snug.

"That clinches it," approved Jimmy. He took out the sheet on which the broker had written all the information and read: "Built 1763. Originally a snuff factory, later used as house and shop by a cobbler. Six rooms, 2 baths, large sleeping porch." Jimmy paused and then read dramatically: "Fireplace, artesian well, fine landscaping including boxwood, flowering bushes, herb garden, perennials and berry bushes."

"Let's go in!"

We crossed a front porch that ran the length of the house. We stepped into a small hallway off which was a powder room, and turned right into a beamed living room—with a fireplace. Beyond was a small dining room with windowed walls on three sides.

"It's like a doll house!"

"It's a perfect gem."

I had discovered something that filled me with envy. I invited their attention. "Observe the floors—all of them—the original boards with their wooden pegs." I looked up—"and the original beams. What stories they could tell."

We trooped up a narrow staircase. Two bedrooms and a sleeping porch around two sides of the house. Closets and the bath. On the third floor, one large bedroom and a big walk-in cedar closet. Everything was dry and there was that sweet odor of time that only really old houses have.

Rory skipped out to investigate the barn. We stood in the dining room watching. Dusk was dimming the colors and the north side of the barn was in shadow. We could just make out Rory's figure. Suddenly he stopped and stood still as a statue. For a full minute he didn't move—just stared ahead. We pressed to the windows to discover what so riveted his attention. Not ten feet from him stood a splendid buck. Rory must have spoken then, for the buck wheeled and vanished into the woods.

"That *really* clinches it!" said Jimmy.

"Let's get home—quick—so we can call Russ." Gloria was all but hopping with excitement.

She reached him on the first try and rapturously and minutely described the house and land.

"What did he say?" Jimmy asked when she had hung up. She smiled impishly, "Not much."

"Well—what?" I urged.

"He said, 'All this and heaven too!' "

Practical Jimmy. "But does he want to buy it?"

"Tomorrow."

When we were alone Jimmy said wistfully: "That would make a wonderful honeymoon house."

I answered more tartly than I intended: "Don't even *think* such a thing. The last word from the church lawyers was as hopeless as the first."

"Oh, God! If there were only something we could do!"

Shopping around for furniture for Russ's house was a welcome diversion from the ever mounting problems of the national cerebral palsy organization.

When I had drawn the Certificate of Incorporation for this organization it had been with two ideas in mind: that this organization should perform those functions beyond the scope of the local groups—mainly research; that the national group could assist the locals but *for only so long as that assistance was needed;* and that there *must* be *local autonomy.* Further, that the national organization was only a *vehicle,* and the prevention, education, and treatment of those with cerebral palsy—the *goal*.

During a trip to Yorktown to deliver a couple of end tables, I had a time of uninterrupted quiet in which to analyze and evaluate the present operation of the national association. I sat on an orange crate in Russ's living room, took a large sheet of paper and drew a line down the center. Under headings—"PRO" and "CON" I listed item after item.

The conclusion was inescapable and unbearably painful. On October 27th, I wrote my letter of resignation from the United Cerebral Palsy Association, cherishing the hope that the local groups would, where necessary, be the loving parent that disciplines the child.

This letter of resignation, giving the reasons for my action, I sent only to the members of the Board of Directors and despite considerable pressure from members of the press, I did not release it. Jimmy pointed out, lest I be tempted, that I did not have the right to protect my reputation at the risk of undermining public confidence in even one local group.

In the months that followed we set up our own foundation —not an organization—eschewed all publicity, and went on to help where we could. We incorporated under the name of the Karen Foundation and had two provisos.

1) Karen and her family could never use any of the Foundation funds.

2) *No monies could be spent on administration.*

This last stipulation put a considerable strain on Jimmy's salary and my royalties, but looking to the future we considered it essential.

November was a momentous month. . . .

Rory discovered dandelions blooming. . . .

Karen brought home a report card on which the lowest mark was 83%. Her average 88%. This success had to be shared and she made innumerable telephone calls. "Isn't she bragging?" Rory asked Jimmy.

"Yes," he answered, "and I think it's good . . . in this isolated instance," he added carefully.

In this month Karen gave a demonstration of superb objectivity. A visiting youngster asked her what was the matter with her legs. A good healthy approach. Karen answered that she had cerebral palsy. The youngster wanted to know what it was. Karen explained that C.P. was any injury to the brain (and could happen to people of all ages) that affected the control of muscles. "What was your injury? Why do you have it?" asked the visitor.

And Karen replied: "They won't know for sure until they do an autopsy."

It was in this fateful month that we met Father Dominic Rover, who was to be so much help in some turbulent days ahead. . . .

We came to know and love Grace Oursler who was to have an enormous influence on all our lives. Her first note to us read in part: ". . . and one of the nicest gifts I have had from the Lord this year is knowing you. Please kiss each of the family on the back of the neck tonight for—Your Grace." She was a beautiful woman of fine intellect, humor, great sentiment and no sentimentality. I never saw another woman walk with the consummate grace that was peculiarly hers. It was Grace who took Karen to the theatre frequently and *without* mama and papa; she who introduced Gloria, Marie and Rory to the New York of Meyer Berger. She arranged for us to meet Phil and Carla Wallach and it was Phil who agreed to 'manage' me when Grace persuaded me to yield to the urgings of Stu Daniels and become a professional lecturer. As a result of her confidence and tender badgering, I began to write pieces for magazines and a few newspapers. A writer herself, she was what every writer needs, dreams of, and rarely finds—that companion who by questions, silences, interest, and enthusiasm evokes from the author ideas, plots and characters whose presence he never suspected. She loved us all, but being a woman of great perspicacity, she loved Jimmy best.

And at the end of the month momentous, Ed Doll came to stay with us for a few days. On his trips East, Ed usually arranged to make our house his last visitation, perhaps because the days with us made such demands on his energies and his time.

Any family can profit through a close relationship with a

sane psychologist, but how much more do the families of exceptional children need loving as well as wise counsel. With time we encountered constantly shifting situations which required continuing readjustments of attitudes and aims on the part of each member of our family; and with time, the strands of interfamily relationships became more and more intricately interwoven and complicated. Informed anticipation prepared us for new developments, thus insulating us against mistakes and disappointments.

We had family meetings with Ed, and individual consultations. He took Rory and Karen separately on long walks during which confidences were exchanged and counsel given. Ed went to Good Counsel, had meetings with Karen's teachers and delivered himself of rhapsodic praise of these nuns.

He reiterated to Karen a piece of advice which she shared with all of us: "Cooperate with the inevitable."

One afternoon, Ed and I were comparing notes on a book about which we were mutually enthusiastic when I received a call from Sister Mary Arthur, Rory's teacher.

"Mrs. Killilea, this is Sister Mary Arthur."

"Good afternoon Sister."

"I want to talk to you about Rory's sneakers."

"His sneakers?"

"Yes. *When* he has them for gym, they are without laces."

"Oh?"

"I told him today to take some of his allowance and invest in a pair of laces."

"Sound suggestion."

"That's what I thought, but your boy replied, most respectfully, that his allowance was for little pleasures, and that practical things like clothes and shoelaces are his father's responsibility." She gave a small laugh. "His logic was *formidable*. Will you please assume your responsibility and see that he has shoelaces for Wednesday?"

The last night of Ed's visit I came upon him alone in the living room. Looking up from his newspaper he said: "For a psychologist, this has been a most challenging visit." He rose and walking into the dining room he beckoned me to follow him. He pointed at the staircase to the second floor. "Observe!"

I had noticed, but now I saw for the first time the marvelously intricate arrangement of ropes and strings that our son had arranged through the balustrade, in, out and around the spindles, and garlanded to whatever piece of furniture served his purpose—whatever that might be. There were cymbals attached to the newel post, drumsticks to table legs, and more mazes of string, like gargantuan spider webs, from door hinges to frames and beyond.

Ed commented: "It makes moving about the house hazardous but ever so interesting." He sidestepped skeins woven of brown wrapping cord and nylon fish line. "Do you have a flashlight?"

A definite uneasiness galloped into my consciousness. "I'll fetch one."

He took the light, went to the window and shone the beam in the air at eye-level. There was a breeze and just beyond the pane, dancing in macabre glee, was a shrunken head.

My uneasiness grew. Perhaps I hadn't paid enough attention to Rory's activities. What would be the psychological implications of the head? the complicated, irrelevant festooning? There was the familiar tightening and freezing of my leg muscles as I turned to my counselor for a professional opinion. "What does it mean?"

Slowly he faced me letting his eyes run over the stringed designs. His expression was serious. "It means . . ." he paused portentously.

"Yes—" I urged, searching the rough-hewn face for a clue.

". . . that he's a perfectly normal boy." His laughter exploded as he handed the flashlight back to me.

There was always a letdown when Ed left to go home, and I was glad that on the eve of his departure Jimmy and I, the kids, Joe and Russ were going to the Rodeo at Madison Square Garden. Dale Evans and Roy Rogers were the stars of the show and Rory and Karen entertained an unrestrained admiration for both. We had a box seat at the ringside and the younger children held their breath as they waited for that moment when Dale and Roy would ride slowly around the ring, close to the rail, to greet the children in the audience.

There was a blare of trumpets, the floodlights dispersed even the smallest shadow; a sibilant gasp of anticipation, then the two figures rode through the great doors at the end of the arena. Slowly their horses high-stepped close to the railings and the two idols smiled and waved at the cheering mob. I saw Karen throw a surreptitious kiss to Roy as he passed in front of her and then lean forward eagerly as Dale came abreast of our seats. Dale, who is more beautiful in person than she is on camera, looked to the rows above us and slowly let her eyes travel down to our box. With an imperceptible gesture she stopped her horse and an expression of delighted surprise lighted her face. She stood in her stirrups, leaned toward us and said to our astounded daughter: "Why I know you—*you're Karen.*"

Color flooded Karen's face. She opened her mouth but no words came out.

Dale continued: "I just finished reading your mommy's book and I think you're a wonderfully good girl. I must go now, but tell your mommy I should like to meet her. God bless you!" She rode on.

When she had gone round the whole ring, instead of leaving through the gates, she put her horse into a canter, rode up to Karen, and horse and rider executed a deep bow—then cantered away. A gracious salute—from a gracious lady.

Early in December, Winter made a premature and dramatic entrance. Although heating costs soared as the temperature dropped, and getting around in snow and ice was something of a problem, Jimmy and I were happy for this was the season we loved best. Spring, Summer, and Fall are predictable, their tranquillity only occasionally interrupted by storms. One knows on awaking what flowers will be blooming and what changes to expect in the tint of the leaves.

Winter is an adventure with the daily excitement of the unexpected. A bright sun can be suddenly obscured by drifting flakes that will make the world immaculate and still. As suddenly, there can be warmth and rain—then a freeze that glazes the soft swell of mounded whiteness and encases the smallest twig in a silver cocoon. A wide grayness of sea and sky can be usurped by heavens of startling blue on which are hung sunsets, brightly soaringly gold. Winter more than any other season is the delight of all the senses. The smell of snow before the first flake falls, the fragrance of thawing mud mingled with the heartiness of wood fires and the sharper scent of the salt sea. The sound of wind soughing through the marsh grass, the cacophony of gulls, geese and ducks, the crunch of snow beneath the feet, the treble tinkle of falling ice, and the bass grating of floes upon the rocks. There is nothing more pleasing than the ballet of feathered cedars curling and flowering in the wind, and the writhing silhouettes of trees. Nothing more invigorating than the bitter bite of winter gale upon the cheeks, the pleasant numbness of fingers and toes, and nothing more comforting than the enveloping heat of a great black stove.

Christmas Eve was sharply still and cold. Jimmy rigged up the loudspeaker on the porch and once again the carols tumbled across the water and crept up the streets. Inside the house all was bright and warm as we gathered round the tree, not yet decorated but standing tall and full in all its natural beauty. We were ready for the ceremony that made the tree an integral part of Christmas—the blessing. Monsignor Madden stepped forward.

I glanced at Jimmy over the bowed heads of his girls, and Rory, Russ and Joe. Happy patriarch.

There was only one unhappy incident to mar the holiday. The previous Christmas Rory had carefully selected a gift for me. He couldn't wait for me to open it so he had untied the ribbon, torn off the paper, lifted the lid and thrust the unveiled beauty into my hands: a pair of earrings, easily an inch and a half long and three quarters of an inch wide, patently purchased at the Five and Ten. "They have every kind of a jewel!" He had knelt before me peering expectantly up into my face. "—Diamonds, pearls, rubies, emeralds, sapphires! And set in solid gold!"

"They're the most beautiful jewels I have ever seen!" Apparently my enthusiasm rang true for he grinned ecstatically.

He had sidled over to Jimmy and said in a stage whisper: "You won't believe it Pop, but I got them for thirty-nine cents."

Jimmy had swallowed twice and gasped: "No!"

I was wearing them now. I had worn them almost daily for a year attracting more than a few startled glances from hosts on T.V. shows.

Now my eight-year-old, attired in his Christmas gifts, i.e., all the equipment for riding the range, came quickly forward and handed me a small box. He smiled impishly as I opened it. I inhaled sharply and exclaimed, "It's gorgeous!" I held up the treasure for all to see—a pearl ring so large that it extended beyond the knuckle and so wide the pinky was pushed out. "It's too beautiful to wear every day, but I'll wear it every time I get dressed up."

I went to kiss Rory who pulled abruptly away. "Oh, Mom," his voice reflecting disgust and disappointment, "It's a joke! . . . I have better taste than that." Deeply affronted he left the room.

I sat engulfed in bewilderment and guilt.

"Well honey," said Jimmy comfortingly, "your boy is growing up."

"I just wish he'd cue me in."

ॐ

chapter eleven

The steeliness of winter gave way to the softness of Spring.

Gloria and Russ continued to live according to the terms they had imposed on themselves. No "dates" as such, just family visiting between houses. Glo never went to Russ's house except with another couple and always left with them. There were many well-intentioned people who addressed themselves to the matter. We were frequently appalled at the way individuals, normally respectful of the private lives of others, would advise, question and criticize. Jimmy and I seethed and Gloria remained collected. She was advised that if Russ were wealthy, or had connections with the hierarchy, the case would be quickly disposed in his favor; that her single state was unnatural and could only result in a breakdown; that if she really loved Russ, she would forget her 'scruples' and give him a home and a family; that in the end the Church would give a final "no" and she and Russ would capitulate and get married anyway, so why not now—"while you're still young?"

If she was depressed or discouraged we saw no evidence of it, quite the contrary, of all the family, she was the gayest. Even in repose, no shadows dimmed the piquancy of her face.

We were in complete ignorance of the status of the case. Russ, as well as all the witnesses called, took an oath that he would not discuss the case with anyone until two years after its termination. The only part we played in the affair was to propose to him the names of people who might be valuable as witnesses. In this connection we suggested a doctor in New Mexico who was in the position to give testimony of the validity of the marriage. Together, Gloria and I went to the Chancery office where we secured a list of the questions to which we hoped the doctor would give answers. Russ, being new to his job, was unable to take the time necessary to make the trip, so one wild March day, Gloria enplaned for New Mexico. She left buoyant with hope, and returned four days later, literally sick with disillusionment. She had travelled as far as she could by plane then, without pause for sleep, had boarded a bus which, after a miserable eight-hour-trip, had brought her to the small, dusty town where the doctor lived. The house was not clean—neither was the occupant. He listened intently to her explanation, then took the sheet and studied the questions. He put the paper in his lap, scratched a stubbled chin with a dirty fingernail, and said: "I think I can answer these questions to your satisfaction . . ." he paused and picked up the sheet, waving it back and forth ". . . *and mine.*"

It took Gloria a minute or two to grasp the significance of his remark. She was shocked and her voice trembled as she told him: "We want only the truth."

"You want to get married, don't you?" he asked crudely. "In your interest—and my own—I can give satisfactory answers."

Gloria was greatly agitated as she recited this interview to us. Jimmy went over and put his arm around her. She looked up at him, her eyes brimming. "You know what this means?"

He nodded.

"It means that although I believe this man to have in his files the very information which might in itself prove the case in Russ's favor, I have to report to the Chancery office that I know him to be venal, and to tell them he *must not be believed*."

When Russ came that evening, Gloria controlled herself admirably as she repeated the story. Apparently Jimmy had exhausted his control in the afternoon, and in a shaking voice raved at this doctor, employing numerous pithy and colorful references to the physician's antecedents which left me stunned. Never had I seen him so give way to anger.

Russ sat back in his chair and spoke briefly. "As you say, you must report that under no conditions is this man to be believed. It's true we have lost what looked to be our most valuable witness. But—" he looked at Gloria and spoke with simple conviction: "All is not lost for one very good reason—God knows I'm telling the truth."

A few days later I left on a three week lecture tour. The kids were envious that I was going to see so much of our country—poor deluded babes. I saw—air terminals, railroad stations, hotels, radio and T.V. stations. I saw clouds beneath as I flew by day and nothing as I trained by night. Mass at the old Cathedral on the banks of the Mississippi and a brief visit to the St. Louis zoo were all I could report to my family of "seeing our country."

Their disappointment was slightly alleviated when I told them that a not infrequent introduction was of "Mrs. Kill-a-flea." They brightened a bit more when I told of the woman who bought my book and asked for my autograph. As I finished signing I said to her: "I hope you'll enjoy it."

She had answered quickly: "Oh, I'm not going to read it, but where else can you get a decent present for $3.50.

132.

I saved the best story for the last. It was on a T.V. show. The director was new to television and forgot to give me my camera cue. While the interviewer, who was also a neophyte, waited for the belated appearance of her guest, she stared glassily into the camera and chanted: "We have a wonderful guest today—a really wonderful guest. A woman who has all kinds of stories to tell us—all *kinds* of stories. . . ."

At this point I took a Glenn Cunningham start for her desk, without cue. As I approached, she chattered: A woman who has had *remarkable experiences!* A woman who has *four children!"* then triumphantly, as I sank into a chair opposite her, "I give you *MISS Marie Killilea."*

As soon as I unpacked, Karen and I went for a walk. She was stepping better than when I had left, and had increased her pace. She was voluble about all that had gone on during my absence. Shanty conducted only limited investigations of trees and bushes less than ten feet from Karen. Her steps grew slower.

"Come on. Step along." I urged.

We walked a little farther. "You can do better than that," I prodded. "Hurry a bit."

By the time we got back to the house, Karen was walking very slowly and dragging her toes. We had dinner and I went off to the shore to think the thing out. I thought in circles for a long time and then, by some holy inspiration, I came around to an examination of conscience. Here I found the answer — not palatable — but authentic. Mother nagged. Mother was not content with her daughter's rate of progress; she nagged for more. Mother's step was quick; she nagged that her daughter's might more quickly match it.

I looked at my whole self more closely. Mother had gotten in the habit of nagging about many things. Karen, walking with me, was emotionally taut (this was in the last year), her muscles reacted in kind and my "urgings" created a physical difficulty for her and, I was willing to wager, some rebellion whether conscious or otherwise. It was high time to draw a line between correction and encouragement, and nagging. For reasons of mental hygiene as well as physical considerations, I'd better reform. It would take some honesty

133.

to establish the line, and self-discipline to toe it. I thought about this in relation to Jimmy and the kids. They didn't need to reform for they were innocent of nagging. Well, I'd better watch my P's and Q's or I was going to push Karen into further difficulties. Funny, how easily and erroneously I had considered my maternal pattern of behavior to be virtuous. I'd better do some refocusing on the 'whole' child. The moon was high when I finished. Walking back across the sand I recalled and *rediscovered* something that Ed Doll had said so often in helping us to make appraisals: "Is it too expensive?" I had to do much measuring against a question ruler: What the gain? What the cost? Is it too expensive? Father McSorley had given us a similar gauge: "What is the net result?"

When the forsythia burst again into golden tumbles, the weather was clement enough for the children to resume horseback riding. We never did totally conquer some small quakings at the sight of Karen's diminutive form astride a horse that stood fourteen hands, but the riding was doubly important now since her therapy schedule and school work kept her busy indoors from 5:30 a.m. in the morning until 10:00 p.m. Calculating the "net result" we called a moratorium on all therapy and work on Sundays. Everyone needs time in which to just "be."

Rory and Russ had bachelor week-ends at the Yorktown house which more and more resembled a farm. There were a Labrador Retriever, cats, goats, and a goose. Russ had an uncanny rapport with animals. He would walk up to his goose, announce he was mad and the goose would shriek at him. Russ would then speak very quietly, telling the goose he was sorry and add: "Whisper that you forgive me." The goose would move as close as possible to Russ, stretch his neck and make tiny murmuring sounds deep in his throat.

The goats followed him around like puppies, never straying from the property. It was comical to see them watch Russ when he went to the station wagon and opened the back. They'd freeze, and wait for him to say: "Do you want to go for a ride?" then bound into the car. He had a rowboat which he kept turned upside down in the yard. When Sonia, the matriarch of the herd, wasn't getting enough attention, she'd leap on the inverted boat bottom and rock it wildly, bleating the while. If this ruse failed, she'd circle Russ, then snuggle her head under his arm.

Russ had quickly trained his Lab to field work and in the new light of early morning, the two bachelors would tuck their rifles under their arms and with the dog, go off into the woods. Our boy, who had trouble getting out of bed at 7:30 a.m. for school, had no difficulty rising before the sun to hunt with Russ.

One Sunday night, after a day with us on the beach, Shanty lay beside me stretched out in happy exhaustion. I was working burrs out of his coat and my hand was arrested at his shoulder, the one he had injured in his leap from the car. Under my palm was a lump about an inch high and five inches in diameter. My heart skipped a beat. The next morning as soon as Karen left for school I took the dog to the doctor. He walked a few steps ahead of me and I noticed he was limping. Bob Clark put Shanty on the table and while he examined him I stood silent and scared. The dog's large body extended over the edge and I supported his head in my cupped hands. In the sunlight streaming through the windows his coat was like burnished copper and his feathers gold. He lay quite still under the gently probing fingers.

Finally Bob straightened. As he spoke his hand caressed the silky coat. "He has a tumor and the sooner it comes out the better. We won't know exactly what it is until we've done a biopsy."

I decided quickly. "If I leave him now can you operate today?"

"This afternoon."

"What time?"

"Two o'clock."

"Good. Karen is going to a basketball game today and won't be home until 6:00 p.m. He should be reacting from the anaesthesia by then and you may have some news."

"I think we'll know by 6:00 p.m."

"I'll be praying while you're working." I bent and kissed the velvet cheek. Shanty responded by beating a tattoo with his tail on the table.

Most days the girls came home from school at 3:30.

Shanty must have had a clock in his head, for at exactly 3:30 he always took up his post at the end of the driveway, watching up the street for the cab. Nothing could entice him from this spot until the car pulled into the driveway, even on basketball days when it was two to three hours late. The first thing Karen called as she drove up was: "How's my angel—did you miss me?" The reunions were no less wild for occurring daily.

I was standing in the driveway when the cab drove in. "Where's Shanty?" Karen asked peering through the gloom. Then: "Hi Mom! We won!"

I handed her the crutches. "Where's Shanty?" she repeated.

I picked up her books. "He's up with Walter and Bob—"

She stood rigid, studying my face.

No time for hedging, I thought. "He has a growth on his shoulder and Bob removed it this afternoon. He will be calling soon to give us a report."

Typically, Karen said: "Don't worry, Mom Pom, he'll be all right." She was a staunch little figure as she walked slowly toward the house.

Gloria had made her peerless lasagna for dinner but we just nibbled waiting for the phone to ring. Finally the call came and Bob reported: "We removed the growth. It's hard to say if we got all of it. It extended to the rib cage. He's reacting nicely and is in good condition."

I waited, holding the phone away from my ear so Jimmy and the kids clustered around and could hear.

"The growth was malignant. This may be the end of the trouble and it may not. We can only wait and see."

"And pray," whispered Karen. Her face was bloodless.

When the dishes were done and most of the lasagna put back in the refrigerator, Jimmy came up with solid distraction. Gloria and Russ had both been born early in January and we always felt that they were gypped on proper remembrance, for who isn't broke right after Christmas. We had long talked about changing their birthdays so tonight Jimmy fetched legal paper and pen and proposed that we draw up an impressive document officially changing their birth dates. Gloria and I, drawing on our considerable experience in law offices, invested it heavily with jargon and managed to make it not only lengthy but fairly incomprehensible, which of course made it sound authentic. There was some lively discussion and heated argument from Russ who disapproved of the whole idea. He continued to squawk like a mallard but with typical Killilea benevolence, we ignored him.

At the end of several hours we had three pages which boiled down to

BE IT KNOWN TO ALL THESE PRESENTS THAT:
Gloria Killilea was born March 17
and
Russell Lea was born March 19

The whole thing was a lot of nonsense but it relieved a good bit of Karen's emotional strain that evening, and a little financial strain in the years to come.

A week later there was another wrench when Bob and Margaret Chambers left us to move permanently to British Columbia. For days Karen's eyes filled with tears every time she looked at their gift of the television set through which she had traveled during her weary months of incarceration. I felt especially bereft, for all the friends we had, none had so successfully identified with our difficulties, or so extended themselves to ameliorate them. But in the curious design of Providence, what was a great personal loss to us became a great blessing to many, many others.

In May, during a long visit with Father McSorley, he gently suggested (Father always gently suggested) to Jimmy and me that we might think about the advisability of a long vacation. "It might be a good investment," he said trenchantly. I looked at Jimmy and wondered how I had failed to notice how very tired he looked and how drawn.

"Jimmy and I have always thought that parents should get away alone some time during the year—that they need a vacation from the kids."

Father smiled: "And it's good for the kids to have a vacation from their parents."

We spent the next few weeks poring over encyclopedias. Rory thought we should go West to the cowboys. Karen thought South, to the Old South, Gloria thought the mountains and Marie plugged for a dude ranch. Joe said: "I don't think it matters too much as long as you go leaving no thoughts behind you."

We finally decided on a trip that would keep us away three weeks. We were pretty excited for although we had had lots of vacations, this was the first time in twenty years of marriage that we were going to really spend some money.

On a hot, still morning in July, while the fog shrouded the rocks and water and the foghorn wailed like a disconsolate puppy, we started for Canada. The air was heavy with the odor of privet and loud with the burring of locusts' wings playing their single note.

We had beautiful days in the Laurentide Park, took the boat down the Saguenay, and at St. Simeon crossed the St. Lawrence River to Rivière du Loup on the Gaspé Peninsula. Our last adventure before starting home was to be a day on Bonaventure Island, the largest bird sanctuary on the North Atlantic Coast with its feathered population numbered in hundreds of thousands.

The morning was bright, a good sea was running and the waves were just a trifle under the height that would prevent our small craft from making the trip. Bonaventure Island was three miles off shore. In shape it resembled a slumbering whale. It was three miles long, one mile wide, and sloped from a rocky shore to a precipitous rock cliff four hundred feet above the water. It was on this cliff we would find the birds.

We disembarked and walked through a gently rising pasture to a meadow where the ground was literally blanketed with wild orchids, some only an inch in diameter. We found Queen Anne's Lace tall enough to shelter me under its diaphanous parasol. The rise grew steeper and steeper as we walked across the island to the cliff. In the distance we could hear small sounds from the sea and the varied calls of sea fowl. After an hour of climbing we came to a comparatively clear area that extended some seventy-five feet to the edge of the precipice. Here the force of the gale was so great (fifty miles an hour) that we had to get down on our stomachs to crawl close to the edge. Birds nested everywhere, the mothers holding the fledglings securely under a strongly sheltering wing. They watched us warily. Above our heads and out over the sea the air was pulsing with thousands upon thousands of winged creatures, soaring, coasting, dipping, diving deep below the surface of the water. There was constant quivering sound, crooning in the nests, the combative cry of antagonists in flight, the raucous jeers of the victors, the sobbing of birds foreign to us, and always—the whistling wind. There were herring gulls, auks, crested cormorants, sea parrots, gannets, kittiwake gulls, even penguins. We shared our lunch with them, then crawled around among the nests for strange eggshells and feathers to take home to the kids. The mother birds watched us apprehensively but not one left her nest.

Reluctantly we started back. As we came down through the meadow we spotted chimney smoke from one of the few houses on the island. We were thirsty and decided no one would object to giving us a glass of water. We walked through a herd of cows, some of whom moved languidly out of our way, across a stretch of saw grass and knocked at the door of a house. There was no answer. Jimmy knocked again. Still no answer. We waited a few minutes and Jimmy knocked once more, quite loudly.

Silence.

Then a voice called: "Come in."

We entered and stood hesitantly inside the door. Twenty feet beyond was a kitchen, bright, sparklingly clean. Seated with her back to us was a woman. Her elbows were on the table, her fisted hands supported her chin and her head was bowed over something before her.

We waited. She didn't move. "She probably thinks we're neighbors from the mainland," Jimmy whispered to me. He raised his voice: "We're strangers, and we'd be grateful if you'd give us some water."

"In a minute—in a minute!" the woman called impatiently without raising her head.

We stood and looked in puzzlement at each other. "Maybe we'd better leave. . . ."

"Thank Heaven!" The woman ejaculated, sat for a moment longer, then rose and turned to face us. On the table was an open book. She came across the kitchen, tall, hand-

some, smiling joyously. "I'm sorry—sorry to keep you waiting, but . . ." she gestured toward the table behind her, "I'm reading the most wonderful book," she spoke rapidly with a delightful French accent, "and it's about a little girl who had the big heavy braces and when you first knocked she had just fallen out of a boat." She wrung her hands in remembered anguish. "I couldn't put the book down—I had to find out could they save her." She ran her hands through her hair and continued breathlessly. "Both her mother and father dived overboard for the rescue but they stirred up a lot of mud. . . ." She threw up her hands with fine French eloquence.

I could not resist. I looked directly at her and said: "I could have told you what happened."

Her eyes lighted. "Oh! you have read it?"

"No—I didn't read it—"

"Then—how . . . ?"

"I wrote it."

"*Karen—she is yours?!*" She looked from me to Jimmy, stupefied, incredulous.

We nodded. "She's ours."

Impulsively she embraced us in turn. "Come in! Come in!" She backed ahead of us into the kitchen. "Sit down. Sit down—if you please." She sat sharply in her own chair, staring at us in disbelief. "You'd like some tea." She jumped up. "Oh, I forgot," she turned in pretty confusion, "I'm Mrs. Donohue—and you, Monsieur, you would like some nice cold beer?"

Her appearance was typically French, so was her accent. Mrs. Donohue! This was not uncommon on the Gaspé. In the middle of the nineteenth century there had been considerable immigration from Ireland. We had seen the monument to the one hundred and eighty-seven Irish immigrants from Sligo "wrecked here April 28, 1847." Throughout our trip we had been enchanted by such names as Jean Baptiste Flannelly, François Whelan, Marie Jeanne O'Reilly.

Our hostess moved across the kitchen, dropped to her knees, opened a trap door in the floor from which blew a gust of icy air. She put her arm down in the opening and came up with a bottle of beer. She placed it in front of

Jimmy and busied herself with tea things while she bombarded us with questions. "And my little one—she is well? and happy? and the legs work better? She is fourteen now—yes?"

"Yes—"

"And the boy—he must be a big fellow of ten, yes?"

"Yes—"

"How I would love to see them all. Are Gloria and Marie still so sweet, so good to Karen?" She shut her eyes in concentration. Gloria is twenty-six—Marie is seventeen—always so good to their little sister!" She wheeled on Jimmy. "And you, *mon Dieu,* what *you* do for that child! How you do work! How you do sweat! How you do love! How you do keep the patience! *Mon Dieu!*" She turned to me. "And you —you are a good mother too, but oh! so lucky, so *blessed* that he is your husband!"

Until the last warning toot of the boat whistle, we lingered in Mrs. Donohue's kitchen answering questions about the kids, Shanty, the rabbits, the cats, the old, old car. As we stood at the door and regretfully bid her farewell, she ran back into the house and returned with a cannonball which she said her husband had dug up in his field, an eloquent souvenir of the battle of the Island between the English and the French. "For Rory," she said handing it to Jimmy. Then she said to me: "It would be good for your children to have a change. Here all is happy and healthy. My husband can build anything that Karen might need." She put her hand on my arm. "Maybe you would send all of them to us next summer." She hurried on, not giving me a chance to speak. "Maybe you would think about it. We would love them and we would have fun."

ॐ

chapter twelve

Before leaving on vacation we had arranged for Karen to have a swimming instructor. We'd had the great good fortune to find Barbara Cunningham, a pretty young girl with a talent for teaching and the holder of many records. The Sunday afternoon of our return, she and Karen invited us to the beach for a demonstration. "Red sun in the morning, a sailor's fair warning" and sure enough by afternoon we were having a gentle summer rain. We went to the beach anyway. There were a few hardy adults and a little less than the usual complement of children cavorting like otters. As Jimmy and I followed Barbara and Karen down to the water, we reminded each other that three weeks was a pretty limited time in which to learn anything. It was true that Karen started ahead of the gun, for years ago Jimmy had taught her to hold her breath under water for an unconscionable length of time. It was a good thing he had or she would have drowned at the time of that boating accident in Millbrook.

Ahead of us Karen moved slowly on her crutches (no braces) through the sand and into the water. When she had reached a depth of about two feet she let go of the crutches and fell face forward into the water. The crutches floated gently away and Jimmy picked them up. Barbara stood next to Karen and we watched with happy amazement as our daughter executed a few strokes of the crawl. Then tiring, she turned on her back and floated—all without assistance.

"And that's not all," Barbara said as Jimmy and I submerged to get warm.

Karen went on to do a back stroke and a breast stroke. She was never going to make Johnny Weissmueller look to his laurels, nor for that matter, would she ever pose a threat to the ten-year-old swimming past her to the float, but she did have the rudiments of three strokes and could float until she was waterlogged. This last was perhaps the most significant for it required a degree of total body relaxation most difficult for one with spasticity. It was all possible, Barbara told us for two reasons—Karen's desire TO DO; and no fear. And, lest we underestimate the accomplishments, Barbara pointed out that Karen had only about five per cent value from the leg motions of her kick.

The exhibition had attracted an audience of small fry. The little girls chattered, and the little boys stared with that silent absorption typical of males from one year to ten.

Barbara turned her back on Karen and walked some distance away signalling us to follow. "She's perfectly safe," said teacher reading Mother's mind, "and this little ruse just demonstrates my confidence." She turned and called to Karen who was floating: "Over on your stomach, six strokes and that will be enough for today." She stayed where she was and Karen turned over, put her face in the water, and took her strokes. The left arm was quite good, the right much less so because Karen was still unable to straighten it in spite of years of occupational therapy.

Jimmy walked over and picked up Karen. "That's a noteworthy performance. How would you like to dive?"

"I'd love it."

He told her to extend her arms, put her head between them, and point down. Then, lifting her high, he threw her up and out, and she hit the water with a commendably small splash. As she surfaced she grinned a little too soon, inhaled some water and began to cough. At this moment Jimmy was assaulted from the rear. A boy of seven, a trembling figure of wrath, threw himself at the unsuspecting father and pummeling him about the thighs with hard little fists he screamed: *"You're bad! Darn you! You're wicked!"* he was sobbing with anger, *". . . to throw that poor crippled girl!"*

Back at the house, Barbara told us that Karen had had to make a very difficult choice in our absence—to swim or ride. She explained: swimming requires long, lean muscles, and other sports, like riding, short hard muscles; the longer Karen rode, the less able she would be to make progress in swimming. Karen hadn't made up her mind overnight, but when she did decide, the matter was settled and she never mentioned riding again.

Without any talk about it, Marie and Roy quit going to the stables. Whenever we suggested a ride they made some excuse. I would have urged them but Jimmy said if they volunteered such a sacrifice for Karen they should be permitted to make it.

Barbara had a lot of questions about what she should and shouldn't require of Karen so I called Dr. Fay. The next day he hopped a train in Philadelphia and came to Larchmont for a conference with teacher. On the beach with a host of undressed adults, he did look dear in his dark suit, white shirt and black shoes. He perspired freely, sloshed around in the wet sand and enthusiastically approved the program. He praised Karen lavishly on her "spectacular achievement" and no Olympic medal could have meant more. He said that swimming was the best, the very best exercise that Karen could have and that we should keep it up during the winter months. "Find a heated pool," he told me. Not only did Dr. Fay consider nothing impossible, but in the years I've known him, he acknowledges no difficulties. Needless to say, we found a heated pool; we wouldn't dare to tell him we couldn't. After much searching we applied to the New Rochelle Hospital where Karen and Barbara were welcomed any evening that Barbara was free. When Karen had only been able to stand the colder water of the Sound for half to three-quarters of an hour, in the pool she spent an hour and a half to two hours. In six months she was swimming twenty-five yards without resting and with coordinated breathing.

The irate young man on the beach was not the only one who considered us heartless and criminally careless when we left Karen alone. Nor was this the only cause for criticism. Shanty was getting on in years and no one could say how successful had been the surgery for cancer, so Jimmy and I decided that we would occasionally have to tie the dog in the house and let Karen get used to going out alone. Her solitary safaris around the neighborhood (which had no sidewalks) precipitated a visit from an indignant neighbor. This man came yelling to our kitchen door one evening and most fortunately Jimmy wasn't at home. He was quite beside himself and screamed at me that we didn't deserve to have children; that parents who allowed a child as unstable as Karen to walk out alone should be held responsible by some authority and proper steps taken. He so took me by surprise that it was only after minutes of the wild tirade that I began to recover my wits. I asked him to leave. He grew more abusive and in this spate of words charged we were breaking zoning restrictions by taking in boarders—"no one would have that many young people around unless they were getting paid for it. This was a nice neighborhood until you people moved in, and *you'd better get out!*" He was gasping for breath to start his attack anew.

My heart was pounding and my mouth was dry. *"Get out of my house. GET OUT!"* I was standing rigid with my fists clenched. He took a step forward. I raised my fist and would have struck him if he had not stepped backwards out of the door. From ten feet away he continued to spew forth his vituperative stream. I was shaking with anger and shock. "If you're not off my property by the time I count ten I'm going to call the police. I am also going to charge you with defamation of character if you say one more word."

He hesitated to the count of "five," then turned and left, still ranting indistinguishably.

I was trembling so violently I couldn't stand and fell into a chair at the kitchen table. In the past we'd had a few unhappy experiences with people but never anything like this. I gave way to tears of rage. After a fine emotional binge I began to think. I was being completely unrealistic to expect people to understand a situation which they have never experienced. It would be like saying to Karen "I know how you feel when you need braces and crutches to walk." Absurd. I couldn't *know* how she felt unless I also needed braces and crutches to walk. By the same token, no one, other than the parent of a disabled child could possibly *know* how we felt, nor the need for our decisions of prudent withdrawal. The parents of non-handicapped children do not live daily or hourly with the thought that their time with their youngster runs out; that they will not be here always; that every day must be used to bring the child to its maximum potential. Therefore, they could not possibly *understand* the decisions we make nor *know* the reasons behind them. In the face of criticism it is both easy and unintelligent to become bitter. It is also easy to become self-righteous. They are equally damaging. There will be no temptation to either bitterness or self-righteousness if *we* understand that *they* cannot possibly understand. I realized that the larger measure of intellectual effort should properly be ours.

There was a comical aftermath of this incident. Ordinarily Jimmy took the bus when he got off the train in the evening then walked two blocks to the house. One night it was raining so hard that I decided to drive to the station and meet the train. Just after I left Jimmy called to say he had missed the 6:08 and would take the next one. I was parked beside the platform and waited until the last passenger came down the steps. I was about to drive off when I saw the Man of Indictments, as we had come to call him, standing on the platform. The bus had gone and there wasn't a taxi left. I had a nice struggle with pride and a few other unworthy, relevant emotions, then drove over to him and asked if I could give him a ride home. His indecision was at once ludicrous and pathetic. He looked at me with repugnance and at the torrential downpour with loathing. Without a word he got into the car. And without a word we drove the six minutes to his front door. I stopped the car. He fumbled in his pocket and, as he slithered out of his seat, he half turned and extended his hand. Who am I to refuse a proffered gesture of peace? I put out my hand but instead of taking it he placed a dime in the palm. The price of the bus!

He slammed the door, scooted through the rain, and I laughed so hard I wept. We're on quite pleasant terms now. When we meet on the street we comment on the weather and occasionally he smiles.

Morford Downes, the builder who had encouraged us to buy the house, and his wife Ann, continued to hover over our abode like birds over a nest. His gimlet eyes could find a loose shingle or a sagging board at a glance. They were interested not only in the nest but in the fledglings it held.

We were still hoping that Karen could learn to negotiate steps and Morf applied his engineering skill to this project. In many clinics there were several sets of stairs with risers of graduating heights. Of necessity they were large with a broad base and took up a great deal of space, which is always at a premium. Mort devised a set of stairs which would take the place of four sets; they were adjustable and the risers could be changed from a depth of three inches to seven inches. At the top there was a three foot square platform. This set was light and easy to move. We quickly dubbed it "Jacob's Ladder." We persuaded Morf to start patent proceedings which he did in the name of the Karen Foundation. There was a very good reason for this. Previously, a number of people had developed devices for aiding the handicapped and they had been available at cost. Then some enterprising therapist, seeing the possibilities of a quick buck, had patented the product (although having had nothing to do with its development) and the price had skyrocketed. One item went from fifteen dollars to fifty-five! It was our purpose to see that this did not happen with the stairs, as had been our purpose when we patented some of our other ideas.

Joe suggested we have a party to christen Jacob's Ladder. Glo made a wonderful (but sneaky) rum and vodka punch and for the christening Jimmy brought home a split of champagne. We invited Monsignor Madden (the kids couldn't have even a birthday party without their Uncle Leo), Grace Oursler, Joe and Eleanor Gagliardi (she was Rory's godmother), the Schnirrings, Phil and Carla Wallach, Mr. King and Shirley, the inventor of the Ladder and his wife, and a bunch of Marie's and Karen's friends. Russ and Joe were never invited—just automatically included.

We had some brisk days in September and Jimmy turned on the heat. Within a few hours the house was permeated with the most sickening sweet odor imaginable.

"It smells like dead chloroform mixed with rancid, cheap perfume," Jimmy pronounced as he probed and prodded from cellar to attic looking for the source. He found both attic and cellar innocent.

A.M. came in, "Phew!" she greeted us with feeling.

"Can you guess what it is?" Jimmy asked frantically.

"I don't have to guess. I know. Mice. Lots of mice. Billy used to keep them."

"Mice?" Jimmy stood aghast. "We don't have mice."

"We don't any more," I said cheerily.

"What do you mean—*any more?*" Jimmy turned to me threateningly.

"Well . . ." I hesitated.

"This is going to be good," decided A.M. and sat down, putting her handkerchief over her nose.

"It's like this, sweetheart," I began placatingly. "When Mike came home from his summer of laboratory research, he asked me if he could leave his mice here 'til he went away to prep school."

"Where's here?"

"Well . . . I suggested the garage and he said it was too draughty. Then I suggested the cellar and he said the temperature fluctuated too much. . . ."

"Where *did* you house them, love?" There was an edge to Jimmy's voice. "Where?" he repeated.

"In—in the guest room," I blurted.

"So that's why Joe has had to share Rory's room." He gave A.M. an imploring look and bowed his head in his hands. His shoulders began to shake. A.M. gave her hoot of laughter which Ruth Weed had once likened to the strange cry of a sea fowl. Jimmy raised his head and bellowed with her.

"Naturally," he crowed and roared some more.

"They were valuable from a scientific point of view," I defended.

"How many?" He wiped his streaming eyes.

"Twenty-four, to start. . . ."

"And to finish?"

I had difficulty getting my voice through my throat. "One hundred and eighteen." I waited for him to say something but he just looked at me as if he'd never seen me before. I decided to make my summation: "The whole thing was both interesting and instructive for Karen. Mike took her upstairs every day when he came to tend the mice and make out his reports. She had some fine lessons in genetics. Besides, Mike kept them spotless and they've been gone a week, so how could they be responsible for the smell?"

Patiently my husband explained that the cleanest mice have an odor and that our hot air heating system had drawn the air and the smell from the guest room and circulated it throughout the house and out of all the vents. "It's very simple." He sighed a long sigh.

"And so am I?" This was a bid for understanding.

Jimmy said: "I guess it was pretty important to Mike and to Karen." He looked at me and smiled. "I guess I'm even glad you did it. Now I'll turn off the furnace and open all the windows. Bundle up—it will be a long, chilly seige."

Halloween the kids were dressed and ready to go out for

'trick or treat' when Russ arrived unexpectedly. It was always Glo who had the ideas for their costumes and this year she had hit her peak of inventiveness in Karen's. Our daughter was riding in the wheelchair, dressed in her Daddy's football referee's uniform, hair tucked under the cap, right arm and left leg in splints, her face a mask of multiple bruises and contusions. "That's a classic!" Russ enthused as Rory, dressed in football uniform pushed the wheelchair out the door. Karen carried a medical kit for treats.

As soon as they left, Russ said temperately that he had some encouraging news—his wife had given testimony. We were bursting with questions which we could not ask, or rather which we could ask but which he could not answer, because of his oath. Jimmy and I had been wondering about the attitude of the lawyers with whom Russ met. We knew that Russ would present his case with absolute matter-of-factness and with no hint of pathos. That evening we questioned him about the lawyers. We were scarcely prepared for his answer.

The first priest Russ had seen, shall be called Fr. Alucard. Russ related: "I told him the whole story. He listened without comment or question. When I had finished, Father Alucard rose abruptly and said: 'The case sounds hopeless. I don't see any point in pursuing it, for when we get a negative answer you two will just go off and get married anyway.'"

"My God!" Jimmy exclaimed.

I was too shocked for speech.

Gloria jumped to her feet her eyes blazing. "How dare he! How dare he decide that anyone is going to do wrong." She paced up and down in front of Russ. "It would seem to me that this would be the best way to push people into such action." Her voice rose. "Who made him omniscient where souls are concerned?"

I was about to add my indictment to hers when Jimmy gave me his 'keep still' look.

Glo stood in front of Russ with her hands on her hips, "What did you say?"

"I just said I wished him to proceed with the case."

"Didn't you have a few choice words about his assumption of our future sin?"

"No. I didn't," answered Russ equably.

"For Heaven's sake—*why not?*"

Russ took a thoughtful time before replying. "He seemed young to me. I don't mean in years necessarily. My guess is that he was brilliant in college, sent on to do graduate work, perhaps for several years, and then put in a chancery office without ever having worked with people."

Gloria stamped across the room and back. "How can you be so understanding? You make me wild."

"It would have been purposeless to let him make me angry."

She retorted: "Your patience is insufferable and your tolerance unendurable. How can you be so horribly *calm?*"

Russ reached for his pipe and carefully tamped the tobacco in the bowl. "It doesn't do any good to get mad."

"Well it does me good," Gloria shot at him and flung out of the room.

Jimmy followed her and though his words were indistinguishable we could hear his deep, soothing voice.

Russ and I sat in silence which, for me, was just short of heroic.

In time we learned that Russ's guess about Fr. Alucard's background was correct, but time did nothing to gentle this priest and Glo and Russ suffered much at his hands until the case was taken over by Father Kelly. He was a wise and experienced man—a man who in all things was truly "father."

ॐ
chapter thirteen

Karen's days were full—too full—I began to feel, and every minute choked with maximum physical and/or mental effort. She even used the time in the taxi to school for study. She was up at 5:30 a.m. and it was always 11:00 p.m. before she was through with schoolwork and therapy. She still contended day and night with pain. I welcomed the start of a four-day vacation during which time we decided to skip the plaster casts at night, forget all therapy, and hide the school-books regardless of protestations. She needed a rest. A rest from all the grinding things. Jimmy needed a rest too, for he was up with her at least six times during each night, adjusting the casts, adding more cotton padding.

I was awakened at dawn by a flock of crows in raucous disagreement with a flock of equally raucous gulls. The fog-horn was sounding its melancholy warning in b, then sliding to b flat. Contrapuntally came the hoarse blasts of ships' horns. When I was a child living in Rye, my father had invited for the week-end, a friend from the city who had never spent a night on the shore. All night there had been a heavy fog and the foghorn blew its throaty chant. At breakfast the next morning my father had inquired of his guest if he had slept well. "Not very," the friend had responded, "I felt too sorry for that poor cow—in such pain."

The gulls and crows had terminated their debate but I was wide awake. Not wishing to disturb the family, I tiptoed down to the kitchen for a cup of coffee. The sun was just beginning to light the house. As I walked from the dining room to the kitchen I imagined I heard voices. I am always comatose for several hours after rising and when I came to the door I paused and blinked. Before me was a tableau, so unique, that it would have been hard for me to adjust even if really awake and alert.

I glanced at the clock. It was 6:00 a.m.

Karen sat at one end of the table in her coral corduroy peignoir chatting amiably with a strange man who stood beside her. He was slight, gaunt, and obviously had not shaved for several days. His jacket and trousers were shabby, his shoes so worn that there was only a hint of their original color. On the floor beside him was a banged-up cardboard suitcase tied together with cord, and leaning against the wall, a five-foot-long, narrow package wrapped in newspaper. I clung to the door frame trying to orient myself.

Karen looked up and saw me. "Good morning, Mommy," she said brightly, and turned to her companion. "This is my friend, Corporal Franklin Pierce." She made her presentation with all the formality of a Garden Party at Buckingham Palace.

I barely resisted a responsive curtsy. "How do you do Corporal Pierce."

He came across the room and extended his hand. "I'm very, very happy to meet you," he said earnestly. His handshake was firm and warm.

I smiled and inquired: "To what do we owe the honor of this visit?" In the atmosphere my daughter had created, the words did not sound the least bit stilted.

"After I read your book in Germany, I wanted to meet Karen. I'm on leave."

"He just dropped in." Karen gave him a sweet smile.

"Dropped in from where?" I asked, seating myself carefully.

"Syracuse," he replied.

It took a moment for me to calculate the mileage—two hundred and fifty miles from Larchmont. "How did you travel to arrive at this hour?" I thought two hundred and fifty miles is quite a 'drop.'

"Oh, I walked."

"You *walked?*"

"Yes, ma'am."

"From *SYRACUSE?*" I grasped the edge of the table. Steady on, old girl, I told myself.

"Yes, ma'am."

I rose, thinking I needed a cup of strong coffee. I busied myself with the kettle. "Will you have some breakfast?"

Karen answered me. "I offered him breakfast, Mommy, but he's already had it. The cops got it for him. Wasn't that sweet?"

"Very." My mind was staggering under repeated assaults.

"They were very kind," Corporal Pierce took up the tale. "They stopped me on the Post Road about 2:00 a.m. this morning. They asked me what I was doing in town and I said I had come to see Karen. I asked them to show me the way to your house. (I was sure you'd have a garage I could sleep in 'til you got up.)"

Karen took up the recital. "Those dear policemen, they even gave him a bed in a cell!"

"Was it comfortable?" I asked foolishly, thinking that maybe coffee wasn't strong enough to see me through this.

"Comfortable and clean," Corporal Pierce replied. "I was most grateful."

Karen was studying the long, newspaper-wrapped package. "What's in that?" she asked.

"Fishing poles. Many a days I 'caught' my meals on the way from Syracuse."

I poured myself a cup of coffee and said to Corporal Pierce. "If you'll excuse me for a few minutes—"

"Certainly ma'am."

I went upstairs to dress and inform Jimmy that he would find a slightly bizarre situation on the first floor. He grunted over the noise of his electric razor.

When I returned to the kitchen, Karen was alone. "Where's your friend?"

"He told me to tell you he was sorry but he had to leave. He's on his way south but I think he felt he would be in the way when you were getting Daddy's breakfast."

"He seemed ever so nice." I put the bacon in the pan.

"He is. He told me he had been praying for me ever since he read the book." She wheeled her chair around the table and got out the silver. "I woke about 5:00 and when I pulled up the shades—there he was sitting on the back step leaning against the kitchen door. I can't wait for Daddy to come down so I can tell him."

"Daddy's short on time this morning," I put bread in the toaster. "Besides, it's such a wonderful story, I'd save it for the whole family at dinner." Jimmy was a strong character and almost awake when he left for work, but this was a little much to hurl at a foggy head that had to concentrate on catching a bus to catch a train to catch a subway.

In the mail that morning was a letter from Dr. Moore replying to my last report that Karen still had a good deal of pain and her nights in the casts continued a purgatory. I had told him that I had called off everything for the duration of the vacation and that we waited and prayed for the day, or rather the night, when she would be released from her plaster cage. "That day is here!" he wrote.

I made the announcement to Karen. The immensity of my relief was not only for her but for Jimmy who hadn't had a solid night's sleep in almost a year. She looked at me in wondering disbelief. "It's true," I assured her and read the words on the page, then handed it to her so she could read them for herself.

She bowed her head, closed her eyes and whispered: "Thank God!"

Shanty was getting whiter and whiter around the muzzle and Jimmy and I had to face up to the fact that he wouldn't be here forever. Several steps were indicated; send Karen out more without him. This grew increasingly difficult both for dog and young lady. We soon had to stop using the word *walk*, he knew what that meant and would become frenzied. We got away with spelling it for a week and then he caught on to that. We switched to *ambulate*, but in a couple of weeks he was wise to that too. It became awkward fun to have to stop and think and for 'walk,' substitute a-m-b-u-l-a-t-e.

The second step we determined on was to get another dog while Shanty was still around. We thought Karen would then accept the dog for itself and not think of it as a substitute—for such could never be. We were tempted to get another Irish Setter but voted this down on the basis that we would always be comparing him with Shanty. It wouldn't be fair to inaugurate any creature into a home under such a handicap. We wanted a breed that was above all intelligent, calm, affectionate, docile, and hardy. It also seemed a good idea to get a dog that would enjoy the water which was practically at our doorstep. We decided on a Labrador Retriever. I called a classmate of mine from Mount St. Vincent, Lorraine Swinn, who was married to Dr. Michael Donohue, a veterinarian in Cornwall. She approved the choice of breed and promised to see what she could do about finding us just the right dog. A week later she called me back and we made arrangements to meet at Tuxedo Park with a Mr. Ralph Hellum. It is curious to note how many, many times, a special need has led us to those who have become special friends. Ralph Hellum was such a one. A man of great gentleness, dignity, and understanding; he had a unique ability, or more properly genius, for working with and training all kinds of animals from an otter to a hunter. He was most interested in our particular requirements in a pet and through his good offices Karen became the recipient of a Lab bitch puppy, six weeks old. She was named Highland Lark and was a black, shiny beauty of fine breeding (dual championship), of engaging rascality and sentimentality. For a week or so Shanty sulked, then his natural protectiveness and chivalry asserted themselves and she shepherded the pup from the dangers of cars, bicycles and strange cats. He so far forgot the dignity of his years as to play tag and hide-and-seek, facing defeat stoically when the black ball plunged under the sofa, a space too small to accommodate even his great head. Pups, like children, are imitative, so in no time at all we had a beautifully behaved pet. By the time Lark was three months old she was 'saying Grace before meals.' Rory trained her to sit while he put a biscuit on her nose and to stay motionless until he finished: "Bless us, O Lord and these Thy gifts . . . through Christ Our Lord, Amen." The pup would drool and quiver, but move not, until the "Amen." Then she would toss her head and catch the biscuit in flight. So smart was she that the second time around she would advance the toss to the preceding word 'Lord,' the third time to 'Our.'

We were all impressed by the Lab's gentleness and caution with Karen. She would slow to a walk when she came to the crutches, go carefully around them, then dash off on some wild pursuit. Karen's attitude was: "Isn't Shanty unbelievably smart to have taught her so much!"

Karen was blossoming. We hadn't anticipated the metamorphosis brought about by competition, association with her peers in scholastic endeavors, socialization unrelated to the home, a new regimen, and the nuns so openly loving.

When Karen had started school, the Siamese cat had attached itself to Gloria. Karen reported this shift of attention in one of her frequent letters to Ed Doll.

"Etcetera, who now has black satin stockings as well as a black satin mask, has become Gloria's shadow. He even sleeps with her—head on pillow. When she reads in bed he gets quite jealous and insinuates himself between her and the book. If he wants to go out, he uses his teeth to pull the bobby pins from her pin curls. If this doesn't produce the desired result, he gets up on her dressing table and with his paw deliberately knocks over her bottles one by one. He talks but I don't expect you to believe this until you hear him. When he is put out in the rain or snow, he swears. He also says 'thank you' when he is let in. His eyes are blue like Daddy's and Mom is glad that something in the family has Daddy's beautiful blue eyes.

School is great!

I miss you. I love you!"

The writing of this letter took many hours, for Karen's script though much improved was still slow. Ed realized this and wrote to me suggesting we get Karen an electric typewriter. For the first, and I think the only time, I did not go along with his suggestion. I replied: "Even in this mechanized age, I believe good handwriting to be important and I don't want Karen substituting a machine for an art. I am sure that if she had a typewriter she would no longer struggle to improve her script."

Days were so crowded with events that they stumbled over each other. There never was a day when one could finish the tasks enumerated in the morning. I enjoyed correspondence—but there was so much of it; I enjoyed therapy (most of the time) but it was so constant; I really did like housework—but it was never finished. This week Jimmy and I were driving to Providence, Rhode Island, for a lecture. We were leaving Gloria and Marie with a full house: the younger kids, a bird, two dogs, and two litters of kittens for both Ash Wednesday and Yum Yum had proudly presented on the same day—one in the linen drawer in the pantry, and the other in the bottom drawer of my desk on a dozen hard-won manuscript pages. The roster of feline offspring read: Ounce, Bounce, Pounce, Abigail, Johnson (whose purr sounded like an outboard motor), and Tempest

156.

I. In all our inspired appellations, however, we never approached A.M.'s genius when she named her male Siamese "Hey You!" and her female—"Who Me?"

The furnace was still on though it was the middle of April and that meant shoveling coal. "The girls won't have to lift a bucket," Jimmy said as we drove up the parkway, "there will be enough young men around during the day who will welcome the opportunity to be chivalrous."

My talk was Saturday night and when we left the hall we couldn't believe our eyes. The city was white! and getting whiter each instant. A real old-fashioned blizzard in Spring.

The following morning we left the hotel to go to nine o'clock Mass, Jimmy in a topcoat and I in a suit and topcoat and patent leather pumps. No rubbers, no boots, not even the polo coat that was standard car equipment for going any place at any time.

The church was blessedly warm. Just before Communion I experienced a familiar and most distressing sensation—at once physical and mental; an *oppression* rather than a *depression* (though the effect was depressive); a heavy weightiness in my chest that had no confines, stimultaneously with a sense that was a *knowing* of coming disaster. Before the last prayers I whispered to Jimmy that I wanted to leave. As soon as we were outside I explained. Long ago there had been a time when Jimmy was apt to cock a skeptical eye at my presentiments but experience had taught him that they were well founded.

I said: "I'll find a phone and call home and you get the car. I'll meet you here in front of the church."

He strode off quickly, without question, through deepening snow. The telephone lines were busy because of the storm and it was some little time before I reached Gloria. She too knew the validity of my 'hunches' so I did not mention it but just asked if everything was O.K.

"Why wouldn't it be?" she asked smartly. "We can shovel snow with the best of them and besides it's good for the figure. Oh, Lark ate a golf ball but everything came out all right. Isn't the snow beautiful!"

I agreed that it was and hung up before my voice should

157.

betray my anxiety. I went back to the vestibule of the church where I could watch for Jimmy by peeping out the door. I took off my shoes and rubbed my icy feet. My oppression grew. I remembered well the weight and the growing that I had experienced during my months of my pregnancy with Kathryn Ann—a foreknowledge that had been crushing. A few hours after the birth of Kathryn Ann, healthy and howling, a nurse had come into my room. She had gone to the window and partially closed the venetian blinds. I had said: "I can spare you the telling—I know my baby is dead."

Now, I saw the car skidding a little as it came down the street. I slipped on my shoes and ran out. We crawled out of the city frequently halted by cars stuck in the drifts or piled up due to a skid. It was still snowing heavily as we started down the parkway and the driving was difficult and dangerous. Instead of the usual forty-five or fifty miles an hour we fought our way along at an average of fifteen miles an hour. The wind was at gale force and the visibility was very poor. Our car radio urged everyone to stay at home and strengthened the appeal by reporting on accidents due to the storm. We not only didn't have chains or snow tires, but our regular tires were as smooth as a baby's bottom. We had several bad skids, one of which landed us in a drift, and it took Jimmy half an hour to dig us out. Some of the Connecticut hills are very steep and on several occasions we worked our way up these by dint of using a bucket of sand and a shovel that Jimmy had had the foresight to purchase before leaving Providence. We made one stop for gas, coffee and sandwiches. Back in the car we took off our shoes, stockings and socks. Fortunately the heater was working well. Every time we passed a service station with a phone booth I wanted to jump out and call home but we decided we couldn't give the kids the anxiety of knowing that we were driving through the storm. Darkness came early and made driving even more dangerous for the headlights illumined the swirling flakes and the visibility was reduced to a few feet. Jimmy drove and I rode much of the rest of the way home with my head out of the window watching the edge of the road so I might guide him. It grew colder and colder inside the car. We said the rosary aloud, and got some real 'hot' music on the radio which was so noisy and so irritating that it helped to keep us from becoming mesmerized by the falling flakes and fatigue. Ordinarily the trip took five hours. It took us sixteen hours and it was 3:00 a.m. in the morning when we pulled into our driveway.

We left the car as fast as we could on numbed feet, and Jimmy's fingers were so stiff he had trouble getting the key in the lock of the back door. After an eternity he had it open. Inside the kitchen we turned immediately to open the closed door of Karen's room, flicking the light switch as we did so. At that moment the oppression left me. A rush of coal gas enveloped us from Karen's separate heating unit. Jimmy ran to her outside door and threw it open and I wrenched open the windows. We bent over Karen. Her face was deeply flushed, and her breathing was deep and slow. Jimmy snatched her from bed and rushed into the living room. He put her on the couch and I got a heating pad and bundled her in blankets. Jimmy was on the phone to the doctor. Dr. Haggerty was out of town and by the time the alternate arrived Karen's color was fading and her breathing was more normal. She behaved like someone reacting from anaesthesia "which," said the doctor, "was to be expected because in a real sense, that is exactly what she is doing."

Jimmy's voice was trembling. "She's going to be all right?"

"She's going to be all right," repeated the doctor reassuringly, then added: "I wouldn't have given much for her chances if you'd found her a little later."

ॐ

chapter fourteen

"All of life is *becoming*," Ed Doll had once said.

It was so for all of us, but more particularly for Karen, Gloria and Russ. It can be painful as well as heartening to watch youngsters becoming. Karen's life was lived to an accompaniment of pain. When the plaster casts were no longer worn at night the braces were substituted. With much effort, she could then turn on her side, but the spasms continued. Jimmy and I would watch her manipulating in the braces and on the crutches, see the grimaces of pain and ask: "For what?"

The answer: "Independence—as much as possible."

Late one afternoon I was in the kitchen getting dinner. Karen was in her room not ten feet from me. She was standing in front of her mirror practicing posture and balance. I heard her speaking low and I stopped the egg beater to listen. "It hurts a lot today," she was almost whispering, "but I'll try to handle it nicely, and ask You, Lord, to help Glo and Russ get a 'yes' on their case."

As with all growth there are many phases and one of my jobs was to ever encourage Karen, manifesting a constant hope. Because of her attitudes this was not hard to do.

The love between Gloria and Russ became stronger and deeper as anguished month followed anguished month. Although the lawyers gave them repeated "no progress" reports there were times when I perceived a strong surge of hope in my daughter. It was something I got through the process of osmosis, or perhaps was based on preknowledge. For her to entertain such hope was contrary to reasonable thought. I knew too well the trauma of hope repeatedly blasted, and I had to acknowledge that if something were not done, when the final "No" came from Rome, Gloria's temptation to defy it would be that much greater. Greatly troubled I went to see Father McSorley. In his loving wisdom he handed me an undertaking that was the most difficult I should ever be called upon to perform. I should be watchful, he said, and, when necessary, I must speak words that would quell the rising emotion and yet help to sustain in Gloria the theological virtue of hope. As one year faded into another I can only say that it was like periodically operating on your own child without anaesthesia. That this child survived the procedure without a real hostility for her mother is little short of a miracle, but I was always conscious that I was gambling a relationship as precious as any two people could have. Looking back I can see that my fear was an unwarranted reflection on both her character and her love.

Russ knew that witness after witness was either being called to appear or being visited, some in states far away. His confidence that somehow all the facts would be brought to light, and that eventually Rome would decide affirmatively, was unshakable. Again this was something we perceived, for he did not articulate it. Emotionally he was steady as the rocks I could see from my windows, and constant as the tides. So far as we knew, he only wavered once and this we learned from a mutual friend. Before Russ had left the Air Force he was taken ill and rushed to a hospital. The only available bed was on the maternity floor. After the first day Russ insisted on being moved even if his bed had to be in a corridor on another floor. He confided to a friend that listening to the cries of the newborn was just too difficult since it might never be for him.

We had enjoyed a hiatus in unpredictable medical problems and expenses. There were times when a whole week would go by and I would forget to appreciate their absence. Then, on September 15, Jimmy had a thyroidectomy.

I am not loath to admit that my husband is a paragon of virtue and possessed of the most endearing personality— when he's well. I am only slightly loath to admit that when he's ill or recuperating he would try the patience of three saints working eight-hour shifts. I was doing a fourteen-hour shift and a far cry from a saint. In all humility, I reminded him on several occasions that only through *my* practice of heroic virtue was this marriage going to be saved during his recuperation.

Cards and letters helped to dispel the patient's gloom. A lengthy epistle from the Chambers in British Columbia was a positive boon. When they had first left us to move out there, Jack had gotten the Kiwanis Club interested in cerebral palsy. One of their first efforts was on behalf of a boy named David Stone. Jack wrote:

. . . Early Friday morning David was taken over by more capable Hands. As I followed the little white cof-

161.

fin to the grave it occurred to me that this small boy had not lived in vain by any means. Because of David, thirty men in Duncan have become intensely interested in C.P. work; others will go to Vancouver and the Kiwanis Clubs in both Courtenay and Victoria are sending requests to me to speak to them on the subject.

Further, I intend to press for the setting up of a clinic here and I shall be justified in doing the same for Victoria when I go there. I also cherish the secret hope that the mother of one of our children might be persuaded to take a course in therapy (she is already a trained nurse) and become active in such a clinic.

In the meantime, we are raising funds by the sale of salvaged newspapers. Our members are all in business locally and in these parts this means that they own trucks of one sort or another. We have had as many as five trucks turn out on a Sunday afternoon, driven by Kiwanians and with these have collected many tons of paper. They are dumped in a large empty barn where we sort out magazines from newsprint. After this we push the newsprint through a hay-baler and makes bales of it. One of the members trucks it down to Victoria for nothing and last quarter we made $500.00. Properly developed this scheme should earn much more, say $4000.00 per annum. This is our target for the coming year. Our membership is thirty. . . .

We send our special love to Karen who started all this. We send her our thanks also.

In the same mail Karen received a letter from Ed Doll which she read to Jimmy with some pride. "If Smokey's foal (due in a couple of weeks) should be a 'she,' would we be sued for anything if we named her Karen? I dreamed of a palomino filly the other night—silken hair, lovely disposition and a 'willing horse'—so that name seemed right. We are shopping for announcement cards." In such wise did Ed repeatedly manifest his faith in Karen and the lasting effects are imponderable.

To Jimmy he wrote:

162.

"As for Karen's delight at school, make the most of it and share it. I'd like to be there to let my eyes shine into hers with happy enthusiasm for something so precious and prized because so long denied and perhaps, secretly despaired of. I'd like to be present to applaud and counsel but perhaps I am? For Lo! the spirit at least, is with you and her and all the family."

A many candle-powered beam of light came into Jimmy's room with an examination paper of Rory's. Question: What are the chief products of Italy? Answer: Olives, spaghetti, grapes and the Pope. The brilliance was enhanced by my report that his son wished to help the family budget and had decided to do so by cutting his own hair. Rory walked in, turned slowly for Jimmy's approbation and announced: "Daddy, I saved a whole buck." When Rory had left, Jimmy grabbed his throat in painful hilarity. "It looks—" he gasped, "as if the moths had been at it!"

A few hours later Jimmy sustained another shock. Marie was going to a formal dance with Joe and when she tripped into the living room Jimmy stared in dismay. Her hair was *up*. No longer in braided loops on her shoulders but dressed most beautifully in a chignon. She looked so grown-up that I, too, felt a few pangs.

Joe was delighted with the coiffure and the tiny pearl crown. His eye didn't miss a detail of her long white gown with its bouffant skirt (for this was the time of multiple petticoats). White was the perfect complement for Marie's dark hair and eyes and she did look beautiful. She carried herself like a queen as she walked over to Jimmy to kiss him good-bye.

"Have a wonderful time," he said, "and you do look lovely."

"She looks like a fairy princess," said Rory.

Marie kissed us each in turn and floated off. The door closed behind her. Jimmy blew his nose furiously and Glo and I burst into tears. I've never quite understood why.

But the day was not yet over. When Jimmy and I went up to bed we found a present from Yum Yum, another litter of kittens on the couch in front of the window. One of this litter turned out to be such a variety of unattractive colors that we named it Bilgewater. Morf and Ann Downes put in their bid for her, to go with their boat—the Ugly Duckling.

Sunday, the swimming awards were being given out at the Larchmont Manor Beach. We were all present and cheering lustily for the winners. Then the voice over the loudspeaker announced: "The staff and the children have voted for the swimmer who has made the most improvement this year." There was a weighty pause. "The gold medal is awarded to —" a hush so deep I heard an oak leaf blow across the patio, "to—*Karen Killilea!*"

There was a tumultuous shout from the crowd. Karen had won by dint of swimming without pause or break in breathing from the float to the steps. Barbara Cunningham was as proud as we, and not the least bit ashamed of dropping a few tears. Gertrude Ederle never had a moment like this. Karen glowed, accepted the medal graciously, and said simply: "I had the best teacher in the world." We stood happily watching Barbara and Karen being congratulated. It was quite a Scene on which to close the Summer.

My pride on this occasion brought me to the consideration of a question—the answer to which in the years to come, would serve both as a guide and a check as I encouraged Karen in her efforts. "How much of what I feel is purely for Karen and how much because she is the extension of my ego?" I'm not keen on trying to see myself as I am, but rather as I want others to see me or as I would wish to be. Once again I had to be grateful for our special situation which necessarily required frank, if distasteful, evaluation on my part.

In the soft days of early Fall Jimmy and Karen spent hours on the beach training Lark to obey hand signals in the water. She learned quickly and by the time Jimmy was able to return to work, the dog was diving, and one hundred feet off shore she was responding to the movements of the hand that meant "go left," "go right," "go out," "come in." She retrieved faultlessly bringing her fetch to Karen, and sitting at her feet until relieved of her carry. There was quite an audience for these performances, for wherever we walked the six cats and Shanty walked also. Shanty ran less these days and sitting beside Karen he resembled nothing so much as a benevolent and mitred bishop.

During his convalescence, Jimmy took over some of the correspondence, and when A.M. came to ask if there was anything she could do for the invalid, he handed her a stenographic pad and pencil. With our team doubled the output grew encouragingly. The anguish of so many of the letters caused A.M. to weep and also to give up much swimming and bowling to help in answering them. We lived to the rhythm of typewriter keys. One evening after A.M. left, I found a note to her children she had inadvertently left behind.

Dear Billy and Suzy:

I want to thank you very much for all your cooperation. It was delightful to come home and find you had:

Emptied the garbage

Made your beds

Fed and watered the animals

Brought in the empty Coke bottles from the front lawn

Tidied up your toys, blanket, etc.

Put perishable food in the icebox

Brought in the glasses from the front porch, and

Made yourselves tidy and as attractively dressed as the other children.

Since you are not home at 6:00 o'clock, which in case you have forgotten, is the time I like to have you back from your various hardworking days, I take this opportunity of informing you that you can cook your own dinners. And be damn sure you wash up after them.

—Love,
MOTHER

For months we had been wrestling with the problem of how to deal with the many letters written to us in a foreign language by the readers of *Karen*, all save the Dutch, for Kaasi Slezak was translating these and our replies. The solution was offered by Father Louis Dion, Assumptionist, who was later assigned to Moscow. He suggested that we forward the foreign language letters to his college, Assumption, in Worcester, Massachusetts, for translation. Here there were priests who spoke and wrote in many languages. In the curious way that so often obtains, we thus established a relationship that was to play a significant part in the future.

I had gotten away from writing a juvenile book of *Karen* which we titled *Wren,* and Grace Oursler was patiently prodding me to return to work. She frequently spent weekends with us and Rory called her his "Best Girl—after Mommy, Glo, Marie and Karen." Hers was a charismatic personality and the children, out of their admiration and deep love, strove to be like her. She was the age of the company she kept at the moment and of similarly suitable interests, whether it was a young boy, a captain of industry, a struggling author, a mission priest, or her laundress with family problems. Everyone seemed to have an unconscious response to her enthusiasm, curiosity, sincerity and unhampered love of people. She had a gentle wit and was a natural psychologist. This latter talent she brought to bear on me to get back to work on the book. A note from Grace: "Darlin' —Loved the new sign in your guest room—'IF THERE'S *ANYTHING* YOU NEED—*ANYTHING* YOU WANT —DON'T CALL ME—HELP YOURSELF.' Am having it printed for you. How about getting back to the book—a lot of kids need it and they're growing up." A week later: "Don't you think it's time 'the wren fledgling' left its nest?"

I succumbed and went back to *Wren* and found the going most difficult. For hours I sat before the typewriter and blank paper. The keys stayed quiet and the paper stayed blank. Some writers call this being "dry." For me it was more than that—I was parched and paralyzed. I finally resorted to the tactic of letting myself be distracted, on the theory that, if ignored, an idea like a child, eventually will demand your attention.

Our kittens proved a fine distraction. They surrounded me, scampering, leaping, attacking, retreating, twisting, rolling, always in flawless ballet. The thought came to me that the grace and charm of the creature must derive from the Creator; then the further thought that the Creator who made kittens so enchantingly playful—must *be* playful. (I think it was Chesterton who said that the creation of the hippopotamus proved that God has a sense of humor.) Both ideas are as valuable as they are intriguing because they afford one a wider concept of God. I was about to pursue this concept of Playfulness in relation to the planets when, sure enough, an idea presented itself, not subtly, but boldly. The keys began to click and several hours later I was still going great guns when the kids rushed to tell me there was a hurricane on the way.

When you live only a couple of hundred feet from Long Island Sound, this is significant news indeed. If the storm comes in from the sea there is nothing to break the force of the wind that sweeps down from Block Island a hundred miles away. There is always the wondering: what is the quarter of the moon? how high will the water rise? These questions were not our special concern since our house was elevated but even so, a tide rise of five feet would bring the water only twenty feet from our steps. I hoped the water would stay away from Mr. King's door, a few feet above sea level. His house was up for sale and a flooded cellar would scarcely increase its marketability.

For us the coming of a hurricane meant a big job of battening down. Joe and Russ arrived within a half hour of each other and we put them to work. On the porch there were ten heavy pieces with large pillows, all of which had to be carried down the steep front steps, around the side of the house and stored in the cellar. The iron tables with glass tops, the kerosene lamps, innumerable ash trays, two large jardinieres, assorted milking stools, and crickets we brought into the house. Rory's job was to find anything loose in the yard and put it in the garage—the outdoor grill, rakes, lawn mower, two stone statues, benches, metal chairs, clothes dryer, bike, even the garbage cans. If the predicted one hundred-mile-an-hour gale hit us, such objects would sail through the air and could easily be blown through a window. Marie and Gloria were in the attic rooting through Christmas boxes for candles and holders. It was a cinch that there would be an electrical failure. Russ and I took off as many screens as we could and all breakable objects in proximity to windows were moved. Piles of newspapers were readied for when the storm struck; some windows would be opened slightly in order to equalize pressure.

We called Shirley and suggested that at the first rise in the wind she and Mr. King come to our house, but Mr. King elected to stay home.

Joe trimmed the wicks of the lamps and we put in a supply of kindling and wood. Our mad daughter, Gloria, baked cookies—"We'll have a party during the storm—"

As I went from one snugging task to another I recalled a hurricane of not so long ago. We had weathered it well and were thankful when it blew away in time for us to leave for Connecticut for a wedding. As we drove up in front of the church, the storm reversed itself and came back with greater force than before. The wedding was a memorable ceremony. The words of the minister and the bride and groom were swallowed up by the roar outside, and above us, grindingly sharp, was the sound of the steeple as it was being wrenched loose from the roof. We had excused ourselves from the reception, which was at a shore club, and that was a prudent move for the tide came up, surrounded the club, and the entire wedding party was marooned for the day and the night and finally evacuated in rowboats. The hazards of our trip home had been multiple—falling branches and trees, live wires writhing across roads and dangling above us, blinding rain, and a gale that made Jimmy's job of controlling the Austin difficult in the extreme. Then we had run short of gas, but providentially in front of an old garage on the Post Road. The owner told Jimmy. "Good thing you got stuck here. I have a hand pump. All the others require electricity and that they ain't got!"

This hurricane, sweeping up from the south, moved faster than anticipated. We didn't need the radio to tell us, for prior to its onslaught there came an unnatural stillness of air and sea; even the birds desisted from their afternoon gossiping. The last job was to round up the livestock, a job made most difficult by Mr. King's parrot. Each of our cats had its own whistle and as my pursed lips summoned them in turn, Mr. Hopkins did likewise. Across the lawn, in dulcet imitation, floated varying notes from that blasted bird. Terribly confused, the cats would scamper first in one direction then another. I dispatched Rory to King's to tell them that if they didn't silence their blessed parrot—I would, and forever.

The storm hit with a suddenness beyond our previous experience. Shanty quivered beside Karen as the wind screamed hideously around the house. The trees twisted and writhed and I feared for the elm that supported our wisteria. Looking to the water we saw hundreds of gulls on the lee side of the rocks, their bodies pressed down against the rough surface, and the ducks congregated between the hummocks. The waves grew monstrous, a good twelve feet, and charged the land like an invading white-plumed army. They crashed against the breakwater with dreadful force, hurling their spray twenty feet into the air. The pounding of the rain was like a pneumatic drill.

Inexorably the tide raced in and the sea grew wilder. Some sailors had gotten their boats out of the water, others had removed masts and flooded the cockpits so the boats would ride out the storm partially submerged. Those at their moorings reared, bucked, dove, and strained under the ever-increasing impact. As the storm raged on, many tore loose and were carried like chips by the heavy water and hurled against the rocky shore where they lay helpless and repeatedly beaten.

The noise became horrendous, screeching, roaring, crashing. The house trembled and pictures vibrated against the walls. The chimneys shuddered and window panes seemed about to jerk themselves asunder. Great branches whipped against the roof and tore at the sides of the house, snatching shingles and clapboard. Jimmy, Russ, Joe, and I patrolled the house and Marie and Glo sought to distract the younger children with games. The dark was oppressive and candles and lamps only accentuated the ominous gloom. Rory said, "Our house is a fortress," but his voice quaked and I noticed he had trouble swallowing.

"This house," Karen replied in an unsteady voice, "has been battered by storms for almost a hundred years."

The water kept moving up. It swirled across the road and foot by foot into Mr. King's yard. Over the tearing gale we heard the crash of some object through our garage windows. The water was just short of Mr. King's foundation when the tide turned.

Hour after hour the insensate storm continued and we gathered in the living room and prayed for the repairmen who must be about their jobs in this concerted wildness.

There was a moment when someone said: *"Listen!"* The wind was dropping. We waited for a renewed attack but the next gust was weaker and the next weaker still. The hurricane was moving away. I grabbed Jimmy's hand and squeezed it in overpowering relief.

Some time later, when Jimmy was sure the storm would not reverse itself, we went out to take stock. The birds were chanting vespers; the water was quiet with the stillness of exhaustion; the boughs of the trees hung sodden and limp; flowers lay on the ground, their poor faces battered; from the leaves of bushes water dripped like the helpless tears of the aged. Happily our elm and wisteria were intact but we stood grief-stricken beside our towering two hundred-year-old cedar with twenty feet of its top snapped off.

We went afield and found that the entire front of the Manor Beach pavilion was gone; the breakwater had huge craters; power and sail boats were piled inertly on the rocks, pitifully destroyed; the sea wall in front of Slezak's was hugely gouged. Worst of all—the number of beautiful trees—uprooted, desecrated. We walked back up the street and saw that fences had been tossed about like matches; windows smashed; chimneys topped; great sections of roofs ripped off, and around one house, copper gutters and leaders were strewn like Tinker Toys.

The beach looked like a junkyard littered with masts, planking, the hull of a small sailboat, cushions, deck chairs, several splintered dinghies, two telephone poles, oars, paddles, dead fish, and an enormous man o' war. Jimmy picked up a child's sodden stuffed animal—unrecognizable.

We were a sad and thoughtful procession as we filed back home and paused by our amputated cedar. "We still have a beautiful forty feet," said Jimmy. "We lost a couple of dozen shingles, two windows, and our flowers. I'd say we were pretty lucky."

The damage of this storm ran into tens of millions of dollars and the number of lives lost was appalling. There was an enormous job of restoration and rebuilding to be done the length of the Atlantic Coast.

On our street they had to use a snowplow to clear away the sand, rocks and debris. It took us days to clear our property, small as it was, and we had to scrape the sand from the bay windows before we could wash them. As I worked I could only be thankful that we had come through unscathed —or almost. As soon as the danger of live wires was removed, Rory was released. He took his bike for sight-seeing, and riding down Slezaks' driveway, with his eyes on the sea, his front wheel hit a stone and he catapulted over the handle bars, taking the full force of the fall on his arm, breaking it neatly.

"Am I a storm casualty?" he asked his father as we left the hospital.

"In a manner of speaking—and not thinking," replied Jimmy tersely.

ह৵

chapter fifteen

Our life was very much like a patchwork quilt—innumerable tiny pieces, the edges touching and moving in all directions to make a colorful whole.

I noted in my day book:

Russ, Glo, Karen and Rory went to Playland Amusement Park. When they returned, Karen had little to say about the rides but did remark, "Mom Pom, I never saw so many babies and all beautiful!" She added wistfully, "Do you think God will ever send us another baby?"

Didn't realize what fear Rory entertains for Karen

171.

because of her poor balance and occasional falls. It was revealed today when he confided to Marie that he was afraid for children when they rode bikes, climbed trees, and used roller skates. He said he wished they would all wear protective hats like Karen. He is intrepid about his own activities.

When Jimmy and A.M. returned to their work in New York, it was possible to keep up with only a small proportion of the letters as they came in, about three-fourths of which were from people not connected in any way with cerebral palsy. Of necessity, the balance pleading for help came first and it was impossible to reply even to all of them. Typical, was a letter from a grandmother:

Alicia's mother and dad gave up and I'm afraid now it is too late. She's such a sweet child and it is breaking my heart to know she's facing such a bleak life. And there is so much promise.

Thank you for writing *Karen*, it has helped me so much. I have read it over and over. I am enclosing a picture of Alicia. . . .

I looked at the bright little face, the laughing eyes. We had been sent many pictures of lovely children, happy, alert, but body-bound. I had quite a collection of pictures of adults too, for whom public interest came too late.

Eleven years after the publication of *Karen*, we're still receiving such letters.

The book was about to find two new audiences. 1) I received a letter from Mr. Donald G. Patterson, Chief, Division for the Blind, Library of Congress, Washington, D.C. "We are happy to inform you that we are having *Karen* transcribed into Braille, and also Talking Book. . . ." 2) The book became required reading in many high schools, colleges and universities. This brought an avalanche of letters from students interested in going into the field of cerebral palsy as teachers, doctors, therapists. We answered as many of these as we could and as quickly as we could.

One day there came an envelope in which was a large

sheet of paper and two one-dollar bills

FOR CEREBRAL PALSY
I'VE JUST MET "KAREN"

No name. No address. I had no way of saying "thank-you"
—until now.

All the happy responses to the book were not in letter
form. Our washing machine conked out. Two young men
came to repair it(advanced senility was the diagnosis) and
they did not finish the job until 1:00 a.m. I was working in
the office and Gloria fixed them sandwiches and coffee.
While they ate their midnight lunch she told them of our
work in C.P. When the machine was again purring prettily,
I made out a check, thanked them extravagantly and returned upstairs. The next morning I found the check on the
kitchen table. Across the back was written—"Please use this
for your cerebral palsy work." (signed) Cliff Porter and
Jack Berg.

This was a beautiful Fall. There were days when, as
Karen said, the water looked like taffeta. In the vibrant sunsets the marsh grass seemed to catch fire, its beauty burned
against the rocks until extinguished by a wave of purple
dusk.

Russ and Glo, Jimmy and I were sitting on the rocks. We
had left the house and the younger children to get a report
from Russ on his case. It was five months since he had had
any word from Fr. Alucard; Russ had telephoned him that
morning. To Russ's inquiry, Fr. Alucard replied, "If there
were anything to report I would have called you. Don't
bother me."

Russ told us this with devastating matter-of-factness, but
the insensitive bluntness, the gaucherie of this priest left us
appalled and angry.

"Does he think he's running a casting office—'Don't call
me, I'll call you—'" Gloria asked bitterly.

Our puckish daughter was subdued and silent as we continued our walk, but once back at the house with the kids
she became again a person of infectious fun. For all her ap-

pearance and air of fragility, this young woman was strong as granite. She needed to be. I remembered something Father McSorley had said about her: "Even as the archer loves the arrow that flies, so he loves the bow that sends it."

Monsignor Madden, pastor of Our Lady of Fatima Church in Scarsdale, had just completed his school and convent. He invited us to the dedication, Cardinal McIntyre presiding. We took the wheelchair so Karen could move quickly along the corridors, and the crutches, for her to use in the rectory later. There was an enormous crowd. Glo said it looked like the opening game at the Yankee Stadium. People were packed on both sides of the hallway as the procession came slowly toward us, the Cardinal at its head. Rory was carrying Karen's crutches by using them. We were grouped around the wheelchair, Rory leaning heavily on the crutch handles. Behind me an elderly lady whispered loudly, "That poor woman! She has *two* crippled children!" Jimmy and I exchanged an amused glance and Karen giggled uncontrollably. As the Cardinal came abreast of us he paused before Karen, raised his hand to give her a special blessing, and passed on. Rory had been still for some time and as the Cardinal and his entourage moved north, my son scampered away to the south, tossing the crutches to Jimmy.

From the woman behind us came a cry that echoed the length of the hall. Pointing to the sprinting figure she called in clarion tones: "Glory be to God—a miracle!"

I always meant to write the Cardinal and share this gem with him, but somehow I never got around to it.

Christmas was galloping up on us with the innumerable preparations attendant thereto. Christmas dinner we had ten days ahead of time, following our honored custom of never having a holiday dinner on a Holiday. We dined by candlelight which played peacefully on the crèche set up on the large sideboard and on the assembled guests: Uncle Leo (Monsignor Madden), Father Rover, Grace Oursler, Phil and Carla Wallach, Russ and Joe, Jim Meighan and Dominick Tranzillo with whom Karen was still studying music. After dinner, with Dom at the piano, we had a carol fest which to my prejudiced mind left nothing to be desired.

In the comparative quiet that followed the last song,

Karen walked to the center of the room, Shanty beside her, and prepared for a dramatic announcement. She looked darling in a high-waisted, black velvet frock with white organdy ruching at the neck, her looped braids held by two wide velvet bows. Her cheeks were pink and her eyes bright. "You will notice," she spoke like a professor from a podium, "that I have omitted a customary article of my attire—" She paused for effect. "This is a surprise Christmas present for Daddy, but I wanted to tell him when you were all assembled." Again she paused and pulled herself up tall. She took a deep breath, then in a rush all but sang the words to Jimmy, "I don't need my hat! I hardly ever fall anymore!"

Rory rushed to embrace her; Jimmy's eyes were moist as he walked across the room and put his arms around her. The others, after a momentary silence, cheered and applauded and Dom ran to the piano and played the "Notre Dame Victory March."

"That's a curious selection," I said to him.

"I'm so excited—it's the only thing I could think of."

It was 2:00 a.m. when Jimmy and I finally put out our light. It was 2:15 when the pain struck and a few hours later Jack Hibbard had me on the operating table.

Karen's evening therapy was always done by Jimmy; now, while I was in the hospital, he rose an hour and a half earlier and did it in the morning as well. Rory assumed the job of putting on the braces and he and Karen figured out a way to make it easier—lay Karen on her side, put the pelvic band against her back and roll her backward into it. Karen, to save Jimmy time in the morning, started doing the "spread" exercises herself, and with knees bent was getting fifteen inches with no assistance. She was also doing the knee-up exercise by herself. My operation then, was a blessing in disguise but as Kitty Collins remarked some time later, "What I'm looking for is a blessing that is not disguised."

Another piece of home news which accelerated my recovery was that for the first time, Karen brought a book to the table to read with her meals. Dr. Guibor had said that with her eye difficulties she read by "brute force," and the fact that she was now reading for pleasure was a milestone of great significance.

Dr. Hibbard released me from the hospital on Christmas morning. Once again Karen's wheelchair came in handy. It had for some time been used to bring driftwood home from the beach, ride little ones around the zoo, transport the grocery bags from car to kitchen; now I rode into the house in style. Waiting for me was a Christmas letter from Ed Doll in which he said, ". . . and the happiest of our Christmas Greetings are those in Karen's own *script*—the perfect spelling paper (but how unfeminine) . . . a surge of gladness that we know you all. . . ."

During the Christmas vacation Karen counted the days —only so many left until school starts. "I can't wait."

Rory looked at her as if she were daft.

January brought successive snows that delighted the eye of the beholder, and we discovered an unexpected and to us, inexplicable result of Karen's operation. She could now steer a sled herself! To Shanty this represented the ultimate in hazards. His initial attempt to frustrate such a dangerous mission was to seize Karen's jacket in his teeth and drag her off the sled before I gave the final push. Foiled in this he would race barking beside her to the bottom of the hill and snatch her from the sled the instant it slowed down. One fine day, he had his left foreleg run over when he tried to stop the sled by blocking it with his body. Nevertheless he limped along executing his custodial duties. He permitted Lark to race along beside him but did not allow her near the sled. When she tried to move close to it he blocked her with his shoulder and pushed her away. Lark, gentle female that she was, would retreat with a puzzled set to her ears and an expression of hurt bewilderment in her dark eyes.

One afternoon we had a visitor who was both stuffy and pious. For the most part he talked to Karen, and in a most patronizing manner. On two occasions he oozed pity as he referred to "the terrible cross you have to bear." We'd all had about as much as we could take. There was a lag in the conversation and I was mulling over a tactful way to ask him to leave when he said to Karen: "Tell me, child, where is your wonderful dog?"

Karen managed a sober expression but her eyes twinkled.

She answered in a dulcet voice: "He's chasing a bitch up the street."

That ended the visit. Poor fellow, he was unfamiliar with the vernacular of dogdom, and shocked into departing by what he took to be vulgarity of this sweet-faced young lady.

"That was brilliant," Gloria congratulated Karen as she closed the door firmly behind our guest. "What inspired you?"

"He gave me a pain in the neck," Karen answered trenchantly.

Due to the weighty accumulation of medical expenses, our finances were at a low ebb that winter and spring, so there was not only no theatre for the children, but darn few movies. A week before Valentine's day we got a scrawled note from Grace: "Come with me to Never-Never Land— all of you——" And so it was that the kids got to see Mary Martin in "Peter Pan." I had seen two previous productions of the play but there never was a show for "young people of all ages" as delightful as this. The following week Grace sent them the album of the show, which she had had the stars autograph.

One evening we were playing the music and Rory and I, and Gloria and Joe were dancing the tarantella. Just a little weary, I sank down beside Karen who had her arm around Shanty. She said in a small voice: "Mommy, the lump is back."

I placed my hand on the silky coat just below the shoulder. It certainly was and apparently had been growing very rapidly.

"Let's do something right away." Her voice was tight and loud with fear. It carried over the music and the family stood shocked. They looked at me and the dog, and I nodded. They moved over to Shanty who acknowledged this attention by rhythmically thumping the floor with his tail on which the 'feathers' glinted like gold. Joe bent, kissed the top of Karen's head and suggested: "Let's roast some chestnuts. He seems to like them as well as steak."

"Yes." But Karen spoke listlessly.

"Good idea." I commended Joe in the kitchen.

"Roasting chestnuts have a comforting fragrance." He began to slit the shells.

When I talked to Grace later in the evening I told her about Shanty. The next day she mentioned it to somebody who mentioned it to somebody else who was a doctor, had read *Karen* and knew what the dog meant to our daughter. As a result within twenty-four hours, there was a call from a doctor at a hospital which did a great deal of work in research and treatment of cancer. If we would bring Shanty to the hospital he would receive the finest and most complete medical care—roentgenologist, surgeon, the works. It would cost us nothing.

I said we would bring him the next day.

Early the following morning, Karen, Rory and I took Shanty to the beach. Lark we left home when Karen said: "Shanty should have all of our attention." Watching him rout ducks we realized that he had lost a lot of his usual ebullience and was making but a token effort. The tide was halfway in and white-plumed waves shepherded the rocks. Rory pointed to the moorings that stood up from the water in irregular lines. "They look like cornstalks after the harvest." He picked up a stick and threw it into the water. Shanty retrieved it, not rapturously but dutifully.

"Just let him be," I suggested. "Let him meander as the spirit moves him."

Slowly we walked back up the street. Rory pushed the chair and Shanty walked beside it so Karen's hand could rest on his head. "In a couple of weeks you'll be as good as new," she told him, but I could taste her fear as well as my own.

Joe was in the kitchen waiting for us. He said to me: "I though you might like to have a chauffeur, so I cut classes for the day."

Gloria said to Karen, "Let's make a black cake for Daddy with chocolate icing."

"Fine," replied Karen dispiritedly. She leaned over, gathered the dog's great body to her and covered his face with kisses. Gently I disengaged them and we left. The look on her face was almost more than I could bear. She didn't say good-bye.

Joe had dinner with us that night and the conversation at the table was feverish to say the least. No one wanted any quiet moments in which Karen could think.

"Daddy ducks like a fighter when he's shaving," Rory offered.

"Why?" Joe responded.

"I don't know. He gets cut like a fighter too."

"I'm glad you brought this up, son." Jimmy cleared his throat.

"Little idiosyncrasy?" I inquired sweetly, having a pretty good idea of what was coming.

"You see, children," Jimmy spoke in measured phrases, "your mother is a very busy lady and just a little absent-minded—"

Marie broke in: "A little? Don't you remember when she put the carrots in the hat box and the hat in the hydrator?"

"Precisely," said Jimmy when the laughter subsided. "And because of this peculiarity of hers—" he allowed me a pitying glance, "she has to make notes to remind her of things, and then because she's *so* busy she forgets to look at the notes." He struck a professional attitude.

I glanced at Karen. Jimmy's peroration was a fine distraction.

He went on: "Now, no woman forgets to make up her face, which means she *has* to look at a mirror. *Q.E.D.* Notes written in soap on the bathroom mirror have to be seen. There are many mornings," he turned to Karen with expression and gestures inviting her pity (I thought he was overdoing it a little but she wore a look of tender understanding), "—many mornings when I don't have two square inches of unblemished glass." He sighed dolefully. "The mirror's like a checkerboard and I have to move from one clear spot to another. It's very trying." He dropped his head in mock despair.

"Daddy's a clown," Rory chortled.

"So's your mother."

"You really shouldn't, Mother," Marie was serious. "It's dangerous. Daddy might sever an artery."

Glo: "There are no arteries in the face."

Karen: "He might get an infection."

Rory: "or— tetanus—"

Joe: "No horses—"

Rory: "Too bad!"

Daddy: "That little remark is subject to misinterpretation."

Mother: "Oh, for Heaven's sake, I'll get you a shaving mirror."

"Fine," applauded Jimmy, "then you'll have two glass notebooks."

"Why don't you handle your notes the way Grace does?" Glo asked.

"You mean putting slips of paper across the floor?"

"Exactly. You'd be so irritated by the untidiness you'd do the job to get rid of the paper."

"Please—" pleaded Jimmy, "that's a wonderful idea."

"All right," I agreed magnanimously.

Karen asked wickedly. "Did you tell Daddy about going to Mass Wednesday morning without your skirt?"

Jimmy threw up his hands. "I believe it."

"I discovered it right after I got out of the car," I defended. "I felt chilly. I don't think anyone noticed."

"I pray not." Jimmy folded his hands devoutly.

"Make a note on the date of my Confirmation, Mom. I wouldn't want you to forget that," Rory said.

Joe offered: "Let's talk about saints and their names and maybe we can help you make your selection of a patron."

"I've already made it." Rory looked around the table. "I've selected two—'Michael Mary' " He added quickly: "Do you think the Bishop will give me any trouble on 'Mary'?"

"It's quite common in other countries for boys to be called by some variation of Mary," Joe told him. In Spanish speaking countries, Maria for a man is not at all unusual."

"Good." Rory was reassured.

The girls and boys got up to clear the table. As Glo piled the dishes in the sink she said to me: "Tell them about the woman who came on Monday."

"Oh, yes—you'll all love this! There was a knock at the door and I opened it to a most attractive woman who was selling an encyclopedia which I coveted but knew we couldn't afford. In the course of our conversation, she told me about her three children, one of whom has violent red-orange hair, and according to her, his whole body is covered with enormous, bright freckles. She said the boy's face looks like a perforated mask, and it disturbed them because it made him so *different*. When she was leaving she asked me for my name so she could record the visit. I spelled 'Killilea,' for her.

"She paused in her writing and without looking up asked, 'Are you the Mrs. Killilea who has the girl with cerebral palsy?' I answered that I was and was pleased that she used the medical phrase easily. Quite a forward step, I thought.

" 'Where do you keep her?' she asked bluntly.

"I gasped but quickly recovered. 'My husband built her a snug little house in the back yard. Where do *you* keep your redheaded son—he's different too.'

"She whispered: 'Forgive me' and turned scarlet.

"I felt sorry for her so I told her it was quite all right but it might be helpful to remember that everyone is handicapped in some way—the only difference being that Karen's—and her boy's—showed."

"Neatly done," commented Joe. "What did she say then?"

"She said 'thank you' and meant it."

Joe dried the last dish and put it in the closet. (I still haven't figured out whether Joe doesn't wash dishes because he wears French cuffs, or if he wears French cuffs because he doesn't like to wash dishes.) "Karen, let's leave all these dull people and go to the movies."

I asked Jimmy. "Therapy now or later?"

"Skip it," he decided wisely.

Karen laughed: "We'll leave the slaves to their salt mines."

After they left Jimmy said: "Joe is amazingly perceptive. He knows that for all of Karen's brave front she's scared to death for Shanty. A good movie will help a lot."

"He's a lamb," said Marie with feeling.

It was late when Karen got to bed and we turned on the speaker in our room. This was an electrical device whereby we could hear every sound from her room on the floor below and at the opposite end of the house. By depressing a key we could converse. The last sound from her room that

181.

night was a choked: "Dear Lord, please take care of my four-footed angel and bring him safely home to me!"

Two weeks later, Shanty came home. The only after-effect of his surgery that seemed to bother him was embarrassment over the large shaved area on his side. If someone pointed to it he would shrink out of the room. "Poor baby," Karen would comfort, "don't you know you're the handsomest dog in the world."

The doctors had inserted radium and this caused large collections of fluid in the area. Several times a week a doctor came up from New York and tapped the fluid. Shanty stood beside the large basin, patient and unwhimpering throughout the procedure. Karen, white-faced beside him, murmured caressing reassurances. The big dog was back on the job full time with an interesting result. When Karen dropped something, either from her chair or while on crutches, she couldn't pick it up, and long ago Shanty had started doing this for her. Now that he was back to retrieve I noticed that she dropped less than she had while he was gone. The reason was obvious—when she had him to recover objects she didn't worry about dropping them, so she was more relaxed and consequently dropped less.

At irregular intervals, Russ went to the chancery office to give further testimony. About what and to whom, we never knew. He was able to tell us however, that the lawyers after a two-year search had finally located a couple who had shared an apartment on the base with Russ and his wife. There was every reason to hope that their testimony would advance the case.

I once heard Father Gannon say: "True joy lies in well-ordered effort and happiness in self-control." Gloria was deeply happy and joyous in spite of the desolation that must have swamped her heart. There was only small reason to hope that her marriage to Russ could ever be.

The New Year brought change, growth, and significant new friendships—Grace was to leave shortly for Formosa where she was going to do a book with Madame Chiang Kai-shek. None of us looked forward to the separation—

Marie wore her hair up all the time, not just for parties—

Loretto and Jim Kelly moved to Larchmont with their

four beautiful daughters when Jim was named Agent-in-Charge of the New York office of the F.B.I. At first meeting there was rapport which burgeoned into a rare friendship. Jim was tall, blonde, handsome, and serene. Retta was slender, dark, beautiful, and volatile—

The sleeves of Rory's shirts receded rapidly toward his elbows as the cuffs of his trousers climbed toward his knees. He was growing in other ways too. He took over more of Karen's therapy and, working hard against resistant muscles, commented: "This is sure good—it exercises both of us!"

One morning as he sat on the bed resting after a particularly strenuous half hour, he and Karen talked about Glo and Russ. "It beats me," Rory said, "why we pray so hard for them to get married. We're praying *against* ourselves, because then she'd leave us."

"I know," answered Karen, "I have trouble meaning such prayers with my whole heart."

Just before February 22 (Rory thought it was so nice that George Washington was born on *his* birthday), my son presented himself at the kitchen door, battered, bruised, and bleeding.

"What happened?" I asked as I gently bathed his face. I knew he didn't like fighting.

"He was bigger 'n me."

"Well—"

He looked up at me. "You know, Mom, I was so mad I forgot to be scared."

"What were you mad about?" I put some antiseptic on a cut cheek.

He winched, swung around—mad all over again. "He called a colored kid a 'nigger'—"

"Good boy!" But he didn't understand in the least why I kissed him.

"Sister said to show you this." He pointed. "Where the circle is."

Framed in red pencil: Question: What happened in 1497? Answer: Columbus did not find India.

He looked at me without guile. "Sister said I should look up 1497—and I should show you this to brighten your day —and I don't understand her at all."

183.

The following week, Eddie Brothers enplaned for distant points and although he wrote regularly, letters were no substitute for his visits.

In conjunction with the publication of *Wren* I made the usual guest appearances at book and author luncheons and radio and T.V. shows. I took Marie with me to one show, that she might observe the intricate, inner workings of a television studio. Halfway through the program, the interviewer invited Marie to join us. He asked her some questions and I was gratified by her self-possession.

"What's the most exciting thing that happened to you this month?" he asked.

My teen-ager answered promptly. "The Father-Daughter Dance at Good Counsel." I glanced at the monitor. Marie photographed beautifully. "Daddy is a wonderful dancer and waltzing with him is a dream—"

Our host failed to conceal a smile at the ingenuousness of the reply. He next asked Marie: "Your sister Gloria is twenty-three; why do you think she hasn't married?"

I thought—'what an unfortunate question!' and hoped Marie would not attempt an explanation of the complications. I underestimated her. She dealt with the question basically.

"I guess Gloria compares every man to Daddy and then she's not impressed."

She winked at me and as we left the studio remarked: "I saw no point in mentioning that Russ measures up so well."

Tex and Jinx asked me to bring Shanty with me to their show. He was an out-and-out sensation. Not only was he glorious in appearance but the crew almost broke up when the dog followed hand signals from the director—sitting, standing, and turning from Camera 1 to Camera 2. He was quiet and regal and totally enchanting, but the whole thing was a mistake because it provoked a fresh avalanche of fan mail—for *him*.

I was keeping my day book faithfully so that my reports to Dr. Moore between our regular visits would be accurate. Ed Doll received a report on everything that happened in the family and for him I would just copy my notes *in toto* and send them along without editing:

It has rained almost every day for six weeks. Sun out today. Jonquils beaten down by heavy downpours. Lilies-of-the-valley about four inches high. Jimmy and Rory moved cherry tree.

Misty Morning, that patriarch of our cat family, grows feeble and can no longer manage the leap to use the knocker when he wants to come in.

Lark grows smarter, stronger and more handsome. However she has made a decision—SHE IS RORY'S DOG! Karen has sent for all Lark's papers and is going to have them framed, together with a Transfer of Ownership, and give them to Rory for Christmas.

House ailing—trouble with its iron intestines. Jimmy ministering nights and week-ends. Has progressed from plumber to Master plumber.

APRIL 20
Lilies out and magnolia in bloom. Easter vacation. Karen, without braces, gets self into wheelchair. Rory taught her how. Takes self to bathroom and to bureau and to closet and puts away all her laundry.

APRIL 21
For first time since operation, Karen dressed herself completely today!
She has bad blisters on heels. Can't seem to get rid of them. She sleeps on stomach, can't have heels touch the bed Jimmy put chair at foot of bed and drapes sheet over that as even that much weight is too painful. Over speaker at night we hear her whimper with pain. This is a purgatory for Jimmy, especially when it follows a day that is never over until 10:30 p.m. I think he loves his children too much.

Marie translated fifty lines of Latin without help.
Saw a friend *carry* Karen across the lawn the other day. I asked her: "What's the big idea?"

She smiled and answered: "But Mom, it made *him* feel so good!"

APRIL 22

KAREN STAMPED HER FOOT TODAY!! This gratifying physical accomplishment was provoked by Abigail, most enterprising kitten, upsetting Karen's file basket for the third time. I gave kitten saucer of cream as reward. Karen's braces tear her clothes, Nicest dresses have holes. Glo has started lining skirts. Makes all the difference.

Etcetera has become "kitten-sitter." Karen whistles for him when mothers leave kittens. He climbs into basket, gathers kittens in with forelegs and washes them assiduously. Karen started to use camera to record such tender scenes. Developing finger control impossible before surgery. Why?

MAY 15

Karen filed her own nails into perfect shape.

Have decided that it is very important for parents of exceptional children to realize that there will *always* be new situations to deal with.

Mr. King not well so don't see much of Shirley. The kids planted a religious medal in his yard and asked God to send us a family with children. Hear there's a family named Kerr interested.

Received a beautiful hanky from Grace today with a card: "Dearest—here's a 'think-of-me.' "

Our most recent letter from Ed, acknowledging the above hodge-podge make a very good point. Jimmy and I discussed it at length. As a matter of fact we still discuss it. ". . . Not just children change, but parents as well, and we want feedbacks on our own changes."

Commenting on the school rejection of many bright youngsters with cerebral palsy Ed said, "Examinations not valid because of the expressive inability for formal procedures."

"It will take some doing to sell that idea," was Jimmy's comment.

At the end of the school year Karen was on the Honor Roll. She wrote the news to Ed Doll, in script. He replied: "We've known all along that you could but it is reassuring to have one's confidence vindicated. You should be proud of yourself as we are all proud of you."

To us he wrote: "We must now be concerned with adolescence and pre-adult needs. Also anticipation of adult status. Until we get together, let us mull over these questions: What are we working for? What values are at stake: How best to achieve them?

ઠ✍

chapter sixteen

I hold with many others, that it is easier to believe in Providence than coincidence. What is especially intriguing is that the machinations of Providence are usually visible only in retrospect. Certainly we could not have anticipated the dividends with which our prayers would be answered when we planted that medal under Mr. King's splendid rhododendron bush and asked for a family with children, nor was the full significance of the response to be appreciated for some little time to come.

The Kerrs did buy Mr. King's house but only after overcoming some solid obstacles and facing more than a few difficulties, not the least of which was a fire which destroyed an entire wing the week they took title.

There were four Kerr boys. There was a wire-haired fox terrier. They had been in occupancy some weeks before I met them. I'm dull in the morning, fairly alert in the afternoon and early evening, and then come really alive about 11:00 p.m., when normal people are retiring. On a soft June night I was walking alone, trespassing on Kerrs' wide lawn. The sky was heavy with clouds and the only sound was the silken swish of the waves as they brushed the shore. The only sound, that is, until from about twenty feet away I heard a female voice say with sweet reasonableness: "Kelly, if you have to bite someone—go bite a Killilea. I understand they won't sue."

This could only be Mrs. Kerr speaking. I knew she wasn't addressing her husband, his name was Walter, I well knew, for I saw it daily as drama critic in *The New York Herald Tribune*. I assumed, reasonably enough, that the four boys were in bed, therefore she must be addressing the terrier. A shrill bark and a hurtling white form confirmed my assumption.

"Kelly! Come here!" commanded a male voice. As lovely a voice as Jimmy's, I thought.

Apparently the Kerrs were sitting on the wall 'exercising' their dog. I went over and introduced myself, "I'm the one who won't sue." We chatted for a while and I found Jean Kerr as helplessly humorous in conversation as she was in her writing. Several nights a week we had nocturnal visits. We later learned that we had passed each other daily on the beach; we didn't speak because we hadn't yet *seen* each other. Around our kitchen table, we had referred to our new neighbors as Mr. and Mrs. Raccoon, the Night People.

My meeting with their five-year-old twins is not easily forgotten; they presented themselves at the kitchen door, their faces shining with eagerness—John, round-faced and cherubic, Colin, elfin. They proffered for purchase a lovely bouquet of flowers for $.62. Ever one to encourage enterprise in the young I took the flowers and counted out the coins. It wasn't until later in the evening that I discovered just how enterprising they were. I went out to water my garden and established beyond a reasonable doubt that I had bought my own flowers.

Over the past year, we'd had a warm correspondence with a minister from Iowa and had suggested that if he were ever in the neighborhood he should call us. One beastly hot Friday afternoon he did come to call with his wife and sister. They were in the neighborhood—Rochester to be exact, a scant three hundred miles away. They were as dear and sweet as we might have expected though I felt I shocked them when I smoked a cigarette. They met all the family and commented on what a well-bred boy we had. I invited them to stay for dinner and went to the kitchen to attempt an interesting disguise for canned tuna fish. The Reverend followed me and we chatted comfortably while I made a sauce. He was seated, facing the door of the back stairs and, as I turned to him, I saw the door swing slowly open. We stared, transfixed at the vision confronting us. It was posed leaning languorously against the wall, body tilted backward. There was a garishly colored scarf on the head, pendant earrings, and several pounds of make-up on the face included violet eye-shadow, lashes heavy with mascara, rouge, and a carefully painted mouth that was revoltingly, greasily red. A peasant blouse exposed the neck which was hung with a dozen strands of beads. There were as many bracelets. The waist was cinched tight and a full red skirt fell to the feet. The apparition raised a languid arm and we saw bejewelled fingers place a cigarette in the mouth. With swaying hips the figure gyrated slowly, then turned and vanished up the stairs. My guest was thunderstruck. With great presence of mind I went over, shut the door and spoke with what I hoped was a convincing chuckle. "One of the neighbor's daughters— they're rehearsing for a play." Such a character would properly belong only to Tennessee Williams and I hoped my visitor hadn't been to the theater lately. "I hope you like fish?"

He faced me slowly, moistened his lips and collected himself with an effort. "Fish—oh—ah—fish? Oh yes, yes indeed —I love to fish."

I awaited Rory's appearance at the dinner table with considerable trepidation hoping he knew enough to use cold cream to remove all that paint and grease. He bounded in, face shining, innocent of all save soap and water. I turned quickly to the minister; not a shadow of suspicion darkened his clear blue eyes. The sauce turned out just fine, the conversation around the table was stimulating, our parting warm on both sides—then I escorted Rory to his room. I shall draw a veil over the ensuing interview.

At Dr. Moore's suggestion we had given Karen a five-week sabbatical from exercises. When we resumed therapy we did only a few exercises a day, gradually increasing to the full number, and only five days a week. This procedure paid off and Karen now had very little fatigue and fewer spasms. The blisters on her heels were healed and our major concern now was the non-use of her right hand. She was left-handed and the right arm was more severely involved than the left. As a result she didn't want to use it much and consequently the arm was bent at the elbow and she was unable to straighten it completely. We did all kinds of occupational therapy to correct this situation but it wasn't until a year or so later that we found an activity requiring the full use of the arm with consequent improvement.

However, this summer we had lots of fun. Jim Kelly bought an aluminum rowboat which he kept in our yard. It was so light we could carry it to the end of the street and launch it. I strongly doubt that Jim, as Agent-in-Charge, had any illusions about the amount of time he'd spend on the water. I do not doubt that Karen figured in the arrangement. She loved to fish and this summer we happily rose many mornings at 4:30 a.m., coasted silently through the morning mist, and on two occasions had a school of porpoise perform for us. Some days we had a fine catch, others days were not so fruitful, but this was of secondary importance. It was healing for all of us to be far away from a telephone, from mail, from routine. There was only the squalling of the gulls as they followed us for remnants of bait; the pat-pat of the water against the side of the boat; the occasional splash of a leaping striper; and the soothing whir of a cast line. In the heat of midday we would come home refreshed, serene.

The outside of our white house was looking a little seedy on the first two floors as a result of storms and rain, so we washed it. Our family made a crew of six and Rory had friends eager to splash around with brushes, soapsuds and no restrictions on the use of water. For such an undertaking the garb was simple—a bathing suit. And of course barefoot. We were all thus profitably engaged one Saturday when a V.I.P. arrived. I had forgotten he was coming to discuss, nay urge, my appearance as guest speaker before a large and distinguished group. A stranger came up the steps and I waved from the top of a ladder where I had acquired a good part of the grime I had removed from the shingles.

Standing well away from flying suds and coursing water he called above the din: "Is Mrs. Killilea at home?"

I eased myself down the ladder, bucket over one arm, padded across the wet porch floor in dark grey feet, smiled engagingly and said: "How do you do. I'm Mrs. Killilea."

The gentleman gave a startled look, muttered, "There must be some mistake—" and scuttled away like a scared fiddler crab looking for his hole.

And that was the last I heard about that speaking engagement.

At this time we had received over eleven thousand letters and in their perusal a number of things came to light. Not infrequently, men had more trouble adjusting to an exceptional child than women. We certainly were in no position to draw conclusions but there were some clear indications. Another thing that became increasingly clear—the three C's of any marriage, Communication, Consideration, Compromise, were more necessary where there was an exceptional child. Also, of more than a few workers in the field of cerebral palsy, we could say with Caryll Hauslander: "The unexamined motive is not to heal suffering but to disinfect it."

And *mirabile dictu!* People who had donated to, and worked for aid to the cerebral palsied were now writing that subsequently, they had had a child with cerebral palsy; how little did they dream they said, at the time of their giving, that they were building for their own son or daughter.

A.M., Gloria and I were working on the porch at a large table on which we had placed carefully divided piles of correspondence. In the yard there was a great commotion and Yum Yum and Ash Wednesday scooted up the steps and across the porch, Kerrs' terrier, Kelly, in pursuit. He pursued them up on the couch and thence to the work table scattering papers in all directions, then through the door into the house in full cry with me in pursuit of the pursuer. Across the living room we charged, tore across the dining room and plunged into the kitchen where this beast treed my two nursing cats atop the stove. I yanked them spitting and trembling, from under his noisy mouth, shoved them in Karen's room, closed the door and went to the phone to call

Kelly's mistress. "Your damn dog just chased my cats all through the house to the top of my stove!"

There was a pause, then Jean's calm voice asked: "Is it lit?"

My anger evaporated in laughter.

The quarry out of the running, Kelly left and I went back to work. Karen was reading and looking up from her book and said: "Glo, I'm thirsty."

Immediately Gloria got up.

"Sit down," I said sharply. To Karen I suggested: "If you're thirsty, go get yourself a drink." I locked the braces, handed her the crutches, helped her to her feet. "You're on your way."

When she was well out of earshot I remarked to Gloria: "Do you realize that this is just one of many requests Karen makes of you during a day?"

"I love helping her," she answered.

"That's just it. You're not helping her. You're spoiling her."

"Now really—" Gloria began with more than a hint of annoyance.

"Really. Now you listen for a minute. You've worked just as hard as we for Karen—to make her independent—and now your kindness, and a kind of selfish love (because it hurts you to see her struggle), are robbing her of the desire to be independent. All you kids offend in this respect, but you most of all." I offered her a cigarette and lit one myself. "Although you're younger than Jimmy and I, you're not going to be here forever either. What applies to us as her parents, applies equally to her siblings. Father McSorley taught me a long time ago: 'A good mother will grow up to be useless.'" I spoke gently but firmly. "A good sister will grow up to be useless also."

Gloria looked out over the water with an obstinate set to her lips. "I could get her a drink in less than a minute, and it will take her fifteen minutes to go to the kitchen, get that drink and come back."

"Glo, darling, you're not really thinking about what I just said. Think on *destructive* kindness, and *selfish* love. You must love her enough to let her take those fifteen minutes to

192.

do something for herself. Tomorrow it will be fourteen minutes and in a day or so, maybe even a week, it will be thirteen, and in a couple of months, she'll do it in five or six minutes—*if she's allowed to do it!*"

"But it's so hard for her—"

"And for you," I said softly. "This is not an isolated instance. I count a dozen or more each day. The trouble with all you kids is that helping Karen is instinctive. Well, you're going to have to curb your instincts. For her sake."

"I'll try." Her eyes were flooded with tears as she picked up her stenographic notebook.

Grace had not been well when she left for Formosa and was even less well on her return. She was on her way through the lobby of her hotel when a youngster careened into her and knocked her down. Her hip was fractured and there began long weeks in bed. I went in to see her as frequently as I could.

The evening of December 15th we were sitting in the kitchen with a friend who had driven up from New York. We wound up a political discussion and the third pot of coffee about 11:30 p.m. and he rose to go. Prompted by I know not what I said to him: "If you'll wait a minute I'll get my overnight bag and go with you. I want to see Grace."

Jimmy said with sweet succinctness: "At this hour! You're crazy."

I hesitated, then hurried upstairs and was back in a matter of minutes. "I don't know how I know—but she needs me."

"If you must, you must," Jimmy said with resignation as he kissed me good-bye. "Kiss Gracie on the back of the neck for me. Several times."

I arrived at the apartment shortly after midnight. The nurse admitted me and I walked to the door of Grace's bedroom. She was lying, with the head of her bed elevated, in an oxygent tent. Her eyes were closed. As I stood quietly in the doorway she said, without opening her eyes, "Dear Marie! I knew you'd come! I told the nurse so."

I looked to the white figure. She nodded.

Speaking had exhausted Grace and she said little during the long hours of the night, but what she did say I shall not forget. "In that closet," she pointed, "are the Christmas presents for the kids. I did my shopping early." Her breathing was labored.

"Hush. Don't speak. Save your strength."

"Those presents," she persisted, *"must be opened with gladness."* The words had a whispered emphasis.

The following afternoon Grace left us.

In the days that followed her family was deluged with telegrams, letters, mammoth floral tributes from heads of state, captains of industry, artists in all fields of endeavor, from people she had helped—whose names were unknown even to her children.

I took the box from the florist that was most eloquent. It was not impressive. It was slight and it held blossoms that were white and delicate and fragrant with the eternal hope of Spring.

White lilacs.

ॐ

chapter seventeen

We would indeed be lacking in mother-wit if we didn't take cognizance of the providence which summoned Grace from our family circle and simultaneously linked Jean to it. Where the children had turned to Grace for confidences and advice, they now turned to Jean. She didn't creep into their hearts, she galloped in. There have been few relationships in their lives so meaningful. Or in mine for that matter. Jean, like Grace, knew that the most important thing one has to give is one's ears—to be a listener is to give truly of one's self.

We went ahead with the regular preparations for Christmas, making a valiant effort to do it with the "gladness" Grace had urged. It was especially hard for Jimmy who missed her cruelly. Marie was working on the candles she made each year, beautiful pieces of varying shapes and colors. There were great heavy green ones in the shapes of trees

194.

weighted down with tiny shimmering decorations like the diamond sparkle of ice on fir; slender white ones that rose delicately with burdens of infinitely tiny pearls. This kind of fine handwork she had taught herself years ago when confined to bed with tuberculosis and rheumatic fever. The year she was eight, she had made for us, from pipe cleaners, a ballet group dressed in gossamer garments and arranged in lovely postures on a mirrored floor.

While Marie was engaged in the candle endeavor, working in the kitchen was hazardous. There were pots of boiling paraffin on the stove, buckets of ice water on the floor, and clotheslines strung from wall to wall for hanging the finished candles to harden. She paused in her work to look out the window. "Come quickly, Mom," she summoned me, "it looks as if there's a great ice floe in the Sound."

Two hundred yards off shore, about thirty yards wide, I saw it extending a quarter mile from Umbrella Point to far below Slezaks'; it was moving slowly to the east and as I watched, I realized that this floating whiteness was composed not of ice but of pulsing sea gulls. Thousands of gulls in an unbroken white blanket moving so uniformily in quiet harmony that they seemed not to move at all. We called the other children and phoned the Kerrs. I've never seen anything like it before or since. We stood entranced, then, as though a great rushing wind tore the blanket from the surface, the birds rose in enormous whirring platoons, hundreds at a time, in flawlessly executed sequence until the last white wing disappeared into the encroaching dark.

The last light of day swept a cloud-ridged sky and Rory said softly: "It looks as if God had started plowing."

"All this and heaven too!" Gloria whispered.

Practical Karen said, "There are people that scrimp and save all year long for two weeks with a view that we have every day."

"That's *right*," affirmed Rory, he often spoke in italics. "We don't have much money—but *boy*, are we *rich!*"

Jimmy and I had for some time been discussing Karen's need for competition away from school. We thought and thought, trying to come up with some area of activity where she could compete with nonhandicapped people on their own level. We knew that an essential part of growth is learning to win and to lose gracefully. In vain we applied our best mental efforts to this matter. Not only was there no bright light of illumination, there was not the feeblest glimmer. We were also constantly mindful of the bent right arm, but again failed to come up with a solution.

For Gloria and Russ this was a happier Spring because Father Alucard moved out of the picture and Father Kelly moved in. Now they had a priest who appreciated their conduct in the present, and manifested every confidence in their conduct in the future, no matter what the outcome. He was Christ-like in his understanding, compassion and kindness. He was never too busy to talk to them and for as long as they needed or wished. It was obvious that he *cared* for them as individuals.

The interviewing of witnesses continued.

The budding of hyacinth and crocus cast small spell this year for Shanty's lump had come back and was growing at an alarming rate. He limped badly when he walked. I called his doctor friends and they said, "Bring him back to us!" But they warned that there was little hope that this surgery would have a happy outcome. There was much comfort in the fact that he would be with friends, not abandoned to strangers. After all, the first time at the hospital he had been taken by one of the doctor's to live in his room and that same dear man had called Karen one night, given the medical report, and then added, "I thought your dog should see Park Avenue, so he and I just took a lovely walk."

It was Thursday of Holy Week. Jimmy decided to go with me when I drove the dog to the hospital. Shanty's behavior as we made ready to leave caused my heart to bump with fear. There had been all the good-byes, Karen clinging to him so fiercely that Jimmy had gently to pry her arms from around the dog's neck. Shanty followed us to the door, then turned, and limping back to Karen, he sat before her resting his great head on her knee. He looked into her face with unquestioning adoration. Jimmy called him, gave his short whistle, snapped his fingers. The dog didn't move.

Jimmy waited.

Karen leaned down so that her face touched Shanty's. "I love you with my whole heart. Thank you! Thank you for loving me so." She raised her head, her face was ashen. She placed her hand on his head and curled her fingers in the silky ear. "Go with Daddy."

He looked long into her face, rose, and walked away.

We never used a leash for Shanty because he 'heeled' perfectly. As we entered the lobby of the hospital, rode up on the elevator and then negotiated miles of corridor, we were frequently intercepted—well, not we, but he. I don't remember anyone speaking to *us*, but many doctors halted our trio and addressed our companion: "You look handsome as ever, old boy." "Poor fellow, it hurts to walk doesn't it?" "That's a nasty lump, but we'll take care of it." "Getting a little grey around the chops aren't you?" "Must say you carry your age well."

They permitted us to stay with Shanty until he was anaesthetized. We were torn between remaining at the hospital to see him after surgery, and being home when the doctor called Karen.

We went home.

It was eight minutes to 7:00 p.m. when the surgeon called. His voice broke as he said: "Tell Karen we did everything we could—all of us. He didn't suffer. I was with him when he died."

About midnight I went back into Karen's room. I lay down and put my arm around her and kissed her. Her face was wet. In the communion of grief we lay silent for a long time. Then she turned her face to mine and spoke in a voice that was tight with anguish. "Mom, Holy Week is the time of Our Lord's greatest suffering."

"Yes, darling, it is."

There was a heavy silence before she asked in a whisper, "Do you remember during Holy Week last year, I had that badly infected finger and it was so painful?" She seemed to be thinking aloud rather than talking to me. "And this Holy Week, He took Shanty. Mom, isn't He good to let *me* share His suffering?"

I stayed beside her long after she slept. When finally I left I went for a walk on the beach and my own longing for the big red dog was unbearable. What must it be for her? Across the darkling waters of the Sound, Execution Light threw the brightness of its beam; its swift stabbing was like the insightfulness of Karen's remark. Many things became clear to me with a sudden, sparkling clarity. I must write them down before I lost the precise wording that seemed to grasp, and to hold the whole essence, the 'becoming' of my fifteen-year-old. I hurried back up the street, tiptoed into the kitchen, listened at her door, then sat at the table and wrote:

She grew beneath a night that spanned the years
In posture bent.
Nor fear, defeat
Her knees by adoration weighed
In dark so deep
It manifest the light beyond.

Russ also, was trying to find an area of competition for Karen. He came up with the idea of bench-firing, and took Karen and Jimmy and me to his shooting club. With infinite patience he spent the whole afternoon trying to get Karen to shoot—or rather to shoot accurately. It was just no good. Karen has acute hearing, and is most sensitive to loud reports. She managed to hold the rifle well enough, but anticipating the report, she just couldn't help shutting her eyes. Russ was terribly disappointed and with the idea of making him feel serviceable, I asked him to show me how to fire a revolver. Ever the born teacher, he said that before he would let me shoot I should have a course in all the regulations for safety. He gave me my first lesson that afternoon and others on Saturday afternoons to follow. Then, and only then, did he permit me on the firing line. I was just getting the hang of it when Russ's hours of work were changed. I complained to Jim Kelly and he volunteered to take over. We went to the Winchester Police and Rifle Range and Jim set me a fine example with his expert marksmanship. He coached me carefully and got Jimmy interested as well. It was a wonderful sport for us, inexpensive and unlike golf, we could leave the house, shoot until our arms were too tired for accuracy, and be home in less than two hours. I rapidly became an addict.

For Mother's Day, the family gave me a Smith and Wesson 22.

Jimmy and I were driving home from the range one day feeling pretty smug about a really good score. Figuratively, if not literally, I shook my fist heavenward and demanded, "Why, oh why, don't we come up with something for Karen?" We pulled into the driveway and Lark hurled her sleek black body at the car. *"I've got it!"* I yelled at my surprised spouse. "The competition for Karen, *and* with non-handicapped people on *their* level!"

I grabbed Lark and gave her a hug. "A dog!"

"We have a dog. I don't get it."

"A show dog!"

"Ah!—Ah!"

We raced into the house to Karen. "How would you like to get a show dog?"

"Daddy! Could I really?"

"Why not?"

We got a list of dog shows from Ralph Hellum and as often as not, he went with us. Jimmy and I spoke persuasively of West Highland Terriers and Dachshunds. Karen replied carefully: "If you don't mind, Daddy, I'd like a dog I could look up to."

We moved to the benches that housed larger breeds. We agreed that in addition to being a show dog, our choice must be intelligent, gentle, docile, bold. Week-end after week-end, close to home and far afield we wove our way with the wheelchair through crowds of avid spectators, large women carrying small dogs, small men leading large dogs, large men with large dogs and kids under sixteen proudly parading their entries in junior handling. Karen wouldn't be able to take her dog and gait it around the ring, but she could select it, be responsible for grooming it, take care of entries, and keep the calendar of events. The prospect was bright. When I hesitantly mentioned to Jimmy that such a business was going to run into some money he remarked, "So do braces. Psychotherapy can be more valuable than physiotherapy."

We went with Ralph to the Saw Mill River Show at the Westchester County Center. The limit on the canine entry was one thousand, and the limit was there. Ralph and Karen went off by themselves, and Jimmy and I went to watch the German Shepherds. I leaned toward this breed myself, having had shepherds as a child, but for some reason Karen wasn't equally enthusiastic. The judging over we went looking for our twosome. Up and down the aisles, past benches with everything from Maltese Terriers to Irish Wolfhounds, and then we saw the wheelchair, empty in the aisle. We hurried up to it and found Karen on a dog bench, buried by two enormous black dogs. "I've found it, Daddy!" she called around a huge head. "I've found my breed!"

"Newfoundlands!" Jimmy was visibly shaken. There are only three or four breeds that are at all bigger or heavier.

Karen wriggled to the front of the bench and called to a man and a woman standing a few feet away. "Mr. and Mrs. Chern, here are my mother and father. I've told them."

One of the dogs gently placed a heavy black paw on Karen's shoulder.

A most attractive woman and an exceptionally handsome man came over and greeted us cordially. Ralph whispered: "They own the Little Bear Kennels and it's the largest and the best Newfoundland Kennel in the world."

Mrs. Chern said, "We've been having a lovely visit with your daughter."

Karen offered: "Daddy, did you know that with the possible exception of the Chihuahua, the Newfoundland is the only dog native to North America?"

"No, I didn't," answered Jimmy with remarkable composure.

We moved closer to the bench. Our presence was greeted by large tail thumpings and muzzlings. No question the dogs were remarkably amiable. They were also beautiful. Large bodies but of a wonderful soundness. Their coats gleamed with the lustre that bespeaks fine diet and constant grooming. The eyes, well set in broad heads, had an expression that could only be described as melting. The word that came most readily to mind, as I watched one of them fold his great frame in order to get his forequarters in Karen's lap, was benevolent.

"What do you think, Daddy?"

"I think they're large," Daddy answered honestly.

"And so quiet and well-behaved," said Karen encouragingly. "They'd never be a nuisance like a noisy, little dog. Why, they haven't barked once."

"Then they're the only ones who haven't," retorted Jimmy who had to keep turning down his hearing aid to lessen the ear-shattering cacophony.

I asked the Cherns some questions about feeding. "One would think they'd eat more." I said to Jimmy. Before he could reply I added: "And I can tell you after feeling their coats that they'll take much less grooming than most other long-haired breeds. The hair won't mat nearly so quickly."

Jimmy gave me a searching look. "You've kind of fallen for them too, haven't you?"

"Hopelessly," I pushed two dogs aside to make room for myself on the bench. They gave ground gracefully and professed their pleasure at my presence with a few strokes of very pink tongues.

"Daddy," Karen leaned forward over her lapful, "could we go to the Cherns' kennels and just *look* at the dogs?"

"Why not?" Jimmy let Karen think he had been taken in by her guile. "Where are they?"

Karen's answer came in a non-comma-d rush: "They're in Vermont and I hear it's one of the most beautiful states and we could make it a week-end holiday."

Any man who has lived so many years in the company of four women, with but one male to support him, has developed flexibility and the knack of yielding quickly and graciously. Jimmy was no exception. He turned to the Cherns: "When would a visit be convenient for you?"

"Any time."

"How about the week-end after next?" Jimmy asked me. "Fine."

"Splendid," said Mr. Chern. "Plan on staying with us and for as long as you can."

We left for Vermont late Friday afternoon, drove until dark, and started the last lap early in the morning. Karen had elicited considerable information about the Cherns during the hours she sat with them at the show. Vadim had had his own schooner in the North Atlantic and had written a book about his adventures around Newfoundland-Labrador, at that time a Crown Colony. He was Montenegrin and spoke several languages including Russian. His interest in Newfoundlands started with his sailing. In the cold waters of the North Atlantic a man cannot long survive, so the dogs are carried on ships for purposes of lifesaving, and to carry the life-line to shore in case of shipwreck. Furthermore, the captain's bunk was made wide enough for the captain and the dog—for warmth. Karen interrupted her recital to ask: "Can you imagine having a Newf to snuggle up to on a cold winter's night?"

We agreed it would be lovely.

The recitation continued. The Cherns had a home in Silvermine, Connecticut, but had bought hundreds and hundreds of acres in Vermont during the war, so they would have a place for the many refugees they had brought to this country.

"You have all the instincts of a newspaper reporter," Jimmy commented.

"That's not all. Margaret (they asked me to call them by their first names) writes too, and Vadim is also an artist. He's done cuts to illustrate his book. He works on plaster from black to white and makes his own little steel knives. He works in oils too. Margaret said his pictures are seascapes and ships and Newfoundland. They have some of them in Vermont."

"Sounds like it's going to be an interesting visit in more ways than one."

"I can't wait." Karen was quiet for a little then ruminated aloud. "I have the feeling that they're exceptionally good people and that we shall be very good friends."

We stopped in Northfield and asked directions to the farm. "Just up the road a piece," was the laconic reply. We'd spent enough time in New England to know that this could mean anywhere from a quarter of a mile to five miles—and five miles it proved to be. We followed a very narrow, rutted dirt road that snaked a desultory course up the mountain. It was accompanied on its journey by a wide stream, and we passed a few scattered farm houses and rocky fields that seemed about to slide off their steep hills into the pine forest below. We climbed sharply and the air became keen and exhilarating. The last mile we did in first gear and knew we had arrived when we drew up in front of an old farm house and were greeted by the resonant barking of a noble of Newfoundlands—more than sixty of them.

The Cherns welcomed us with warmth. "Our friends call us Margaret and Vadim." We settled down in the large farm kitchen. From the windows one looked into deep valleys, sudden hills and mountains beyond. As with most New England farmhouses the barn was connected with the kitchen. A large table in the center of the room seated ten comfortably. On a great wood-burning stove (I learned as the days went by), pots were always boiling with goodies for the dogs— tripe and liver and kidneys, so rich in nutritive value and so "rich" in odor, and buckwheat and barley. None of your processed devitaminized food for Little Bear dogs.

The tour of the kennels was quite an experience. Many of these dogs had lived in their pens all their lives except when they left to show, and there wasn't a one that was anything but cordial and loving when we went in with them (which we did hesitantly the first few times). We soon lost track of the Champions, there were just too many and the names were not short. We met Raider, the patriarch of the kennel, and James Thurber, who had set the all-time world's record for Newfoundland wins. Karen embraced, and was embraced by every dog and bitch we met, and we met them all. She held in her lap three-pound puppies, warm mounds of black cuddlesomeness, and was charged by their four- and five-month-old cousins. With each new visitation she would exclaim: "Oh, how can I choose?"

Margaret explained that one could not always be sure that a dog would be a fine show prospect until it was over a year old. "But I do love the puppies—what a decision!" Karen was torn between immediately showing, and the fun of raising a little one.

We took the jeep and Margaret drove across the fields to the pens that had been built in the woods along a racing brook. We climbed down to the swimming pool the Cherns had made for the dogs by damming a creek. Carrying Karen, we went the half mile through the pines to Christmas Tree spring where the coldest and sweetest water in the world was drunk from a tin cup that hung on a bough. We went deeper into the woods and saw the well-beaten circles where the deer danced in the clearing. We saw a pair of red fox.

Karen was transported.

While Vadim cooked four-inch steaks on the outside fireplace, we visited the whelping pens and runs built off the house, and the nurseries where ultra-violet lights burned always.

Following dinner, puppies were brought in for Karen's inspection and after watching them romp, play and collapse, she announced definitely, "That's my choice," and pointed to a five-month-old bitch with a most beautiful head. Margaret removed the others and this young lady stayed, and stayed right beside Karen, ignoring the rest of us.

"She's really a good show prospect," Vadim said, "but at this age one can't be absolutely certain."

At 10:00 p.m. we helped feed puppies, then literally fell into bed. We were awakened about midnight by a mighty chorus. My first thought was—I have heard about wolves singing. But it wasn't wolves—it was the dogs. We lay listening for the twenty minutes that the song continued and then I got out of bed, took paper and pencil, and tried to write about it. When I finished, I knew I hadn't really brought it off. The next morning at breakfast I told Margaret and Vadim of my abortive effort and he handed me a copy of *Popular Dogs* with a piece Margaret had written: "Mighty Symphony."

> The first note was sounded by a three-month-old puppy then the refrain taken up by his sisters and brothers and cousins in a falsetto chirp. A bitch repeats the melody and rhythm in a strong steady soprano. Now the voices of dogs and bitches join in groups, repeating and inverting the minor-keyed melody. A quartet of six-monthlings beat a syncopated tattoo in tones as pure as timpani. At last the great basso of Raider rises in thunderous volume. All voices soar in a mighty crescendo. Then an unseen baton must slash downward, for all sound stops at once— suddenly, completely.

Vadim invited Jimmy to take a "little walk up his mountain." They started off with Ch. Broadside and Ch. O'Lady, and came back many hours later having covered over ten miles. While they were gone, Margaret and Karen and I made the rounds of adult show prospects. I could see Karen was yearning over the puppy but she said to Margaret: "I mustn't let my my heart rule my head, and I did come for a proven show dog." Again and again we returned to a pen that held a most gorgeous bitch, Little Bear's Ocean Borne. Margaret pointed out that in judging Newfoundlands, size counted a good deal and therefore a bitch was never going to have the wins that a dog would.

"I want a bitch anyway," Karen stated flatly, "and this one looks impressive enough to win any judging."

"She is impressive. You have a good eye for she is the best bitch we have."

Every time we approached Ocean Borne, she looked quickly around the pen for a 'present' to bring us: a stick, a bunch of leaves, a stone—but she never came up to us empty-mouthed. When Karen extended her hand, the bitch whimpered with delight and pleading. I could see Karen falling rapidly in love. She said: "She's the best bitch you have."

"Yes."

I could tell from Karen's expression that she also was thinking, 'this big girl must be worth a fortune.' Reluctantly we turned away. As we moved along Margaret recited Ocean Borne's pedigree. (She could recite the pedigrees of all her dogs back eight generations without consulting her records.) As she talked I ticked off on my fingers: two forebears that were International Champions, an English Champion, and seventeen that were American Champions. As the recital went on I kept revising upward my original estimate of the dog's value. It seemed that Karen was doing likewise, for she looked back over her shoulder with her heart in her eyes.

We had the pup in the house that night and again the next day. She offered Karen immediate adoration. Karen whispered to me, "I love this one and Ocean Borne equally." To Margaret she said, "I can't leave without this enchanting little one."

"Little one, indeed," snorted Jimmy. "She's as big as Lark right now."

So it was settled. We had given our check and Margaret had made out the transfer of ownership. We loaded the back of the station wagon leaving plenty of room for the pup to move around. I think Jimmy and I were almost as excited as Karen. Vadim had gone off and Margaret stood with us in the front yard as we tried to express our appreciation for all the joys of the week-end. "Come for a week-end next month," she urged.

"We'd love to," Karen exclaimed, "and will you come down to see us?"

"Next week." Margaret promised. "And we'll go into all the details of showing. What fun it's going to be, we'll be going to so many shows together!"

Karen looked across the hill to the field. "Look," she pointed, "Vadim is bringing Ocean Borne to say goodbye."

Borne trotted up, bearing a stick and making sounds in her throat "like a family of mice," said Jimmy.

Karen bent and kissed her. She didn't have to bend far.

Vadim wore a beatific smile. Margaret spoke, "You have a puppy to bring up which we hope will be a good show dog, but we thought you should have a good show dog *now*—we thought you should have the best."

Vadim took the leash and placed it in Karen's hand. "We want you to have her."

Jimmy gasped. I was stunned into speechlessness. There was no mistaking Vadim's meaning.

Margaret spoke up quickly: "We think you're both so special, Karen, that you belong together. Besides, we can tell Borne wanted to go with you as much as we want you to take her."

Karen flushed scarlet. She stammered, "I couldn't! I couldn't possibly—"

I had to swallow hard and I noticed Jimmy's eyes were suspiciously bright. "We can't accept—but you're wonderful!"

Margaret laughed. "It doesn't seem to me that you have any choice. How could you refuse a present that means so much to your daughter?"

"I know," said Jimmy, "but it is impossible."

"You're both so dear," I said, "but you understand that we couldn't accept her."

Vadim laughed. "Nonsense. You couldn't possibly refuse us the happiness of giving her to Karen." He took the lead and started the dog toward the back of the car. I looked at his shining face and Margaret's, glowing with pleasure. I remonstrated no further. Had we known then, what we know now about the value of this gift, we'd have had no choice but to make our refusal hold, daughter or no.

Karen sat as though in a coma. The dog leapt lightly over the tailgate.

It was well after midnight when we pulled into a gas station about halfway home. Both dogs had been lying down. As the attendant put the hose into the tank, Ocean Borne stood up and put her head out over the tailgate. The man, half asleep, took one look, yelled a profane epithet "— — *you've got a bear in the car—*" and took off—

The tank filled and ran over.

The man didn't come back.

Jimmy took out the hose, hung it up, put the money in the office.

We drove away.

ह‍े

chapter eighteen

Rory telephoned news of the arrival of *two* Newfoundlands to Chris Kerr over a private line they had rigged up between houses.

Life with the new dogs was staccato.

Jimmy bought grooming combs and brushes and two kinds of scissors.

Karen and Marie began to groom.

Russ helped Jimmy build a pen forty feet by twenty feet.

Lark greeted the newcomers with cautious condescension that rapidly developed into affectionate camaraderie.

The Newfs accepted the cats as they accepted everything else—benevolently.

Gloria started boiling buckwheat for the pup.

Mommy started housebreaking both Newfs, for although Ocean Borne was three years old she had never been a house dog.

In the past, housebreaking was a task I had undertaken with small puppies that could be picked up and carried out of doors when they made a mistake. At the freight station, Ocean Borne weighed in at one hundred and seventy pounds, so a different technique was called for. It was done in three days! In our experience that was an all-time record. We trained with voice alone. To a Newf, *"Shame!"* is less supportable than a beating; this breed's primary purpose in life seems to be to understand what you want them to do—and to do it.

When the pup was "shamed," she would trot to a corner where she would sit with her back to the room, her head down against the wall; Ocean Borne, "shamed," would wilt into a grieving black rug, head between outstretched fore-paws, eyes running over with contrition.

Finding a suitable name for the pup was a task not lightly undertaken. Karen said it should be connected with New-foundland or water. We consulted maps and the encyclo-pedia. Finally Joe came up with a suggestion that Karen accepted promptly. "Little Bear's Perigee Tide—that being the Spring tide—powerful, strong!" Her call name would be "Peri."

Word of Karen's new 'girls' was rapidly circulated. A.M. embraced them, took off her shoes, ran her feet through their coats and said she'd like to borrow them on a cold night.

Shirley, who was so busy with Mr. King that we saw very little of her, came for what Gloria was now calling a "view-ing."

Eleanor Gagliardi remarked, "They're not dogs—they're bears!" We found this a pretty general reaction.

Frank Burke dropped in. He *said* he was on his way from

Philadelphia to New England. He gasped, then exclaimed with a wealth of feeling, *"Holy smoke!"*

We found that gasping was an immediate reaction, but the dogs, so volatile out of doors, were so quiet in the house that they were quickly forgotten. They'd go off to the side of a room where they'd fling themselves down and as Jimmy said, "Even if you did trip over one, it would be like tripping over a pillow, and nobody would get hurt."

Peri had a wild crush on Joe and he responded in full measure. Nowadays he never sat on a chair but stretched out on the floor beside her. He dubbed her "Peri-Shan," declaring that she was Shanty in a different fur coat.

The Cherns came as they had promised and we scheduled our first show for Pennsylvania, a month hence.

Jimmy, leading his family down the street to the beach, looked like nothing so much as Pa Brown and his cows. There were six or eight of us, the three dogs, and strung out in a line behind, the six cats. Ocean Borne never even paused at the water's edge but walked right in and started to swim. Peri, whose pool in Vermont had been frozen since her birth, was leery. She'd run along snapping at the waves, then beat a hasty retreat when the water touched her feet. I decided on a tactic which, unfortunately, I conducted on a Sunday afternoon when quite a few people were out for a stroll. Peri was not yet trained entirely to heel so I took her on leash down the street and across the beach. When we reached the water, I just kept walking and she kept walking right beside me. I had on a pair of dungarees, shirt, sweater and sneakers, but so far as the gaping witnesses were concerned, I was "plumb crazy." I kept on until I was waist deep and by then the dog was swimming happily. I unsnapped the leash, walked away and she kept right on swimming. That was her introduction to the water and she has swum every day since, breaking the ice along the shore in the winter. More than a few spectator comments on my behavior were relayed to A.M. She was happy to have an opportunity to explain, but reported that she felt not everyone was convinced.

Karen's close friend, Nina Reznick, who lived across the street, undertook to condition the dogs and gaited them

209.

daily. We were most grateful. For the conditioning that Jimmy and I had time for was not enough.

It took Rory just two days to train the Newfs to "stay" at the top or the bottom of the stairs when anyone was going up or down. This was a safety measure.

After a couple of weeks, Ocean Borne no longer swept coffee tables clear with her tail. It wasn't all beer and skittles, however, for Peri, while she was teething, chewed up a new pair of orthopedic shoes that we had had custom-made for Karen at a cost of $40.00. Jimmy ordered another pair, wrote a check, and Karen retrieved one of the pup's teeth and put it tenderly away in a ring box.

Quiet as the Newfs were in the house, one could hardly have three dogs on the kitchen floor while preparing a meal. At the beginning of such preparations I would say: "Go into Karen's room and *stay* while I'm getting dinner." (With these dogs I found myself speaking in sentences rather than one- or two-word commands.) Reluctantly they'd get to their feet and trot obediently through the door. Our initial reservations over having such large dogs around the house quickly evaporated.

Karen asked Monsignor Madden to bless the dogs and she attributed their exemplary behavior in large measure to his benediction. Rory and I felt that we should have a little credit too.

While Peri blatantly wooed Joe, Ocean Borne courted Russ. I knew it would just be a question of time before a Newfoundland was added to his menagerie at the Little Red House, but I hadn't an idea under what unexpected circumstances it would arrive.

Somewhat nervously we were getting ready for our first show in Pennsylvania. Ocean Borne had to be bathed two days previous so her coat would not be fluffy. With the Cherns' list in hand I went to the drug store to make the necessary purchases. "Tar soap, Charles Antell shampoo, atomizer—"

The clerk interrupted: "I'm just out of Charles Antell, how about—"

"It must be Charles Antell—you see all these things are for my dog."

A woman in the front of the store summoned the clerk to the ice cream case. As he approached she said to the dog she had on a leash: "And what flavor does baby want tonight?"

The sale completed, the man returned to me. I shook my head over the woman's behavior and remarked: "How crazy can you be?"

"How crazy indeed!" he answered with a side glance at me. "No Charles Antell!"

For the rather long journey to the show we needed two station wagons to accommodate our party and luggage. Russ, Joe and Nina were going with us. In addition to the hampers, bags, and bundles that we would take to a country fair, Karen had a bag to pack for the dog: choke collar, canvas leash, bench chain, rake, three combs of assorted sizes, two brushes, paper towels, pan for water, pan of ice, atomizer and bottle of stuff, whatever it was, chenille rug for the dog to lie on so she wouldn't get dusty or grassy, and a large bathtowel to be put bib-like under her chin, so that if she drooled she wouldn't mar the beauty of her chest coat, and a couple of safety pins.

It was an outdoor show where the dogs are not benched and this was one reason Margaret had chosen it to start Ocean Borne on her career.

Through Ralph Hellum, we had met Ed Carver, one of the top handlers in the country and he was going to handle Ocean Borne. Ed was a paradox—brusque as Brillo, kind as cream. He and Ocean Borne were most compatible, but then, any dog Ed handled was compatible as long as he handled it.

We had a beautiful day on which to drive through Pennsylvania. The mountains were deeply green, the rivers full, the barns bright in the sun, and the houses of warm, gray native stone looked composed and homely. Cows grazed, sheep stared, swallows stooped, and children went about their solemn businesses of dabbling in ponds, hammering unrelated pieces of wood, or walking purposefully anywhere —nowhere.

Ordinarily, when we drove, Karen kept up a running commentary. Today she said nothing. Not one single word. We found an ideal picnic spot for lunch where the dog could run and we could wade in an icy creek. Karen ate half a dill pickle—nothing more.

We arrived at the show with an hour to spare and plenty of time to unload and put the final touches to Ocean Borne —a last brushing, spraying of her tail, and the careful removal of the smallest wisp of grass. The towel was pinned under her chin. Karen worked in silence. Ed Carver came over to us and almost immediately there was the call: "Newfoundlands to the ring please!"

Ed snapped on a short canvas leash. "Come on, sweetheart," and off they went to the ring, our gang pressing closely behind. We had entered Ocean Borne in Open Bitches and as she took her place in the line I looked at Karen. She sat, hands clasped (in what I was sure was prayer), face taut, body rigid. I had a sudden and violent realization of how much this competition meant to her. I nudged Jimmy. "Wow!" he exclaimed with some dismay. "I didn't think it would be that important!"

The sun struck highlights from Ocean Borne's coat and a gentle summer breeze ruffled her 'feathers' a little. The judge stood in the center of the ring and gave the handlers the signal to start gaiting the dogs around him. Our group was tensely silent and totally still. There were five bitches competing and although we still had much to learn about conformation, it was easy to see that a few of them were tough competition. I glanced at the program. They were Little Bear dogs. I philosophized, 'If Karen loses to a Chern dog it won't be so crushing. But she mustn't lose!'

On command from the judge, the dogs were lined up, and carefully, oh so carefully, he started going over them. Our girl looked glorious—strong, powerful. Her head was spectacular, her front straight and wide; her chest was deep, her top line in flawless parallel; her rib spread impressive and her rear broad. When the judge leaned on her back it didn't give a centimeter.

The minute going-over of all the dogs completed, the judge had them run separately away from him, across the ring, then back. To some judges, as I knew it would be to me, movement was very important. Ocean Borne floated, never breaking gait and seeming to wish to gait on forever.

Despite her breadth of chest, she had a perfect single track.

Having completed this estimate of the contestants, the judge signalled them to move once more, in line, around him. He commanded in turn: "Walk." "Gait." "Walk." It seemed to go on for hours. Karen was now quite pale and squeezing my hand so hard it hurt.

The judge directed: "Now line up facing me." Well, here it was. In a matter of minutes he would go to the stewards' table, write something historic on a paper, turn back to the waiting men and dogs, raise an arm, extend a finger—and point to the winner.

With painful deliberation he stood looking at the line-up. As he studied each in turn my heart thumped so hard I could hear it. It seemed to me that Karen had stopped breathing. Now, with maddening slowness, the judge turned away, walked to the table and wrote. Karen's lower lip was caught tightly in her teeth. Nina moved over and put an arm around her shoulder. We all moved in closer.

The judge straightened, turned, and walked back. I felt as though I were watching the whole thing in slow motion. He raised his arm, pointed his finger—at Ed and Ocean Borne!

Nina and Karen screamed with delight (and believe me this isn't *done* at dog shows), we clapped like mad (one should only clap restrainedly), and hugged Karen in turn. Ed and his winner walked after the judge to the table and the judge held out the Blue Ribbon. Ed shook his head and said something. The judge left him, walked across the ring and handed the ribbon to Karen. She tried to say "Thank you." Her lips moved, but no sound came forth. The judge smiled and said: "Congratulations!"

Ed came over with the dog, who walked proudly. Karen kissed him, kissed her dog. Only then did she relax. "How I wish Maggie and Vadim could have been here! They'd have been so proud!"

Next, Ocean Borne had to compete against the Winners of the other classes for Winners Bitch. Again the agonizing go-around. Our dog looked far superior to us, but would the judge see her so?

He did. And brought the purple ribbon over to Karen.

The next entry was to go in against the Winners Dog. The judge took a good while on that one and finally—again tapped Ed and brought Karen the cherished blue and white ribbon for *Best of Winners!*

Karen alternately paled and flushed. To cop Rory's phrase —I was scared spitless. Jimmy's lips were tight. Glo, Marie, Nina, Rory, Joe and Russ stood like stone statues.

Ocean Borne was now going in against the Champions. She'd come a long way. Could she go to the top—to Best of Breed? Jimmy whispered: "Good thing we all have low blood pressure—otherwise this strain could be fatal." He took my free hand and held it tightly.

"I'll settle for Best of Opposite Sex," I whispered.

Once more the parade, the individual going-over, the gaiting and walking, the lining-up. Hands behind his back, the judge stood surveying the field. Ocean Borne held her pose without moving. I didn't look at the other dogs. The judge walked toward the line, took two steps to the left, and placed his hand on Ed's shoulder.

"Best of Breed!"

The judge brought the purple and gold rosette over to Karen. "Congratulations!"

She found her voice. "Thank you, sir. I think she's tremendous!"

The judge smiled at this most unorthodox comment from an exhibitor. "I think she's one of the best Newfs I've ever judged."

Rory grabbed Karen. "I have goose pimples on my duck bumps!"

Marie, looking wan, said: "I don't ever want to go through anything like that again."

"It was hell!" agreed Gloria.

Joe asked Karen: "How often do you plan to put us through such an ordeal?"

"As often as possible."

Russ stated: "There are millions of people who think the World Series is exciting. I could tell them a thing or two."

Other exhibitors came over and congratulated Karen, and Ed brought handlers to meet her. I began to realize that there was a value to this whole enterprise which hadn't occurred to us. In this field of competition, Karen would meet all kinds of people from every stratum of life and there would be acquaintanceship with a variety of characters and personalities far beyond average experience.

Such a victory deserved a celebration so Jimmy decided to be wildly incautious and take his crew to a swank restaurant for dinner. He chose a charming place, a lovely old house with manicured lawns and lush gardens (the kind that automatically raise the figure on the right side of the menu). It was called Crorfort House.

As we milled through the foyer we saw a man with his arm in a cast and a sling. We hadn't long been seated, when a woman came in using a cane, and before the meal was over, a man in a wheelchair entered. Karen, who hadn't stopped talking since her win, began to giggle and patting the arm of her own wheelchair, said in a stage whisper: "This shouldn't be called 'Crorfort House'—but 'Cripples' House!' "

We spent two hours over dinner, discussing the faults of all the other dogs and rehashing the show. Jimmy ordered several bottles of wine for toasts. The conversation was sprightly:

"Did you see that darling minister showing his mother's Kerry Blue?"

"Did you see the woman who had her hair dyed to match her dress?"

"And the woman judge with bracelets galore on each arm? They made so much noise the dogs were most upset as she went over them. Wouldn't you think a judge would know better?"

"Incredible! And I understand she's been judging for years."

"Did you notice the round woman in the man's suit and shoes? I was told she's very rich and has worn the same suit since the First World War."

"When was that?" Rory asked.

"1917."

"Wow!"

"How about the guy who was hand-feeding his Dane

because the dog was so depressed at losing that he wouldn't eat!"

"He told me it takes that dog two weeks to recover from a defeat."

"I wonder how long it takes the owner."

Karen began to laugh and reached a point where she had trouble stopping. Finally she burbled: "Did you hear about the fellow who got caught putting 'falsies' on his French Poodle?"

"What?"

Karen was again convulsed and it was some minutes before she could explain. "You know that poodles are supposed to have full tufts here and there—well, this one was missing a tuft—here or there."

Joe said: "I am now beyond surprise."

"I heard a group," Marie related, "complaining bitterly about some arbitrary rulings of the A.K.C. One man terminated the discussion by saying: 'Let's face it—you can't buck them—they are all-powerful.' "

"Explain it to me," asked Rory.

"I can't, answered Jimmy, "I'm new at the game. It's all Greek to me."

"Do you suppose it's true?"

"Only time will tell."

"Did you know that the Judge of the Gordon Setters was a District Attorney?"

"And the man who won Open Dogs with his bull terrier was a geophysicist?"

Karen said: "I met a wonderful fellow, Ken Golden. He breeds and shows Labradors and teaches at a New Jersey School for the Deaf."

"I can top all your stories," Joe chuckled. "There was an elderly woman behind me, talking to an admiring group of young friends. Her gestures were made dynamic by the flashing of many diamonds on fingers and arms as she said: 'I have donated as a prize in my breed a $500 urn that poor Teddy bought in Venice the year before he died. I should get some consideration. I never knew what to do with it. It's been in the cellar—it's very ugly and valuable. The judge knows *objets d'art.* I saw to it that he knew the urn came from me. That should carry some weight. . . . Don't you think so?' Her friends," Joe finished, "nodded like so many happy puppets."

"What happened?"

"I couldn't find out. She didn't name the breed."

"It's all very illuminating," observed Karen. "What do you think about all this, Daddy?"

Jimmy raised his glass: "A toast to a dandy departure from routine. The crowd was dapper, dowdy, dour, darling, determined, and a few decidedly demented. It's fascinating and I am looking forward to the next show."

During the ride home Karen never stopped talking, and from the balance of our gang in the car behind, came a good deal of boisterous singing.

It was 1:30 a.m. when the two cars drove into the driveway, bumper to bumper, but before Karen went to bed she sent a telegram to Ed Doll: "REJOICE! TODAY OCEAN BORNE WENT BOB." She didn't consider it necessary to explain that BOB meant Best of Breed. The next morning Ed wired back: "DELIGHTED EXCLAMATION POINT STOP WHO'S BOB?"

Jimmy and Karen and I decided that we couldn't 'campaign' our bitch because this would mean taking her every week-end to Saturday and Sunday shows in different parts of the country. True, it was the best way to go after a Championship and pile up a record of wins, but for many reasons, the approach for us was a show a month. It would take a lot longer for Ocean Borne to acquire the fifteen points required for her Championship, but this way the demands of showing would not spoil the fun of showing.

In training our new dogs, we faced only one difficult situation: amiable as angels, Newfoundlands are still great watchdogs. If, after dark, anyone set foot on any property on our block, the dogs would herald the fact with deep growls and terrifying barks. Our difficulty was provoked by the unnatural hours kept by the Kerrs who, on opening nights, came home in the wee hours of the morning arousing the dogs who aroused the neighborhood. It took several weeks before the dogs allowed Jean and Walter to make late entries into their own house unannounced.

Karen's horizons began to widen in a number of unexpected ways. She became interested in collecting old prints of Newfoundlands and this took her treasure-hunting through antique shops. She searched old books and found a report of a maritime disaster in 1919 when "through seas too rough for life-boats, the Newfoundland brought a rope to rescuers who rigged a breeches buoy and save 92 passengers." She framed a quote from Lord Byron, written of his Newfoundland: "Beauty without vanity, strength without insolence, courage without ferocity and all the virtues of man without his vices." Margaret Chern gave Karen a copy of her book, *The Complete Newfoundland*, for which she had researched for years both here and abroad. This became a fascinating textbook.

Little did we know, the day we found the empty wheelchair in front of the Little Bear kennel bench, what a wide and engrossing interest was to follow.

Karen and Ralph Hellum encouraged Rory to show Lark, and to enter the competition in Junior Handling, although he was completely inexperienced. News item in the *Daily Times*:

> Rory Killilea, Sursum Corda, Larchmont, was awarded first prize Saturday at the Bronx County Kennel Show in the Junior Handling Class, with his Labrador Retriever, Highland Lark. Competing in his first show, Rory received a sterling silver Revere bowl.
>
> His sister Karen entered her Newfoundland, Little Bear's Ocean Borne, winning Best of Winners and Best of Opposite Sex. She received an additional three points toward her Championship.

Further comment on Rory at this time is taken from my day book. "Had a meeting with Rory's teacher today. She said: 'He may grow up to be a bishop if I don't put his head through the wall first.'"

Glo and Russ were now visiting Father Kelly at least once a month. The purpose of these visits were entirely therapeutic. So far there was nothing for him to report to them but they were greatly helped by his interest and affection. All of us continued to assault Heaven with our prayers, roping in our friends for the additional strength of their petitions.

At the close of the school year, Rory got a job as newspaper boy. We had encouraged such enterprise, never giving a thought to our own possible involvement. In the Manor some of the houses are far apart and all of the front doors are a fair hike from the street. The boy must do the route by bike. It was responsible; it was healthful; it was financially productive; we were all for it. What we hadn't considered was—who would do the route if Rory were ill? As luck would have it he contracted several colds and then the mumps. Who took over the route? Gloria and mother took turns. Off one would go in the station wagon leaving the other to get dinner, supervise the first phase of homework, carry a tray to the small supine business man, feed the animals and take care of all the other assorted chores that seemed to pile up at the end of any day. The route took two hours. Rory began a bank account, and we began stomach ulcers and a few charley horses from unaccustomed hurling.

August 18th was Karen's sixteenth birthday.

The week before she made a momentous decision—she would cut her hair. "There are two considerations," she told me. "One—it's more mature; two—I shall be more independent as I shall be able to take care of it myself."

Karen had a cut, a permament, and a set. It was really most becoming. The braids I put tenderly away with a scrap of linen that had caught Marie's first tear, a ring box that held Rory's first tooth, a dried flower from Glo's graduation corsage, Valentines from Jimmy, a snipping of Shanty's feathers, and other embarrassing reminders that mother is a sentimentalist. Karen determined to take care of the expense of "sets" herself and began a silver-cleaning enterprise. She did beautiful work and built up a tidy account.

As one of her birthday presents, Gloria and Russ decided to take Karen out for the day. "What would you like to do?" Russ asked her.

Her answer came quickly. "Let's take a picnic lunch, spend the day fishing, and swim out in the middle of the

219.

Sound. And in the evening let's get all dressed up and go out to dinner."

"You'll be tired after a day on the water."

"Who—me?"

Russ nodded. "That's right, I forgot, you never get tired."

They embarked early in the morning and returned about 6:00 p.m. Russ and Glo dragged themselves in—hot, sunburned, and exhausted. Karen was hot, sunburned, and spry as a cricket. "What happened to your hair?" I asked. The day-old set was no more, there were just wet wriggles all over her head.

"I fell out of the boat," she announced calmly.

Russ collapsed into a chair. "I went over after her, though why I don't know, she was happily swimming away three miles from land, serene as you please. Her only comment when I swam up beside her was 'I just had my hair set. That's five dollars shot.'"

The next evening we had a wonderful Birthday dinner party at Manero's Steak House. Karen invited Dr. John Gundy and his wife, Evie, with the comment: "After all, I wouldn't have had even one birthday if it hadn't been for you." I wondered if many doctors had saved such a tiny morsel of humanity born almost three months early.

During the lengthy dinner Karen told John and Evie all about her dogs. Naturally we spoke about breeding and Jimmy said that Ocean Borne should be in season shortly.

"What do you mean in season?" Karen asked. (Lark had been spayed.)

Rory answered her. "You know, the hunting season, when the male chases the female."

Manero's had a lovely birthday cake for her and the waiters and everyone from the kitchen followed their custom coming to the table and singing. Watching our daughter I decided that she had grown up about three years in one.

The following night there was a birthday party at home with twenty of her "closest friends." Jimmy Dengler played and sang, and Jimmy and I took turns calling parents after midnight to explain that the party was going to last a little longer because the kids had just conga'd out of the house, around the porch, down the stairs, and over to the park.

We had not recovered from all these celebrations when it was time for the New Hampshire Show. Our plan was to spend Saturday night with Bishop Weldon in Springfield, Massachusetts, and leave early Sunday morning for New Hampshire. Our car was acting up so we borrowed Jim Kelly's. The heat was appalling and it was a strenuous trip, but Karen picked up another two points toward Ocean Borne's championship so discomfort and fatigue mattered little.

We had a lot of time to think that week-end and we wrestled with a decision that ran contrary to the advice of Karen's doctors. We had been planning to hold off on this decision until we could discuss the matter personally with Ed Doll, who was coming for a visit in about a month.

While Karen was at the ringside watching Ed Carver show his English sheepdog, Jimmy and I sprawled on a bed of needles in the shade of a pine tree. Ocean Borne lay panting beside us with an ice bag tied on her head. I took from my purse the paper on which we had itemized "Pros" and "Cons." One by one, Jimmy and I went over the lengthy list. This decision was to be perhaps, the most vital we had yet made.

Karen, especially during the school year, had little or no time for socialization because we were still doing three hours of therapy a day. She had been doing therapy for fourteen years. In addition to the exercises, there was walking, sitting, balancing practice. Karen had *no* time in which to read, to enjoy her collection of records and, most important as Jimmy phrased it: "She has no time to just *be*."

So much emphasis on the physical was beginning to impede her total growth. There was no time in which to cultivate the mind, to think, to meditate. I quoted from one of Ed Doll's articles: ". . . the stimuli for learning are provided by the environment of people and things, ideas and feelings, impressions and expressions of social and worldly experience. . . ." Karen had little time for such stimuli.

We lay quietly. We had said all there was to say. The fragrance of the trees mixed with the aroma of Jimmy's tobacco was soothing; the shade deep and cool; a large bumblebee droned slowly by. Jimmy reached over and took my hand, twining my fingers in his. "I think we've decided."

"I think we have."

"It remains to put the matter to Karen, and in such a way that we won't influence her."

Ed Carver wheeled Karen back to us and left for the Working Group. Jimmy fetched a bucket of cool water and Karen bathed her face, neck and arms. "Today is a scorcher," she commented as she splashed the water on her dusty legs. "It was one hundred and two degrees at the ring. The dogs, especially the big ones, are really suffering. Most of the handlers kept wet towels on them until it was time for the judges to go over their dogs. I'm glad we showed early in the morning. Poor baby!" she crooned to Ocean Borne, who acknowledged the commiseration with a listless thump of her tail. "That bed of pine needles looks most inviting, Daddy."

Jimmy took her out of her wheelchair and she stretched out between us. Jimmy spoke: "Karen, Mommy and I have given a good deal of thought to a matter on which you may want to make a decision. You know all of life is made up of alternate issues."

"What matter do you mean, Daddy?"

Jimmy scraped out the bowl of his pipe and spoke with no emphasis. "The matter of physical therapy. We've been considering the pros and cons of continuing or discontinuing it on a permanent basis. What is your thinking?"

Karen looked quickly from him to me, closed her eyes and breathed: "Thank God! Now I can begin to *live!*"

∂✑

chapter nineteen

Early in September, Ed Doll came for a visit. The day before his arrival, Karen and Jimmy and I went fishing. The *blacks* were running well and we had a large catch. The primary purpose of this expedition was to have fresh fish for Ed's breakfast. Karen and I thought it would be nice to serve him on the porch where, to the metallic song of cicadas, he could eat in solitary splendor, read the newspaper, or just enjoy the view. We fixed a pretty tray with a tiny bouquet of shaggy purple asters, made corn bread, and broiled the fish with TLC. I served it with a flourish and retired. A little later I went out with a pot of hot coffee to find our friend and counselor behaving most peculiarly. His body was weaving from side to side, his head jerking and his arms were executing motions similar to Arthur Fiedler in front of the Boston Pops. He was not having a solitary breakfast—he had been joined by a host of yellow jackets which are passionately fond of fish. They floated above and in front of him, swarmed over the tender sweet meat of the Black, skated around the rim of his glass of orange juice, plodded through the marmalade, and tracked about on the back and sleeves and front of his shirt.

"I refuse to yield," he said indistinctly. I guess he was afraid to open his mouth.

"I insist," I said firmly, standing well away from the buzzing horde.

He looked longingly at the fish crawling with yellow bodies.

I cajoled, "I have more fish in the kitchen. Lots more."

"In that case I'll retire graciously and as strategically as possible."

We left the raiders in possession of the camp and maneuvered unaccompanied through the screen door.

We retreated to the kitchen and while I broiled some more fish, Ed sat at the table facing Karen's room. She was grooming Ocean Borne. Ed watched for a few minutes, then got up and went to stand beside her. While Karen worked she regaled him with stories of the 'characters' she had met at dog shows. Ed continued to observe as she swept the comb and then the brush from the dog's shoulders, down the back to the rump.

"If you can leave the fish, I wish you'd come here for a minute," he called to me.

I went in and stood beside him.

"Why didn't you tell me?" he asked.

"Tell you what?"

"Is it possible you haven't noticed?"

Karen and I looked at each other. "Do you know what the good doctor is talking about?" she questioned me.

"No. Do you?"

"I haven't an idea."

Ed looked at us in amazement. "May I respectfully draw your attention to a remarkable development."

We looked at Ocean Borne.

"Not the dog—the girl. *Karen is using her right arm and it is almost straight!*"

Karen looked at her arm as if it were a new appendage, then reached to brush some more.

I watched closely. The arm was not straight, but there was only a small bend at the elbow.

"Well, what do you know!" Karen's arm swept again from the dog's head down the back to the tail. "It *is* almost straight." She addressed Ed who looked as happy as a clam at high tide. "Over a decade of occupational therapy didn't do what this blessed beast has done."

"Blessed beast indeed!" Ed said. Ocean Borne thought he was speaking to her so she put her muzzle in the palm of his hand. "You're a pretty important member of the family," he told the dog. She replied by making little crooning noises in her throat.

After breakfast Karen and Ed went for a walk and didn't return until lunch time. I was sure they had talked about her decision on physical therapy, but I didn't ask and she didn't volunteer. They had lots of secrets.

Shortly after Ed's departure, school opened. Without the therapy Karen was not nearly so fatigued and there were afternoons when she had time to go for a walk, play her records, or read.

Time flew by for all of us. Letters continued to pour in, there were lectures to give, washing, ironing, sewing, marketing, cooking, cleaning and research for a new book, *Treasure on the Hill.*

Thanksgiving, the Cherns joined us for dinner. Quite properly Karen toasted them: "For whom should we be more grateful?"

Right after Christmas we began to plan for *the* show in

February, the Westminister at Madison Square Garden. The Cherns had brought down from Vermont six dogs they were showing. Two nights before the big event was bath night and Margaret called from Silvermine to say that something had gone wrong with their hot water system and they still had two dogs to bathe.

"Bring them down." I told her.

Rory's famous tin bathtub was ideal for bathing dogs because it was half again as deep as the modern ones, and was not slippery. The floors of the bathroom and kitchen we covered with newspapers and laid out a pile of towels, tar soap, and shampoo. We moved most of the furniture out of the kitchen, and Vadim set up a large crate and pointed into it one of those huge dryers that are used in beauty shops. Jimmy added coal to the furnace, turned up the heat, and we donned bathing suits. As we prepared to immerse the first dog, the Del Hagens, who run a delightful gift shop, and of whom I am very fond, called to see if they could drop in for a short visit. "We're getting the dogs ready for a show, but if you don't mind the confusion, come ahead." Of course I neglected to recite just what went into getting the dogs ready. Bill and Louise arrived as the first wet bitch was put in the crate, the dryer turned on, and the second dog escorted upstairs. It is true that they did manifest some controlled surprise at the garb in which I opened the door to them. I just assumed they would relate it to our activity so didn't offer an explanation. We put them in two chairs at the end of the kitchen, offered a small libation, and continued with our work.

Russ was out of town so we didn't have his help; Marie was exempt because of exams and Joe used a similar excuse though I suspected its validity. Gloria, Karen, Margaret and I combed and brushed. Jimmy and Rory washed. Vadim trimmed. This last job is most important and no one but Vadim was permitted to put a scissor to a dog. The kitchen table was covered with a rubber sheet and a freshly washed chenille rug. The dog to be trimmed stood up there and Vadim went to work. Believe me, the coiffure of Mrs. John F. Kennedy is handled with no more care and skill. I think it is a fair statement to say that Bill and Louise were fascinated. They had said they could only stay an hour. I waved good-bye to them about 1:00 a.m. Shaking their heads, they repeated over and over: "If I hadn't seen it—I wouldn't have believed it!"

I can only describe as torture what we went through during the judging at the Garden. A win at the Westminster could mean the world to Karen. True, one of the purposes in giving her this field of competition was for her to learn to handle defeat. But not here, Lord, oh please not here!

Ocean Borne and Ed Carver were undisturbed.

We were anguished, and I don't mind admitting—prayerful. So were more than a few spectators who hadn't taken long to get the picture. Margaret, Vadim, Nina, Russ, Joe, all of us, were literally clinging to each other, lips moving, when the Judge pointed to Ocean Borne for Best of Opposite Sex. Totally forgetful of ringside decorum, we shouted, hugged each other, and applauded madly! Again Ed had the Judge bring to Karen the precious red and white rosette. As he presented it he said something and Karen, glowing in her victory replied: "I've never been so proud!"

"And justifiably so," replied the judge.

Rory said: "I couldn't swallow."

As soon as Ocean Borne was benched, with her ribbon proudly tacked above her, Karen called the Kerrs. "Your prayers were answered and in full measure. Not only did we go BOS, but the Chern's Little Bear dogs won every ribbon in the breed!"

As she went on talking—no, gushing—I thought of the Westchester Show to which Jean had gone. It had turned bitterly cold but Jean stuck it out and had come home with a bad case of bronchitis. I wondered if the germ had been planted by the opposition, for as a certain badly groomed bitch was led into the ring, Jean remarked in a carrying voice: "She looks like an unmade bed!"

The dog pen in our yard was so large that we cut down on the population of the Cherns' hotel room by bringing two of their dogs home with us. One of them was the splendid and valuable Ch. Little Bear's Broadside.

Jubilant, but completely exhausted, we retired. I was just dropping off to sleep when I heard what I was sure was a

Newfoundland bark in the park. I jumped out of bed and rushed to the window. The pen was empty. Ocean Borne the culprit, no doubt. She could open any door in the house and turn on the taps at the sink to get herself fresh water.

"Jimmy!" I yelled, "the dogs are gone!"

"All of them?" he shouted jumping out of bed.

"Yes."

"Not Broadside too."

"Broadside too. And none of them is car-wise."

He raced down the stairs, tore out the back door and jumped on Rory's bike, still not thoroughly awake. "Alert the girls; call A.M." he yelled over his shoulder as he pedalled off in his pajamas, without so much as a sweater.

I roused the girls and called A.M. Marie took her bike, Gloria the car, A.M. in her car, was out in four minutes flat, and I was about to set off on foot to search through hedges and bushes when I suddenly thought: what will the police think, or do, if they see a man pedalling around the Manor in his pajamas and the temperature an even forty degrees. I called the Police station. It was a little difficult to explain. For the first few minutes, the cop on the desk acted as though I were either drunk or off my rocker. I finally convinced him that I was sane, sober, and talking about many thousands of dollars' worth of dogs; that two of them were not ours, were not car-wise, and we were responsible for them. He offered the immediate help of squad cars cruising in our neighborhood.

I threw on a tweed coat and ran across the street. A.M. passed me driving slowly, with a cheery: "I'll never see a black dog on such a dark night. I've got my flashlight. I'm just going to flash it and look for eyes to shine."

It was an exciting search with cars cruising, powerful searchlights probing the darkness, undressed people on bicycles pedalling madly, undressed people on foot walking over strange lawns and up on strange porches. The cops got two reports of prowlers.

Not until three hours later had we rounded up the scattered herd. Ocean Borne we locked in Karen's room until Jimmy could devise an unopenable catch. No one was arrested for indecent exposure; no one got so much as a sniffle.

We let a year go by before we told the Cherns.

Ocean Borne had shown five times and each time earned points toward her Championship. The March show in Washington, D.C. would probably be a major and if she won she would have the required 15 points. Marie said she couldn't miss Friday and Monday school time but we elected to take Rory for the educational value of a visit to his country's Capitol. The Kellys again offered their car. I wrote a letter to Jim Hagerty, Press Secretary to President Eisenhower, telling him the dates we should be in the city. Jim had been a good friend since the days of my lobbying in Albany, when he had been Press Secretary to Governor Dewey. He replied that we should plan to spend as much of Saturday as we could manage at the White House. I also wrote Father Rover, who was born in Washington, and he responded that Monday he would take us on a tour of the city.

Early and bright on Saturday morning we presented ourselves at Jim's office in the White House and stayed with him until 4:00 in the afternoon. He took us on a tour of the building and patiently answered hundreds of questions posed by the children. For Karen, the high spot of the day was to be present at Jim's press conference. For Rory, it was the model missile Jim gave him and the thrill of sitting in the chair of *every* cabinet member—*and the President's.*

The vast high-ceilinged Armory seemed an ideal building for the Dog Show and it would have been if proper arrangements had been made for unloading the dogs. As it was, the entrance gates were so poorly set up that there was a two hour wait. Ed Carver was bringing two of Chern's dogs. The breed showing before ours was almost finished in the ring and Ed had not yet brought in his second entry. With time running out, Jimmy and Rory went off to help Ed through the admittance gate. That left Karen and me at the bench with Ed's first entry, an enormous and powerful male champion, and Ocean Borne who was in season. Time passed, and over the loudspeaker came the urgent call—*"Newfoundlands to the ring, please."*

The boys had not returned, so without assistance I embarked on a trip so arduous, so hazardous, that I tremble even now to think of it. I adjusted the towels under the dogs'

228.

necks so they wouldn't trip over them; I put my pocketbook behind Karen in the wheel chair; the male I secured on a very short lead after releasing his bench chain and with a superhuman effort kept him away from Ocean Borne while I unchained and leashed her. The Champion was keenly interested in this enchanting lady and she was not reluctant. With a leash tightly wound around each hand, and the same hands needed to push the wheelchair, I started off for the ring a good two city blocks away. I had to watch the crowds in the aisles so I wouldn't ram the chair into anyone, and I had to watch both my dogs and other people's dogs at the same time. The big male, ordinarily so docile, was raring to go for he'd been confined on the long drive from Connecticut, and was now so close to an appealing bitch. His prancings and dancings all but pulled my arm from its socket. I struggled to control him and at the same time keep the wheelchair from being tipped over. Simultaneously, Ocean Borne, 170 lbs., was being kittenish, frolicking heartily at the end of her leash. Over the speaker came the voice: *"Last call for the Newfoundlands!"* I gritted by teeth and plowed on, slowly, painfully. Even if I got there in time, only Ed could take the dogs into the ring. Physically I could take them, but the stakes were high and handling is a more perfected art than one would ever guess from watching the apparently effortless maneuverings of the experts. I didn't even know how to "set up" a dog. I risked sliding my eyes for a moment from crowd, chair, and dogs, to look frantically for Ed, Rory and Jimmy. No sign of them. I kept forging ahead and finally, weak and panting and trembling, I arrived at the ringside. The steward came over to me and before I could speak he said, "Lady, you look awful. Are you sick?"

I nodded, then gasped: "Mr. Carver . . for these dogs . . he'll be here in a minute."

He left me to speak to the judge. He came back. "We can't wait much longer."

Karen blurted: "Oh, you *must!*" She was close to tears.

"You must wait," I told him. "The handler was here early but there's a tie-up in the unloading."

He went back to the judge.

"Oh Mommy!" It was almost a wail.

The steward returned. "You see Madam, we're not only holding up the Newfoundlands, but all the breeds that follow in this ring. The judge says he'll wait three minutes—no more."

Karen was wringing her hands and searching the crowd with glazed eyes. "She *might* become a champion today," she said through stiff lips.

I felt that I might burst into tears from nerves, exhaustion and disappointment for Karen. She must have sensed this for she turned to me and said: "Don't worry, Mommy. Ed will make it. We still have a minute and a half."

I pivoted to look once more in the direction of the gate and there, a Knight in brown slacks and tweed jacket, a little pale and glistening with perspiration, was Ed. Wordlessly I handed him a lead. Jimmy and Rory were a few steps behind and I handed them the other. I sat down hard on the floor beside the wheelchair. I didn't have the strength to stand.

Ocean Borne looked sensational as she floated around the ring. She stood perfectly and kept her pose without twitching a muscle. We held our breath as she went from one judging to another. The entry was large, the competition keen. My heart was beating with alarming rapidity when Judge Murr tapped Ocean Borne for Best of Winners.

Karen had a Champion!

There was a great deal of hustling and Karen and Ed and the Judge were in the ring with Ocean Borne as flash bulbs shot off around them. With many cameras recording the Win, Judge Murr presented the rosette to Karen.

As Ed brought Karen out of the ring, she looked up at the big man: "Ed, you're an angel! I can never thank you enough."

He grunted, gave her a special smile and left for his next class.

Ocean Borne put her head on Karen's lap. "Hi Champ!" The plumed tail waved. "I'm so proud I could burst!"

Victory was sweet, and as I watched Karen I thought, more valuable than we could have known.

230.

Easter Week, Glo and Russ had a visit with Father Kelly. We were out in the yard counting the daffodil buds when they came home. Gloria skipped over to Jimmy, gave him a quick hug and announced: "Now hear this—I quote Father Kelly: 'There is a *breath* of hope!'"

Russ was smiling broadly. "His words exactly." He turned to Glo. "However, Father did emphasize the word *breath*, cautioned against too much hope, suggested we pray harder than ever, and promised he would do the same."

Jimmy reached for Gloria's hands. "We'll bombard Heaven and we won't take no for an answer."

Two weeks after Easter, Jimmy took ten days of his vacation and together we drove South for a series of lectures.

We were gone ten days and the family made as much of our homecoming as though we had been on an eight-month whaling expedition to Antarctica. Gloria, of course, had an Italian dinner. Russ brought wine, and Joe some wonderfully smelly cheese. Rose Hurley and Karen baked a cake. Throughout the meal we got detailed, and in Rory's case, dramatic accounts of all that had transpired during our absence. We began to tell the story of our trip as we washed the dishes and continued over innumerable pots of coffee. Because it was Saturday, Rory was allowed to stay up and it was midnight before I finally relaxed gratefully in my own bed. Jimmy fell asleep almost instantly and I was relishing a re-reading of Caryll Hauslander's *The Dry Wood* when I became aware of a creeping headache. It crept for about ten minutes and then galloped into an encircling torment. I eased myself out of bed and using the wall for support I made my way to the bathroom where I took an empirin and codeine. I began to have trouble breathing. Back in bed I lay quietly, waiting for the medicine to have its effect but instead, the pain grew rapidly worse and my breathing more labored. Then minutes later I knew I needed a doctor. Clinging to the balustrade in the hall, on the stairs, struggling for each breath, I made my way to the phone in the living room. It took me many minutes to find the number of a doctor in the village and many more to read the number correctly. With difficulty I dialed. To the voice that answered I simply gave my name and address, speaking now only with the

231.

greatest effort, "I have a terrible pain in my head and—" I got no farther.

"I'll have Jim Johnson, a heart specialist there in five minutes—"

I had given the address at the rear of the house and I realized that if I didn't go to the kitchen and put on the back light, a stranger could spend hours looking for me—even with the light on he'd have trouble. Lark had come to the foot of the steps to meet me and was sticking to my side. Hanging onto one piece of furniture after the other, I made it to the kitchen and flicked the light switch. The door to Karen's room was open and I moved to close it so she would not be disturbed, also so that the speaker would not carry any sound to Jimmy or the girls. I didn't quite make it but became suddenly violently sick and collapsed on the floor. "I hope Jimmy is sleeping on his good ear so he won't hear me," I thought as I struggled to get up. But Gloria had two very good ears and before I had hauled myself to my feet she was there with her arms around me. Karen called: "Is that you, Mommy?"

Gloria answered quickly: "I came down to fix myself a snack—" She eased me into a chair and closed Karen's door.

I couldn't hold myself up in the chair, so almost carrying me she took me to the couch in the living room. Lark lay down on the floor beside me. I forced out the words: "Doctor . . coming . . wait . . back . . door." I was sick again and again and only dimly conscious when the doctor ran into the room and across to me. Lark, barking viciously, sprang to her feet as this strange man approached me. Gloria quickly clamped a hand around the dog's muzzle and kneed her out of the way. She took off the heavy cord of her robe and tied Lark to the brass door lock. I didn't realize until days later how much easier it would have been on Jimmy had I called him, for aroused by Lark's thunder he came charging down the stairs and into the room to find his wife stretched out on the couch, a strange man bending over her, and Gloria, white and trembling, trying to restrain the dog.

I only dimly remember the ride in the ambulance, and nothing of the actions, only the words of the priest giving me the last rites. Finally, there was no *awareness* of anything yet words reached me clearly. One voice: "There's no pulse." Another: "The lungs have collapsed." And another sighing, "My God, I don't want to tell her husband."

The sun on my face was a benediction.

I knew someone was holding my hand. No, that isn't accurate—I knew Jimmy was holding my hand.

I smiled and opened my eyes.

Jimmy put his cheek against mine. "God must have saved you for something very special."

A year later, almost to the day, we found out what it was.

𝔞

chapter twenty

The cause of my attack had been a freak thing—an allergy to some substance in a non-prescription sleeping pill I had taken each night on the trip. My recovery was phenomenal in that it was complete. There was, however, one lasting effect of this experience. Previously I had seen the loveliness of the world "through a glass darkly," but death, in reaching out, had polished the glass; now I had a minute foretaste of eternity in the loosing of limitations of appreciation; the world had a *newness*—the sheen of an ivy leaf, the exhilarating roughness of bark against the palm, the crack of a bat on a ball, the harsh sweet taste of onion grass, the fragrance of soil.

Marie was full of plans for graduation, (Ed Doll wrote her that this was in truth a 'commencement'), summer work, and entering Marywood College in Pennsylvania in the Fall. She was going to earn part of her tuition as a lifeguard at the college pool and during the summer she would have to accumulate a tidy sum for expenses. She was most interested in working with children if she could find a job that paid well enough. She gave Ed Doll as a reference and he wrote:

This is to state that I regard Marie Killilea as a girl of high ideals, earnest effort, and much promise.

She is personable and well poised. She is not only fond of children but is unusually well related to them and warmly concerned about them. She is patient, kind and understanding and plays no favorites. She finds it easy to accept children and identify with them whether they are talented, troubled, or handicapped. She reveals a pleasing blend of the maternal and youth relationships. She is also physically prepossessing with the kind of maturity, interests and aptitudes to which children respond.

I have no hesitation in commending her for a position of friendly and competent supervision or instruction of children. While her professional preparation in academic courses is in the future (she intends to major in child psychology) she has a background of concern and awareness as well as experience in her family circumstances and the use of information and insight as well as procedures and management which are more immediately helpful than formal study. She is popular with her own age peers and she works well with adults. She is conscientious and willing to go the extra mile. She is discreet and displays good judgment.

When Jimmy finished reading this letter he remarked: "It's obvious that Karen has been a blessing in more ways than one!"

To Marie's bitter disappointment, the salaries offered for jobs with children would not meet her budget, so regretfully she took employment as a salesgirl in a department store.

Early in September we had the first break in our family circle when Marie left for college. What did we miss the most? It's hard to say, but possibly it was her laugh, quick, hearty, ringing. The first night of her absence Jimmy buried himself in a book with what I think of as his 'closed face.'

In October when the trees were bedecked and bejeweled in their autumnal raiment, I made several telephone calls to Dr. Arthur Mannix and he finally included a rabbit in his considerations. I said nothing to anyone else. A few days later the telephone rang and a male voice that I can only describe as lilting said: "Marie, this is Arthur. Can you knit?" When I regained voice and thought, I asked him what was my next step. He said there was always a margin of error in such a test and that I should see Dr. Orville Hicky Schell, obstetrician.

I floated out in the yard to Jimmy who was raking leaves and suggested we walk down to the beach—just the two of us.

When we returned Karen looked sharply at both of us. "Is it true?" Her voice throbbed.

"Is what true?" Jimmy laughed.

She didn't answer but looked at us, her heart in her eyes.

"It's true," I affirmed.

"Are we playing true or false?" Gloria asked crisply.

Rory said: "Karen really knows something." He looked at us.

We nodded to Karen. She took a deep breath and announced: "We're going to have a baby!"

The dictionary defines pandemonium—"riotous place, wild uproar, infernal noise or tumult." By all odds it is the most suitable word for the children's reaction. When the tumult had subsided to a hissing excitement, I took the news to Jean. Most people can commiserate with others in time of trouble, but not so many have the gift of wholehearted rejoicing in the good fortune of others. Such a one was Jean.

The next morning, Karen and Jean sat it out while Gloria drove me to the doctor. She wouldn't allow me to drive myself—"too dangerous." It was not until later that I learned that on this day Dr. Schell had afternoon, not morning office hours, but he had given me a 10:00 a.m. appointment "because a woman who has waited eleven years should not have to wait another four hours."

The doctor was in his eightieth year, handsome, straight, slender as a youth and possessed of an old world courtesy. Like Father McSorley, he was aging but would never be aged. He took the complicated history of eleven previous pregnancies and we went into the examination room. When we returned to the office I said: "I'm afraid to hope."

He smiled and said gently: "I would say your hope will be fulfilled in May."

Searching his face I decided he would understand whatever I said. "Doctor, there's just one thing. If there is ever anything amiss with the baby you must tell me right off."

"Of course," he replied, and I believed him. He offered me a cigarette and lit it for me, then sat back, his hands folded composedly in his lap. "You know, Mrs. Killilea, there are some who think the important thing is to have a baby that is perfect mentally and physically, but—" again that gentle smile, "you and I know that the really important thing is the co-creation of another soul to give glory to God."

I felt bathed in serenity. Safe. In all the difficult time to come, I never lost that serenity. I rose to go. He held my coat and told me: "You can call me any hour of the day or night. There doesn't have to be anything wrong. Sometimes you may just need to talk. When you go into the hospital I'll go with you and I'll be with you until the baby is safely tucked in its crib."

Foolishly my eyes filled with tears and I couldn't manage any words.

The coming Sunday was Parents' Day at Marywood and I was not sure I should take the long drive to Scranton. I called Dr. Schell. "I'd rather you didn't," was his answer. So with Jimmy on one phone and I on the other we called Marie.

I said: "Darling, we're so terribly sorry—we can't come for Parents' Day."

She moaned. "Oh, Mommy, why not?"

Jimmy answered: "Mommy's going to have a baby."

A moment of silence and then an uninhibited shout of joy. "When, oh when?"

"May."

"I can't wait. What a lovely month for birth. Oh, I'm so happy—are you all right? I think I better come home—"

"Nonsense," Jimmy laughed. "Everything's fine. Stick to your studies."

"How can I?"

"It won't be easy."

Marie's voice grew thin. "I think I'm going to cry."

"That figures," replied her father.

A choked: "I love you so much—so very much—both of you."

"And we love you."

"Good-bye—Glod bless you—"

"God bless you—double."

Rory reserved the right to call his godmother. "We have some wonderful news—" He squeezed the receiver in his excitement. "You'll never guess—" He listened, and his eyes opened wide in surprise, then clouded in disappointment. "But *I* wanted to tell you—how did you know?" He listened, smiles, and hung up. "Nellie says she couldn't think of anything else that would make me that happy and besides, after so many praying so hard for so long, it just had to be sooner or later. She did say this was kind of later and told me to ask you if you felt like Sarah?"

"She's pretty fresh. You should have reminded her that I'm only forty-three."

"Gee! Are you?" He studied me. "Well, you look fine," he said judicially.

"Gee—thanks. I feel I have a few good years left."

"You better have." He put his arms around me and gave me a hug. "Not many teen-agers can Charleston the way you can—but I guess you'd better skip that for a while."

"That's a good guess."

Russ and Joe treated me with inordinate solicitude. I had only to glance at a table to have one or the other or both leap to get cigarettes, matches, a newspaper. I grew quite weary of their: "Now you relax—what do you think we're here for?" and was at the same time deeply touched.

One morning, shortly after midnight, I was awakened by the terrifying ferocious barking of the Newfs. They were my dogs but even so their vicious roaring made me prickle. I went to the window and looked into the pen. In the dim light I could see the two huge bodies racing from one end of the wire to the other, then snarling, hurling themselves against the barricade. I couldn't believe that anything so benevolent could be so fierce.

I called to Jimmy, "There must be a prowler at Kerrs."

I stepped to the porch outside our bedroom and looked toward the house next door. The dogs continued roaring, snarling and hurling. "That's a warning if ever I heard one," said Jimmy. "It makes my blood run cold." He went to the phone and called the police. My eyes had grown accustomed to the darkness and I saw two male figures race across the lawn beside Walter's study. A voice yelled a curse at the dogs. The men fled across the street and disappeared into the park. One was wearing a dark jacket and light trousers. That was all I could see. We went down to the living room. The dogs quieted. In but a minute or two the squad cars came. Jimmy called, "They went into the park."

In less than an hour, in all those acres of rocks, trees and shrubs, the police apprehended two drunken young men. They had not effected an entry; the dogs had warned in time. "It's mighty comforting," said Jimmy as we went back upstairs, "to know that our two gentle pets can be ferocious in time of danger."

Some time later we had the dogs indoors one evening and the house across Beach Avenue was burgled. One of the cops observed: "If Killileas' dogs had been out we'd have known about it."

November blew in, blustery, arrogant, and the excited sea spoke harshly and pounded on the sand. The children stayed healthy but I began to have difficulties, similar to those I'd had during previous pregnancies. Dr. Schell sent me to bed with the opinion that I might have to stay there for the duration. There were days when I was not allowed bathroom privileges, a visitor, or a telephone call.

Jimmy, of course, wrote Marie, who telephoned as soon as she received the letter to say that she was quitting college and coming home. There was good reason for such consideration. It wouldn't be quitting but rather a year's leave. We had gotten a cleaning woman once a week, but Gloria was now single-handedly marketing, cooking, washing, ironing, making countless trips up and downstairs with trays for me and, most fatiguing of all, driving two round trips a day, forty miles, transporting Karen to and from school. The local Superintendent of Schools had, under the State law, the right to provide transportation, but he refused and we did not have the thirty-five dollars per week for a cab. It did not seem possible that Gloria could carry such a load without assistance. She thought otherwise. "Of course I can do it. There's no reason for Marie to interrupt college. You're being absurd," she said when Jimmy expostulated vehemently.

After repeated arguments she asked, "At least give me until Christmas." Gloria can be very, very stubborn. Reluctantly Jimmy agreed. With equal reluctance Marie agreed to wait on her decision.

I wrote Ed Doll of the super-human accomplishments of our eldest daughter that were largely possible because she had the ability to synchronize and synthesize a large number of disassociated activities. I also wrote of Karen's assumption of new responsibilities. This lassie now rose at 5:20 a.m., dressed herself with no assistance, made her bed and tidied her room. She also kept her bath scoured. She required help only for braces, shoes and stockings, which Jimmy rendered before he left for work. The main burden of my comments to Ed was that Rory had grown up a year in a month and all the family were carrying heavy additional burdens with not only unfailing good spirit but joyousness.

He replied—

It is meaningful progressions that go to make up the life of a family. Families and their composite don't grow by leaps and bounds and when it appears so it is only some catalytic agent which causes a manifestation of what has been developing beneath the surface.

For all I missed Marie and felt that Gloria needed her, I was happy to have her at college. I was happy too in her roommate, Mary Margaret Richardson, who was lovely to look at, highly intelligent and sweet. Curiously enough, she too, had a sister with cerebral palsy. It wasn't long before she became very much a part of our family.

Marie asked Johnny Forsman to many of the social events at Marywood and saw a great deal of him when she was home. We saw a great deal of him when she wasn't home. They did not, however, indulge in the absurdity of "going steady." Gloria being eight years older than Marie, was in a very good position to counsel. This she did subtly and wisely. In addition, Marie had had Gloria as a model from the time she was fifteen. Marie saw firsthand that one can be "different" and at the same time tremendously popular.

The day before Marie came home for Christmas vacation, Gloria put her case to Jimmy most forcefully. "Have I ever been healthier?" Without giving him time to answer, "I never even get a cold. Have I lost weight? Am I happy? Don't I eat well? Sleep well?" Jimmy tried to stem the flow but she rushed on. "It would be pointless to let Marie stay home. More than the rest of us, I think she *needs* to be away from home for a certain kind of growing up." As usual, she was perceptive and practical.

Jimmy yielded.

I was not even consulted.

Since Joe was family, Dr. Schell permitted him to visit me when others were barred. He and Marie pitched in to help Gloria with preparations for Christmas and he took it on himself to prepare my lunch and carry my trays. He and Gloria realized that when one lies in bed all the time there is little appetite so they fixed dishes so attractive that I ate beyond my inclination. Joe would add a touch—a sprig of holly, a cedar shoot. His visits were easy and enjoyable.

Dr. Schell came every other day, whether I was to have an injection or not. I demurred: "You mustn't. You have too much to do. You make me feel guilty."

"And I thought my visits made you feel better," he assumed a face of mock disappointment.

"Oh—they do!"

"Well, that's sound medical practice."

The cruellest deprivation was not being able to go to church. Father Halligan, a curate of our parish, helped me far beyond the call of duty when he brought me Holy Communion three times a week.

I was reading two or more books a day but craving another activity. Father offered a happy suggestion. He knew of my interest in shooting and told Jimmy about an air pistol—no kick and not heavy to lift, less effort than dry firing and far more satisfying. So under the altar on my mantel which faced the bed, Jimmy set up a target and on good days I would fire for several hours. On the same good days visitors were allowed and some fine contests developed.

Twice during the Christmas holidays Dr. Schell permitted me downstairs. Of course I had to be carried and once settled, stay put until I was carried back up to my room. Russ designated himself porter and bore my increased weight with care and ease. The first trip was for Christmas Dinner. The second was to participate in a unique privilege. Because of my long incarceration, Monsignor Madden had secured permission from the Cardinal's office to celebrate Mass in our home. Selfishly, we wanted this Mass most personal and private so we asked just Jean and Walter, Retta and Jim Kelly. The dining room was transformed into a chapel. The large round table was pushed aside and on it the vestments were laid out. The great buffet against the wall was just the right length, width and height to be an altar. It was dressed in linen and lace which fell in graceful folds to the floor. Two old silver candlesticks held the blest tapers. There were bouquets of red roses in crystal vases and above the altar hung a wooden crucifix, the figure pale in a shaft of morning sun. Beside the altar was a small, linen draped table which held a napkin, a bell, two glass cruets for the water and wine, and a little glass basin.

Russ, with the simplicity that was characteristic, had learned to be an altar 'boy,' and he was to serve the Mass.

My family knelt around me. Monsignor's scarlet and gold vestments moved fluidly as he took his place before the altar: *"Introibo ad altare Dei."* (I will go unto the altar of God.)

"Ad Deum qui laetificat juventutem meam." (Unto God Who giveth joy to my youth.) Russ's deep voice made the responses usually given in a boy's falsetto.

The prayers of preparation continued in their eloquent

241.

Latin. "Take away from us our iniquities, we beseech Thee, O Lord, that with pure minds we may worthily enter into the holy of holies—"

"Kyrie, eleison" (Lord have mercy on us)

"Christie, eleison." (Christ have mercy on us)

Each of us used a missal, reading the prayers with the priest; the jubilant swelling of the *Gloria in excelsis Deo* and on to the Offertory with solemn majesty the Mass progressed. Gracefully, Russ's large frame moved in reverent attendance.

"Sursum corda." (Lift up your hearts).

And the reply: *"Habemus ad Dominum"* (We have them lifted up to the Lord).

Then the silence pierced by the first clear call of the bell. *"Sanctus, Sanctus, Sanctus, Dominus Deus Sabaoth."* (Holy, Holy, Holy, Lord God of Hosts).

Around me the figures knelt and the sun flooded the altar deepening the ruby of the flowers.

The Preface completed, we read the Canon and on to its memento of the living, and I prayed as I did at every Mass for "my beloved family, benefactors (known and unknown), associates, friends, enemies, and all those who have written us letters . ."; then the petition for the prayers of all the saints; and the Consecration.

Twice the liquid peals of the bell called us to adoration, and I trembled that *in our home,* the miracle of transubstantiation was being wrought: *"Hoc est enim Corpus meum."* (For this is My Body) ". . . *Mysterium fidei"* (the mystery of faith).

There was no smallest sound nor stir.

We pleaded that This, the Perfect Offering, might be acceptable as were the offerings of "our father Abraham, and that of Melchisedech, Thy high priest, a holy sacrifice, a spotless victim"; thence to the moving, hopeful memento of the dead.

We prayed as He taught us to pray: *"Pater Noster . ."* (Our Father . .)

Sweetly, the bell summoned us to Holy Communion. Like

flowers to the sun our faces lifted, and the Host was distributed with loving gentleness.

God possessed each. Each possessed God.

chapter twenty-one

Week melted into week and there was no scientific reason for being optimistic. Still we were so.

For the first time in my life I had limitless hours for meditation and reading. I feasted on Newman, Knox, Sheed, Hauslander, Halleck, Ward, Tey and a hundred other writers of detective stories. I think it was Newman's words on the difference between rational knowledge and realization that best related to my situation and provided the most fruitful contemplation.

As Gloria whirled her way around the clock and beyond, I realized that her plethora of activities requiring absorptive thought kept her mind pretty much off her own situation. When we did speak of it I prefaced my words with a three-point invocation. "Lord give me the right words; predispose her mind to hear them well; let me known when to shut up."

This devoted daughter was always tranquil, her penchant for nonsense unimpaired by responsibility or fatigue and it shot through the days like a stab of sunlight in a leaden sky.

Phil and Carla were considering a new apartment and gave our name as a reference. We received the usual letter of inquiry. Karen and Gloria drafted an answer and brought it to me for perusal.

Dear Mr. X,

I have known Mr. and Mrs. Wallach for some time. They are kind people; witness the fact that they always rent out a room or two and their extreme charity is manifest in their choice of such tenants—people who need training in habits of personal cleanliness and virtue.

You'll never have to worry about payment ot rent as most of Mr. Wallach's salary is invested at the track and he is very lucky.

When they are settled in their new apartment you must ask to see their exquisite medieval tapestries. Some of these weigh 400 pounds and of necessity must be secured by 5″ nails.

Mrs. Wallach has a host of four-legged visitors in her kitchen because she is such a kind lady and devotes so much time to charitable work that she has no time for the inconsequentials of housekeeping. Her uncle is an exterminator and always services her apartment at no cost.

To my knowledge their cell meetings have always been conducted in an orderly fashion.

Only once have I known them to house anything larger than a Great Dane. They are such rabid Republicans!

If you require further references relating to their interests and activities I suggest you contact Mr. Bernarr McFadden, Mr. Tommy Manville and Mr. William Z. Foster.

If I can be of any further service do not hesitate to call on me.

(Sgd.)

P.S. To quiet vicious gossip I give you my word that since Mrs. Wallach left Minsky's, she has conducted herself like any other lady.

I signed the letter and we mailed it.

Every day at lunch time, Rory walked the mile from school to come home and see me, and save Glo at least one trip upstairs with my lunch tray. He was troubled, as were we all, about the dozens and dozens of times that his sister came to the second floor and the things which I would forego rather than ask her to come upstairs another time. He solved a good part of this problem very neatly over a weekend by pressing Lark into service as a messenger. When he placed something in the dog's mouth, a newspaper, the mail, she quickly learned the command: "Take it to Mother." The big Lab would trot dutifully out of the kitchen, through the dining room, up the stairs, down the hall, into my room and sit close beside the bed where I could easily reach her package. When I wanted to communicate with Gloria, I would whistle for Lark, place a note in her teeth and tell her: "Take it to Glo." This she would do wherever Gloria was, kitchen, attic, cellar or yard.

Glo reported that one morning the man who delivered the beer stopped for his check. She gave the checkbook and the pen to Lark, a command was no longer needed, and the dog promptly turned and left the kitchen. In about a minute she was back. Gloria took the signed check from the book and handed it to the man. He stared at it stupefied then jabbered: "Jeez! Now I've seen everything! *A dog that can write!*"

In the quiet hours I spent much time thinking about Glo and Russ. Russ didn't have time for brooding either. His job and growing menagerie kept him very busy. One of his nannies had had a kid and knowing how much I would enjoy it he brought the little creature to see me when it was only a week old. He stode into my room, the kid cradled in his arms, and put it on my bed. It was lovely; curly hair black as coal, large bright eyes and a gray muzzle. When we put her on the floor she stood with her long legs stiff, angled, looking for all the world like something you would find in the window of Saks Fifth Avenue as part of an Easter display. Back on the bed again, she curled up her legs and nestled softly against me.

Because I was in bed, Karen had to take on still another job that ordinarily I would have done. Ash Wednesday had lost her milk and Karen, with the help of Colin and John, was bringing up three kittens on a bottle. I was glad for every extra chore that took Karen's time and attention. She would have that much less time to worry about me and the survival of the baby.

As time passed I didn't miss Marie any less and looked forward to a visit from Joe who had gone down to Marywood for a dance. In spite of a heavy snow he came the night after his return, walked over to the bed to kiss me, then stretched out on the floor with Peri-Shan. Ocean Borne and Lark and Etcetera were on the bed with me. (I had found that Newf is indeed something to snuggle up to on a cold, winter's night.) We munched roasted chestnuts while he gave his report. "As President of her class Marie is on the Student Council and is doing a very good job. She is popular though as you know, she never makes a bid for popularity, or even gives it a thought. Every time I see her roommate Richie, I like her better. She's a doll."

"She is. We love her."

Joe said: "Marie is going to the Fordham Prom with me."

"That's nice."

"I had the temerity to ask her to wear white."

"I like her best in white too."

"Is there anything I can do for you?"

"As a matter of fact there is. Will you fetch me that prayer of St. Francis that's in the office and hang it on the wall beside my bed?"

"Joe? hang it?" Karen laughed.

"I forgot you don't know how to drive a nail. Well, just fetch it and Jimmy will hang it later."

He brought it and I read it for perhaps the thousandth time.

> "Lord, make me an instrument of your peace!
> Where there is hatred—let me sow love.
> Where there is injury—pardon.
> Where there is doubt—faith.
> Where there is despair—hope.
> Where there is darkness—light.
> Where there is sadness—joy.
>
> O Divine Master, grant that
> I may not so much seek
> To be consoled—as to console,
> To be understood—as to understand.
> To be loved—as to love.

It is in giving—that we receive.
It is in pardoning—that we are pardoned.
It is in dying—that we are born to eternal life."

Joe was quiet when I finished reading and then he said: "You know, that's the way Glo lives every day."

"It is indeed."

"Any word on the case? I don't like to ask Glo."

"Only that there's still a breath of hope."

"I don't know how they stand it. It's been six years."

"Six long years."

"I hate to leave you and Karen and Peri and the fire but I have to spend some time with my books."

February wailed into March and March continued the wild dirge above slamming sleet and seething seas. I made no preparations for the baby. If all went well, that could be done while I was in the hospital, but for the present we did not know what was going to happen from week to week, or, for that matter, from hour to hour. On another occasion, the family had been through the grief of dismantling a nursery and I was not going to risk such an ordeal again. Jean agreed with me, said she had a bassinette, and could do the necessary shopping in one afternoon.

By the end of April the dogwood was blooming and simultaneously the water was dotted with the small boats of those who believed, as do I, that these blossoms presaged an early run of blackfish; the blue water, dressed up in saucy white caps, was as boisterous as children let out from school. Tulip buds burst into color and we left the soft Newfoundland combings about for the birds to line their nests. Each day now brought stronger possibilities of the baby's survival should it come prematurely and hope welled and coursed in each of us like a spring freshet. After all, Karen had come a week past six months and Rory at seven. Dr. Schell decided to do a Caesarean. "I shall pluck the baby like a rose," he said with nice imagery. I was now permitted to be out of bed a number of hours each day. There were just three more weeks to wait. I thought of the family to welcome this baby: Jimmy was forty-five, I was forty-three; Gloria was twenty-seven, Marie—nineteen; Karen was sixteen and Rory twelve. With such a wide spread in ages this baby would be in a certain sense an only child—an only child with four mothers and two fathers.

Through my bedroom windows I watched the silken water and felt the breeze blow freshly sweet. Gloria's laughter trickled up the stairs. Jimmy had left for New York and Karen and Rory were getting ready for school. Suddenly there was pain of considerable strength. I waited a little and when the pain grew even more intense I suggested that Gloria call Dr. Schell. At 8:30 a.m. he arrived and after a brief examination he said imperturbably: "I think we'll take you to the hospital now. I'll go ahead to make the arrangements and meet you there."

Seconds later the intercom buzzed like an angry bee. I picked up the phone and Karen literally sang: "I hear today's the day—THE DAY—I'll take care of things downstairs and Gloria and Rory will come up to help you."

Gloria ran into the room, her cheeks scarlet, gave me a hug and knelt and pulled the suitcase out from under the bed. Her hands were trembling. Five minutes later Rory dashed in. He was a very dapper twelve-year old. He had changed from his school clothes to his Sunday Best and over his arm he had two ties. "Today, with Daddy away, I'm the man of the family—so which do you think is the more sophisticated?" We agreed on a maroon and white stripe and he went to work feverishly packing my overnight bag, mumbling as he worked: "Lipstick, pancake makeup, mascara, comb, brush, books. What books do you want?" The nighties, bed jackets, robes and slippers had been packed for weeks. He snapped the catches on the bags and we went to the car. Rory put Karen in and stowed her wheelchair in the back, for of course we were all going on this little trip. Gloria drove down the Post Road at a consistent fifteen miles an hour, hunched over, hands riveted to the steering wheel. We were still a mile from the New Rochelle Hospital when she inquired for the sixth time: "Are you all right?"

"Fine," I responded happily and added: "A relaxed driver is a safe driver."

"I'm relaxed," she assured me through clenched teeth.

Karen asked: "How soon can we reach Daddy?"

"He should be at the office by the time we get to the hospital."

We drew up under the porte-cochere. Rory took Karen into the foyer and came back for me. "As long as Daddy's not here—I'll admit you." He picked up my suitcase and we went to the admitting office. He eased me into a chair and said to the young lady behind the desk: "I think I can take care of everything." She, bless her, had the good grace not to smile. When the forms were filled out we joined Gloria and Karen in the waiting room and almost immediately a nurse came to fetch me. The children accompanied me to the elevator where the nurse took my bag from Rory and told all of them "no farther for you." Rory was indignant. He was here in his father's place. The nurse explained that fathers couldn't go upstairs either.

At ten minutes past one on May 3, Dr. Schell 'plucked' a baby girl—7 lbs. 12 ozs.

Healthy, howling and beautiful was Kristin.

᳞

chapter twenty-two

I was coming home and this time I was bringing the baby home with me. Jean had done all the necessary shopping and everything was in readiness for Kristin. I called Glo to find out what time they were coming to fetch us. "Your voice sounds funny," I said to her. Apparently I triggered something, for my stoical daughter burst into tears. "Whatever is the matter?" I was really alarmed. Gloria never cried.

"It's the damn dogs and the coffee and the ceiling," she sobbed.

"Hey—give it to me slowly—I can't follow you."

"—and the brownies—" she gulped.

That didn't sound too tragic. "Let's start at the beginning."

"That was last night, about midnight."

"What was last night?"

There was a pause while she pulled herself together.

"The nurses have been so good to you, I baked them a treble batch of brownies—"

"So—"

"So I put them on the kitchen table to cool and when I came back an hour later to package them, those dogs—*those miserable beasts*—" her voice rose hysterically, "had gotten to them and eaten every last one!"

"That's terrible. Just terrible."

"That's not the worst." Her voice trembled. "This morning, after I finished washing and waxing the kitchen floor, I baked three more batches and put them far back on the coal stove. And those Newfoundlands, your hideous Newfoundlands, (like the kids, when they misbehaved they were mine) reached them and devoured every last one and ground the crumbs into the clean floor and I hope they get good and sick."

I could have wept for her and at the same time I was hard put not to laugh. "You said something about coffee?"

"I was so mad I grabbed a large, fat roll of newspaper and began beating them—"

"—the coffee," I coached.

"That's what I'm talking about. Jimmy had wrapped two days' coffee grounds (and you know how much that is in this house) in that paper and as I beat the dogs the paper broke and the grounds flew all over. They're on the ceiling, the wall, the *clean* floor—even in the cuffs of Jimmy's pants the cleaner had just hung on the door. The whole kitchen looks leprous."

"Oh I'm so sorry—so terribly sorry. I'll explain to the nurses and the kitchen needs re-painting anyway."

"You—do—just—that—and be sure to tell the nurses about your marvelous dogs."

250.

"Don't worry about the floor."

"I don't have to. Rory washed it—*again*."

At one in the afternoon, Jimmy and all the kids came to fetch us. As each newborn had been given to the next in line, Kristin was given to Rory to carry. In the fifteen minutes it took us to drive home, there were times when we all talked at once and times when we were all silent, relishing the wonder of it all. As we drove through the Manor, Rory remarked to the bundle in his arms: "Look, Kristin, the world put on her best bib and tucker to welcome you." It was so. The day was warm and bright and the forsythia fell in golden torrents; lawns were dotted with tulips, narcissuses, jonquils, hyacinths brilliant against the young green of new leaves; there were flowing Japanese cherry trees, and the full blown magnolia blossoms were ivory chalices cupping the sun. The air was intoxicating with a blend of fragrances.

Jean, and Pat O'Brien, and A.M. were at the house, waiting to welcome us. Kristin was passed around but nothing disturbed her as she slept with one tiny fist folded under her chin.

The next day the Cherns came to see the wonder child and bring her a gift—a thirteenth century Spanish madonna. We were marveling that they could part with such a treasure when the telephone rang and Gloria went to answer it. She called to me: "One of your many friends with an odd sense of humor."

"Who is it?"

"He said he was Cardinal Spellman, and I said I was Eleanor Roosevelt and I would send one of my secretaries for you."

I picked up the phone. "Hello."

"Oh Mrs. Killilea, this is the Cardinal. I just heard about Kristin and I called to tell you how happy I am for you."

"Who was it?" Glo asked at the termination of my chat.

"Cardinal Spellman."

"Let's not overdo a bad joke."

"Brace yourself—it was the Cardinal."

"Oh Lord, I always have had hoof in mouth disease. Was he miffed?"

"He was much amused."

I fed Kristin, just nosing out my eldest daughter and went up to rest. Gloria went to do the marketing. I was tired but couldn't sleep. Karen's muscle pain was less but there wasn't a day or a night that she didn't have some. Dr. Johnson had given her an anti-spasmodic that helped quite a bit. I pondered a problem she had, more important than pain. She was on her feet and walking but there was a dependence involved that sorely troubled Jimmy and me. To walk, she needed, and would always need, the knees of the braces locked. This meant that when she wanted to rise from a chair and move across a room, someone had to lock the braces and help her to her feet. From then on she did very well, but—when she wanted to sit down again, someone had to unlock the braces. Also, and most importantly, when she fell in braces with knees locked, she could not get up by herself. A thousand times Jimmy and I had talked about what to do. Without being told, we knew this dependence troubled Karen too. She was old enough to baby-sit but if she couldn't get up when she fell, she couldn't take this responsibility. She made one most revealing comment to me: "It's galling!" Kristin would mean so much more to Karen if she were freer.

Marie got home that week-end to see her baby sister. Quite properly it was Rory who made the presentation. Marie handled the baby as naturally as if she'd had a dozen of her own. "How unutterably beautiful!"

Jean came in, looked from Marie to the babe in her arms and said: "Well, Big Marie and Little Marie."

Gloria told Jean and Marie the story of the brownies and the Newfoundlands and illustrated by pointing to loathsome brown clusters that still stuck to the ceiling and upper walls. Jean shuddered and remarked, "We want to get the kitchen done before the christening anyway."

"No deadlines," I begged, "it will be a little while before I'm up to climbing ladders and scraping paper. This room is high!"

Jean answered briskly: "You do the painting and I'll do the scraping. I'll want no conversation and just a few cans of cold beer."

Kristin had been baptized at birth, and Bishop Wright who was then in Worcester, had offered to christen her. We had decided that it would be most meaningful to have the ceremony on our twenty-fourth wedding anniversary which was July 25th. That meant I could put off the kitchen for another month.

The night of the Fordham Prom came and went but it stays green in my memory on two accounts. Richie, regal in a sweeping ball gown, wore sneakers—she just forgot her pumps. Marie wore an unholy amount of pancake makeup —the reason was kept from Mother until the following day. Marie had the measles.

A week later Joe's family moved to Florida and he moved in with us. Jimmy was quite pleased to have two sons. Joe and Russ worked with us on the kitchen and, driven mercilessly by Jean, we finished it just two days before the christening. Of this christening we have a detailed record. Kaasi Slezak took pictures, and Phil Wallach and Walter Kerr recorded every word. Karen and Rory assumed their official positions as godparents since they had not been present at the Baptism.

Kristin at three months was a delight, happy and sparkling. She would stare at one most soberly, then suddenly she would laugh. The family had many names for her. She was Rory's "Princess," Daddy's "second-best girl." (I guess I was still first.) So far as the children were concerned, Jimmy and I need never have done a thing for Kristin.

The summer sped by. Karen continued to improve her swimming and Kristin grew fat and brown. Her constant companion was Etcetera. The night we had brought Kristin home from the hospital we had found the Siamese on his hind legs beside the tiny crib. His forelegs were through the slats and his paws on her arm. He was making strange, soft little noises. From that night on he rarely left her, even when the tiny fists pulled his hair or a poorly directed finger probed a sensitive ear. She imitated the strange way in which a Siamese "talks," and many times we had to look to see if it were cat or baby.

In the Fall, Karen went eagerly back to Good Counsel and Marie, not so eagerly, went back to college. Much as she loved it she had always had a strong pull toward home, and now Kristin made it just that much more difficult to leave. On Kristin's Name Day, Marie wrote the baby:

My Darling sister, Kristin,

I am just sorry, little one, that you will never really know the happiness you have brought to us all.

I am sure that with the wonderful Mother and Father you have, you will bring us much more happiness in the coming years.

Kristin, some day when you are away from home, maybe at college, you will realize just how wonderful are your Mom and Dad and how lucky we are. You won't realize this until you get around and have a chance to see what other parents are like.

Take my word for it, Kristin, you are the luckiest girl in the whole, wide world.

God has chosen us to be the lucky ones for some good reason, even though we won't know what it is, but it gives us a real obligation because we have been so blest.

I love you so very, very much. God bless you,
Your sister, Marie

Other prose came our way that week for Doubleday published Jean's *Please Don't Eat the Daisies*, the sales of which were to be astronomical. One of the first copies off the press Jean sent to Karen with the inscription: "For my darling Karen, who is a joy, an inspiration and a comfort to me— With all my love—Jean."

Early in December we plunged into preparations for Christmas and Rory, who shivered when he delivered papers, took up frostbiting. This is a "sport" pursued by otherwise sane individuals who go out in small sailboats all winter and think nothing of returning encased in ice. It is most suitably named.

Joe drove to Scranton to bring Marie home for the vacation and a few days later we had our holiday dinner. Dr. Schell was with us and his "rose," Kristin, made the occasion memorable by cutting her first tooth on Monsignor Madden's finger. Jimmy bought reels and reels of film for Kristin's first Christmas and Russ came literally before the dawn to do the filming. As Kristin sat on the floor and looked up at the brilliance of the tree, her large dark eyes reflected the wonder that *is* Christmas.

Christmas night as we were going up to bed, Marie put her hand on my arm and said, "Let's have a chat."

We went to the kitchen, put on the coffee pot and sat at the table. I slipped off my shoes and squiggled my toes in the winter coat of the Newf at my feet. Marie was troubled I could see. She began: "You know how grateful I am to you and Daddy for the chance to go to college."

"I know."

"And you know that I love it."

"Yes, we do."

"Well," she spoke slowly, thoughtfully, "if I had a vocation to law or medicine or teaching—it would be different. As it is, I'm pretty sure that my vocation in life is marriage."

I waited.

"I've been doing a lot of thinking and it seems to me that one should prepare for this vocation too. For others it may be college but for me—I believe I could best prepare by staying home and learning to budget and really take over the running of the house. You and Glo know marketing and organizing and Glo could teach me to be a fabulous cook. I'd have experience with a baby and—" she studied my face, "if it's all right with you and Daddy, I think this would be best for me." Her eyes were dynamic punctuation.

"Daddy and I have always been conscious of one thing—it's *your* life. Apparently you have given the whole matter much thought and come to your decision by slow and careful steps. That's enough for us. I don't even have to ask Daddy.

And," I grinned at her, "I must confess it will be wonderful to have you home, especially for Daddy. He's never said anything, but I know he has sorely missed his first-born."

She came over and put her arms around me. "You know, I've just come to realize that one doesn't have to go to college to be educated. You and Daddy didn't go to college and you're still studying and learning."

"It takes a certain amount of discipline—"

"What doesn't?" She asked realistically.

ह✍

chapter twenty-three

Walter and Kaasi Slezak gave us a present—another pet, a mynah bird. "I guess if we're feeding ten, or is it eleven, animals, we might as well feed one more," was Jimmy's unenthusiastic response.

The bird had been given to the Slezaks by Ezio Pinza, in whose household Italian and French were spoken. Walter spoke German to his feathered friend and Kaasi, Dutch. Poor creature, he had to adjust to peasants who spoke only English. I could pronounce Latin fairly well but obviously that would not develop the conversation we were after.

The bird was about the size of a crow, a glossy black with metallic purple on the nape of the neck and metallic green on the rump. He had a sleek dignity and a penetrating eye. We named him Gazebo in honor of Walter's current Broadway hit. There are some who hold that it is difficult or impossible to teach a mynah bird to talk after it's a year old, but the first night we had him he learned to say in a tender basso: "I love you." The second night, Johnny Forsman took Marie to a basketball game. The rest of the family had retired and I sat with the bird in front of me on the kitchen table. I had decided that the first command I should teach him to speak was: "Shut the door, stupid." Anyone with a boy of his own (and especially anyone next door to the young Kerr males) can use an assist in this. In a couple of hours he had mastered the phrase with telling mimicry and as a reward I offered for his nibbling, a round inch-long cracker. Instead of pecking at it, as any mannerly bird would do, he seized and pulled it from my fingers and the whole thing disappeared in one inhalation. In a few minutes he was coughing roughly and I was sure the cracker was stuck in his trachea. I was frantic. His coughing was interrupted by harsh gaspings. I suppose I should have phoned Walter right away, but I knew he was fond of the bird and I kept putting it off until it was too late for a call. Marie and Johnny came in about 11:30, Gazebo was quiet for a minute and then the racking noises started all over again. They sat with me for a while, then Johnny left and finally I sent Marie to bed. I sat up with that blessed bird all night and just when I thought the danger was past, he'd begin to gasp and choke. Several times I wondered if, to save his life, I should attempt a tracheotomy. At 7:00 a.m. I finally called Walter and in a shaking voice told him of the tragedy. I was so tired and upset that I began to blubber. "I'm so sorry—so terrible sorry. What can I do?"

For a moment there was no response and then my ear was all but shattered by a guffaw.

I was stunned. "Walter—wake up! I said I think the bird is going to choke to death."

The guffaw subsided to gaspings (they sounded like the bird's) and finally Walter managed to speak. "Don't worry —he's all right—" He started to laugh again. I became enraged but before I had a chance for a verbal assault, Walter continued in spasmodic bursts of speech: "My father-in-law was here for a visit—he has asthma—(vast gurgle of laughter) and in two days, (more laughter) the bird was mimicking all of his bronchial difficulties.

For some time, I had been bothered by a hard pain in my jaw and finally, at Jimmy's insistence, I went to see Joe Massucco, our dentist. Joe examined me, took x-rays and then asked: "Is anything worrying you?"

"What do you mean?"

"Exactly what I said. Are you worried about anything?"

"No. Wait a minute—" I didn't know whether 'worry' was the right word, but I did know that I never went to sleep without an agonizing wondering about Karen's dependence on others in order to walk, and the acceleration that did not come. The familiar question loomed large at night "where do we go from here?"

Reluctantly I told this to Dr. Massucco. I shouldn't have been reluctant because he is sensitive and understanding, but I guess one just doesn't like revealing too much of one's self.

"That's pretty much what I thought," he replied composedly. "There's nothing the matter with your teeth, and the pain is the result of tension—"

"But I'm not tense."

"Don't interrupt. You are tense whether you know it or not and what you're doing is grinding your teeth at night—and hard. That's the cause of the pain."

When I got home there was a letter for me and a card for Karen from Ed Doll in Hawaii. Karen's was a picture of a bloom called "Cup of Gold." Of this flower the card read "a gorgeous blossom which spreads its golden glory—" Ed had scribbled (his penmanship was bad enough when he wrote carefully), "Karen dear, I give you only one guess on why this reminds me of you. I wish you could see it—it fairly glows. Much love to all, especially my dreamboat pilot."

I read my letter thinking how Ed had been the pilot of our whole family. My most recent report to him was that Karen worked too hard on studies. I told him that when I remonstrated, she had replied: "I can't help it, Mother, I have a fire burning inside." I had asked him if I should compel her to ease off. He answered: "Don't quench it." His letter went on: ". . . As I have said before, I genuinely identify with you all. I would like to point out that there will be difficulties in normal human interrelationships, but there will be nothing morbid in them except the possibility of their becoming so through lack of patience, confidence, and faith based on mutual love and understanding."

On the morning of February 11, I was engaged, as I had been for three miserable weeks, in painting the living room. High on a ladder above snowy mounds and hummocks of sheet-draped furniture, I scraped the ceiling. Outside the gray sky melted into a gray sea and the receding tide lacquered the sand. It was a sight only a little less drab than the moulting room. In the corner beneath me, Kristin, dressed in scarlet overalls and shirt, was the only bright thing as she banged pots against the bars of the playpen. The Siamese at her feet flinched at the noise but stayed, and the three black dogs flanking the pen slumbered undisturbed. The telephone rang and I came carefully down the ladder glad of an excuse to rest on the level.

The Whittington chimes of the Grandfather clock struck ten notes.

"Hello." I noticed even my voice was drab.

"Marie! This is Father Kelly."

Just hearing his voice gave me a lift. "I hope you called to say you're coming in to see us."

"I am. But that's not the prime purpose of my call."

"Oh?"

"Word just came from Rome that Russ and Glo are free to marry!"

The shock was so great that at first I felt nothing, said nothing.

"Hello! Marie . . are you there?"

As realization engulfed me I began to tremble all over. "Yes, Father . . yes . . wait . . Glo's in the kitchen—" I dropped the phone, wriggled a straight course between and over piled furniture, tore through the dining room and drew up short at the kitchen door. Gloria sat at the table cutting up meat for veal paprika. I had decided two things in my forty foot dash: my face and voice must reveal nothing, and Gloria should be alone when she received her news. With a great effort I composed myself and spoke casually: "Glo— telephone." I went back to the living room.

Silence.

A shriek. Then weeping. Then jumbled words.

I waited.

"Marie! Little Marie! Come quick!"

Marie raced up from the cellar.

Glo jumped up from the chair, flung herself on us singing, shouting: "Rome said *'yes'!*"

"I don't believe it!" Marie stood stunned.

"It's true! It's really true!" Gloria cried.

"It's miraculous!"

"I can't believe it." Marie gasped.

Gloria hugged her, then threw her arms wide and caroled: "Happy! Happy! Happy!"

When Gloria got herself under some control she called Russ and, in an unbelievably calm voice, that betrayed nothing, asked him to come to dinner; she said she would meet his train. She then called Jimmy and was told he could not be reached. Next she called Kerrs (and believe me only a statement from Rome would induce anyone who knew them to call Kerrs at 10:30 a.m. which for them is the middle of the night.) Walter answered and Glo asked them to come over right away. What none of us thought of at the time, was that such a summons, at such an hour, would be interpreted as Disaster at the Killileas. In a very few minutes they were coming across the lawn and Gloria watching out the window remarked, "Isn't it sweet the way Walter leads Jean. I think she's sleepwalking."

They came through the kitchen door, their faces reflecting a) determination to hear the bad news equably, and b) to help us in whatever way was indicated. Jean sank into the nearest chair and visibly braced herself. Walter stood protectively behind her.

Gloria sang out: *"Rome said 'yes'!"*

Jean's head jerked back, Walter stood frozen; lightning-quick expressions of shock, relief, incredulity, joy, flashed across their faces. They rallied quickly and there was more wild rejoicing.

Breathlessly Jean asked: "I suppose you'll be getting married right away?"

Gloria answered quickly: "Not on your life! I've never had a courtship!"

Jean's beautiful face (*she* doesn't need make-up) grew dreamy. "What an exquisite bride you will be!"

"Well I won't wear a wedding dress or veil," stated my daughter positively. "I'm too old."

Walter snorted. "You're twenty-eight!"

"I'll be twenty-nine next month."

"You're not making sense," said Jean, "the news has unhinged you."

"I'm too old," repeated Gloria.

Walter, always so sane, forsook argument and offered: "If you really feel that way we'll just cast around you. We'll find someone over seventy to marry you, altar boys in their twenties and attendants about forty. That will take care of it nicely." He punctuated his words with the telling eloquence of his hands.

Gloria laughed and quickly Jean asked: "Don't you know you look twenty at the most?"

"I don't think she ever really looks in a mirror," Marie observed.

I decided to put my two-cents in. "Daddy will want his first bride to look bride-like."

Gloria looked a little wistful at the use of the word bride, so we ganged up on her with more arguments and subtle persuasions.

Walter gave the final push. With a shrug of calculated indifference he said quietly: "I think every man wants his bride to wear a wedding gown and veil."

We let that statement hang in the air.

Gloria stared at Walter thoughtfully. Then yielded. "I hadn't thought of that. You're right."

"And—" contributed Jean, "there's no reason for Russ to know you suffered this temporary aberration."

"Okay," agreed Gloria dutifully.

The bride babbled on. "I know Russ will want Father McSorley to marry us and Father Kelly to say the Mass." She looked at each of us in turn. She sat down. "Can you really believe it?"

Jean said briskly: "I couldn't go through another seven years like this."

After they left, Gloria finally reached Jimmy. Again she heralded: *"Rome said 'yes'."*

We couldn't understand Jimmy's words, but even on the far side of the kitchen we could hear his voice crackling.

Karen and Rory came home from school at the same time. As Rory pushed the wheelchair through the door, Glo swooped down on them. *"Rome said 'yes'!"* I watched Karen closely. Momentarily there wasn't anything to be seen on her face—shock robbed it of all expression. Then with a sob she pulled Glo close and cried: "I'm so happy with you —so happy!"

Glo murmured: "Darling, darling, how much of this I owe to you!"

In a house where bedlam was not unusual and pandemonium not rare, there had never been a scene like this. They shouted, they sang. "Here comes the bride!" Rory danced his big sister around the kitchen, through the dining room and back.

There was more madness when Jimmy and Father Kelly came in. Glo rushed to Jimmy who wordlessly enfolded her in his arms.

To Father Kelly she kept chanting, "Oh, thank you! Thank you! Thank you!"

Kristin didn't get her bath. She was lucky she got her supper.

Jimmy called Mancini's and ordered champagne to be delivered *immediately*.

The veal burned, we forgot the potatoes, and though we did set the peas on the stove, no one thought to put a light under them.

We all kept watching the clock. The reluctant hands laboured slowly to Russ's train time. We held our breath with the chiming of six magical notes and Gloria drifted out the door.

My mind slid back many years to the railroad station at Harmon—Russ waiting so eagerly for Gloria and she speaking the words of final parting.

This time she would be waiting for him.

ह्∾

chapter twenty-four

Russ, when he wasn't 'courting,' had his bachelor house to paint and prettify for a bride. Down county, we were busy with the list for wedding invitations, shopping for trousseau and the frills and furbelows that are more desired by a wife than by a bachelor. Marie took over the organization and administration of the house and younger children, leaving Gloria and me freedom to shop and work on the little red house. We kept telling each other how calm we were in the face of exaggerated activity. Witness: We were shopping for shoes in New Rochelle and stopped at Schrafft's for lunch. The restaurant was crowded but not noisy. There was the usual assortment of men without enough time and women with too much. A smiling waitress did not rush us and we relaxed over a cup of coffee before ordering.

I said to Gloria: "I'm going to call home and ask Rory to wash the car."

Glo leaned across the table and whispered conspiratorially: *"The car is parked one block away!"* She leaned back. "I'm glad you're taking all of this so calmly."

I could feel myself blushing and she, contrite, changed the subject. "Russ got his bill for legal fees from the Chancery Office."

I waited for her to go on, hoping that it was not astronomical.

"What would you guess it would be?" she asked.

"I couldn't guess. But for seven years' work, which included sending people out to interrogate witnesses all over the country, it must be considerable."

"Brace yourself. Total bill—$150!"

"How could that be? That would be low for one year's work. I've worked in enough law offices to know that."

"That's what Russ thought but Father Kelly said that was the usual fee."

"What a happy relief! I had visions of your having to mortgage the little red house to cover the costs."

As we were busy getting ready for the wedding, so were Karen, Rory and Chris Kerr. Gloria (having been persuaded that it was not necessary to cast around her) had asked Rory and Chris to serve as altar boys at her Nuptial Mass, and they were diligently polishing up their Latin pronunciation. Marie and Karen were to be the only two attendants and this meant a gargantuan effort for Karen. Although a processional pace was stately, it was not as slow as Karen's present pace. So hour after sweating hour, and day after sweating day, she practiced to increase her speed. I would come upon her quietly working in the dining room, her face frequently stamped with discouragement which, on seeing me, she would quickly control and remove. One afternoon, Rory said to me: "Mom, when I went out three hours ago Karen was working, and she was still working when I came home. She *never* gives up on *anything*." He bit into an apple. "She makes me feel six inches lower than a snake's navel."

The bridesmaid's dress was most becoming to Karen but she was unhappy over the heavy brown orthopedic shoes which had to be worn with the braces and ill-befitted the frothy organdy. Marie solved this problem as she had so many others, by ordering tightly fitted, zippered shoe covers, which were lined and of the same material as the dress. They looked very chic indeed. Gloria decided not to have a carpet down the aisle of the church as this would provide an additional hazard to crutches.

For all our searching it was Joe who found Gloria's wedding dress. It was a creamy white, Italian silk, delicate. It had a heart-shaped neckline edged with lace, long sleeves, tight bodice and a full skirt with a chapel train. Glo was a size 9 and looked like a flower. Joe's wedding present to her was an exquisite lace mantilla.

As Karen's attitudes toward seemingly unresolvable difficulties had exerted immense influence on Gloria, so Gloria's attitudes over the past seven years had influenced Karen. It was curious, sub-conscious reciprocity.

At eighteen, Karen was faced with what is perhaps the biggest problem that can be faced at that age—the dearth of alternatives; and so far as could be seen, this would be a static state. So it had been with Gloria. Because of her love for Russ and the apparent hopelessness of that love, she too, had been through years of no alternatives. Karen had been fully aware of this. Equally she was aware of the sustaining power that enabled Gloria to preserve intact those elements of her personality which might so understandably have been blighted—the gaiety, humor, spontaneity, selflessness and the absolute negation of self-pity.

It would have been unrealistic to deny Karen's difficulties at this time and she would have been unnatural were they not matters of great moment to her. As earnestly as Jimmy and I might wish to teach, and as diligently as we might apply ourselves to this task, there was no way in which *we* could give Karen what she got through living with Gloria these past seven years. The final underscoring rested on the fact that Gloria was no whit *changed* since the bliss-full word had come from Rome. There had been no tension to ease, restlessness to divert, impatience to subjugate, rebellion or rancor to contest, or self-commiseration to conquer. It was Gloria's *being* that, through the years, had crept un-noticed and unchallenged into Karen—a core of stillness, a reciprocal transmutation—with love—*to* Karen.

Influence is not dependent on presence and Karen would not forfeit her "becoming" because of the change in Gloria's situation and her physical absence from home. Notes from my diary:

JUNE 23
Jean gave a most beautiful shower for Gloria. The patio was ablaze with new roses. Glo remarked: "I don't feel old anymore."

JUNE 24
Today was Awards Day at Good Counsel. Karen came home with the gold medal for the girl with the finest school spirit. It must have been a tough decision for the place vibrates with school spirit. Classes commence at 8:45 yet girls start arriving an hour before. Corridors are still crowded at 5:15 two hours after dismissal bell. Karen's great love for the school probably stems from the fact that here was fulfilled a dream that as Ed Doll had said: "may have been despaired of." Also, and this is most important, at G.C. she was nothing special— just another pupil. In this atmosphere, created by mu-tual affection between girls and nuns, personalities blossom in their own way, unhampered by senseless regimen and equally senseless demands for conformity.

Kristin spoke her first sentence last night. When Jimmy came home he knelt and opened his arms to her. She ran across the porch calling: "Daddy! Hey—beer!"

Kristin anticipates Karen's needs, fetching a crutch as soon as Karen says: "Please lock my knees."

Glo and Russ have taken steps to get on an adoption list if they don't have a baby within a year.

Today Glo and Russ received wedding present from the Cherns—*Champion Little Bear's Valkyrie!*

JEAN IS GOING TO HAVE A BABY IN DECEMBER! I said: "Wait until Karen hears this!" Jean said: "She's known for some time. She was the first and only one I've told up to now."

In four days, Gloria will be Mrs. Lea. They're going to Nantucket on their honeymoon, stopping in Springfield with Bishop Weldon first. They'll be gone three weeks. I won't think of the desolation of this house when she's gone.

It was Monday, June 30, Gloria's wedding day.

The morning was pearly. At the proper time the sun rose with the majesty and beauty befitting the day. From the fleet of small sailboats came the toneless yet musical tinkle of halyards against masts, like the cowbells of a slowly moving herd.

Long ago, Nellie Gagliardi had said that one day she would dress Gloria, the bride. It was not the kind of comment that we encouraged, so although Nellie stopped saying it, she never stopped believing it. She arrived at 8:30 a.m. and took over the third floor with happy efficiency and frequent chicklings of "I-told-you-so's."

Rose Hurley, her dear dark face shining with happiness, came to take over the kitchen for the day. There was to be no 'reception' but rather breakfast for the family, the dozen or more priests who would be on the altar and, as Walter Kerr put it, the "stage hands." He and Phil Wallach were audio and at 10:00 a.m. they left to set up the wires and mikes to record the ceremony. Kaasi Slezak was "cameraman."

Jimmy was unbelievably nervous and I finally suggested he take the dogs for a walk, a suggestion he accepted with revealing alacrity. Marie's calm was determined, and Karen's fluttery as we dressed. Kristin was a bright firefly animated by the sense of what was happening if not the meaning.

At 10:45 Gloria came down the stairs. There was in her face an effulgence of joy almost too bright to be borne. Jimmy's eyes filled with tears as he stood waiting for her. As they walked to the door Glo looked around her and said, "It's a beautiful house—and a loving house." We went on ahead and were waiting in the vestibule of the church when Gloria and Jimmy came up the steps. Our pastor, Monsignor Deegan, was also waiting and as Gloria entered he went up to her. She took her hand from Jimmy's arm, advanced a step and knelt before Monsignor with sweet humility. "Your blessing—" She bent her head, the lace of her mantilla caressed her cheek, the voluminous folds of her gown fanned the floor in a great circle of shimmering white.

Kristin held my hand as we walked up the aisle. She had pranced at the rehearsal, now she stepped precisely, looking not to left or right but straight ahead to the brilliantly lit altar. We took our places and shortly the church was filled with the lovely solemnity of the Processional. At that moment my prayer was for Karen. The church was large, the aisle long. Tensely I watched her dainty figure. She was straight as a sapling, and as she moved I marvelled that neither emotional nor physical strain showed in her face. Her pace was perfect, her steps sure. Behind her Gloria seemed to float, light and ethereal as a spun rainbow.

I have been to many weddings but never to one so charged with emotion. All present had waited with, and prayed with Gloria and Russ; and each had a realization of sharing deeply.

Russ came out of the sacristy and stood at the sanctuary steps. The moment he glimpsed Gloria a smile illumined his face. A step from Russ, Jimmy moved to place Gloria's hand in that of the bridegroom. But here the flawless order of the rehearsal was broken, and the prescribed ritual interrupted, for Gloria faced Jimmy, put her arms around him, and kissed him with all the loving tenderness of her daughter's heart. There was a hushed intake of many breaths, and Gloria turned to Russ.

Father McSorley waited for them on the top step of the altar. Before he read the formal words of the Marriage Instruction, Father spoke a few words of his own, and in his loving wisdom concluded: "I know, Russell, that in the difficult days that come in any marriage, you will need to be, and will be heroic. And you, Gloria, in those same days, will need to be, and will be angelic." There was a holy twinkle in his eyes.

The candle flames burned steadily; the purple robes of the Monsignori were vibrant contrasts to the white surplices, as delicate as the still white flowers on the altar. The sun bored through the stained glass windows and dropped jeweled clusters on the marble floor of the sanctuary. Slowly Father's veined hands opened the book and clearly and solemnly, in a voice that could be heard to the very last pew he began: "My dear friends: You are about to enter into a union which is most sacred and most serious. It is most sacred, because established by God Himself; most serious, because it will bind you together for life. . . It is most fitting that you rest the security of your wedded life upon the great principle of self-sacrifice. And so you begin your married life by the voluntary and complete surrender of your individual lives in the interest of that deeper, wider life you have in common. Whatever sacrifices you may hereafter be required to make to preserve this common life —always make them generously. Sacrifice is usually difficult and irksome. Only love can make it easy; and perfect love can make it a joy. We are willing to give in proportion as we love. . ." Father paused. In a silence that was profound Father pronounced the indestructible words of the Sacrament, and Glo and Russ made their replies. I thought of their sacrifice, their joy, their love, greater for God than for themselves, and knew that the union of their hearts had long ago been sanctified.

At the completion of the Mass, Father Kelly turned to face the congregation. The lines of his Gothic face were softened by the paternal love he felt for these two—his children in a very special sense. He read from a parchment the personal blessing of His Holiness, Pope Pius XII.

About 2:00 p.m. I went to Karen's room on an errand and there found Gloria and Russ closeted with Jean and Walter. As I hesitated in the doorway Jean said in a shocked voice: "This is the darnedest wedding I ever attended. I prayed for years that you two could get married, and here am I at the end of your wedding breakfast—*witnessing your will!*"

I was aghast. Russ laughed: "There's nothing morbid about it. It just seemed like a good day to make sure that we had a share in Karen's future." Shortly after, Mr. and Mrs. Lea drove off. Jimmy and I, alone, stood on the porch a long time after the car was out of sight.

In the quiet of the evening the family sat together. There was a carry-over of excitement and garrulity, and then one by one, we fell silent. A brisk breeze sent a small surf to stutter along the shore. The bell buoy sang its solitary note as it danced in the dark. Rory broke the silence: "I feel as if I'd had a finger amputated!"

Karen said, "I'm happy—and empty."

It was late when we reluctantly separated to go to bed. On our pillow was an envelope, which was no novelty for ever since the kids had learned to write they had left bedtime notes—"I *was* careless about the change. I'm sorry—RORY." Or from one of the girls. "Thank you for the lovely dress."

This note was from Gloria.

I can never speak the gratitude and love in my heart. Love for the most wonderful mother and father a girl ever had, and gratitude for my home and sisters and brother. .

My eyes blurred so I passed the page to Jimmy. When he came to the closing paragraph he had trouble with his voice so I wiped my eyes and read over his shoulder

. . for the riches I found at Sursum Corda, not the least of which was in our friends. From now on, in my daily prayers, and at all my Masses, I shall specifically

269.

mention the Cherns and the Kerrs, who have given so much to us all and to whom I am eternally indebted. As for my beloved family, each prayer I utter, for as long as I shall live, will include you. I love you, I love you, I love you.

Your Daughter

The following morning there was a letter from Jim Meighan.

As of 11:00 a.m. June 30, your crown is dented and a pearl is missing. When born, we might say Gloria was a cultured pearl, but with God's help and a small assist from all your family, she became genuine. You will miss her. I will miss her. But most of all—*Karen will miss her.*

How happy you must be that she married a jewel of a man.

May God bless them and you too.

Love,
Jim

ટ❧

chapter twenty-five

We missed Gloria in a thousand ways. Anticipating the bleakness of Karen's first week-end without her, we had entered a dog show in Massachusetts. Friday, the sun was bright and hot, so I bathed Ocean Borne and secured a large white bath towel around her rump, pinning it under her tummy. The purpose of this was to keep rump coat flat so there would be no distortion of her top line. I walked her from one end of the park to the other until she was dry. Saturday was drizzly and a good day to get caught up on shopping. The forecast for Sunday was for temperatures in the high nineties. I went into a store to get a cool, patterned dress that would not show the soil necessarily picked up in a day at a dog show. In telling the saleslady what I wanted, I merely said, "I want something for a dog show."

With what I took to be kindly interest she inquired: "What color is the dog?"

"Black."

She disappeared and returned quickly with several dresses in 'frosty pink.' "These would be perfect," she said moving toward the dressing room.

"Oh no! You must have misunderstood me—I'm wearing the dress to a dog show."

"To set off a black dog—you would be best in pink." She smiled stiffly.

"I want something that will not show black hair, spilled water, melting ice, some drooling, grass stains or dust."

With an unflattering shrug she left me and returned with a black and green print. I tried it on, it fit, and I made out a check. "Mrs. Killilea," she read the signature. "I seem to know that name."

I assumed that she had read something of mine or heard me lecture. With becoming modesty I kept silent.

"Killilea—Killilea—" she repeated as she boxed the dress. Suddenly she smiled and gave me an appreciative look. "Of course—"

I smiled.

"You're the lady—" she was no longer smiling but grinning.

I nodded.

"The lady who *diapers her dog!*"

We left Larchmont in time to get to Bishop Weldon's for dinner. The plan was to spend the night with him and leave at 6:00 a.m. allowing time for Mass and breakfast on the way. We said good-bye to him before we retired but when we rose at 5:00 a.m. the Bishop was up to celebrate Mass for us in his chapel. A private Mass is somehow a treasure, and this one especially so with Jimmy and Karen and me making the responses, and Kristin adding her voice and sparse vocabulary which of course included "beer."

Following breakfast we loaded the car and just before Ocean Borne jumped in, the Bishop blessed her as well as us. We drove off waving and he stood waving back, tall, handsome, but with new lines of concern and fatigue that must be special to bishops whose cares are inexorable and whose loneliness must be profound. I thought of his hours of sacrificed sleep that he might say Mass for us. I had a lump as big and as hard as a peach pit in my throat.

There is no such thing as an unimportant show and this week-end Karen needed a lift so I wished a little harder than usual. Karen got a whopping big lift, for against stiff competition, she again went Best of Breed. "What did you expect?" she laughed jubilantly, "after all I'll bet Ocean Borne was the only entry blessed by a bishop."

For Karen, the dogs were all that we had hoped for and more. For Kristin they were a number of things—lying down they were soft mattresses on which to curl up, or hills to climb over; sitting, they made fine slides from shoulders to rump; walking, they were superb ponies. At all times they were a means of access. When Kristin wanted to reach something beyond her grasp she would say authoritatively to the nearest dog: "Come!" Obediently the creature designated would get to her feet and walk over. "Sit!" Kristin would command next, then "Down!" then "Stay!" Her stool in place, she would climb up on the broad back, stand on it, and have the desired height. And the dogs took the place of teething rings. I once said to Dr. Clark: "Kristin is teething on the dogs' ears. They whimper but never move. I wonder—"

Dr. Clark shrugged. "My youngster is teething on our dog's feet."

We lined up many shows that summer for there was a high rate of family absenteeism. Joe had gone off to Europe, and Father Rover and Rory again left for Canada and the Shakespeare Festival. Happily for Marie and me, Rory had been able to get a substitute on his newspaper route.

Since the wedding, Karen had been getting up earlier to give more help in the kitchen. When the days were hot, and she and Barbara were going to the beach early, we didn't put on the braces until afternoon. On these days, the only help Karen required in the morning was to have me put on her shoes. Now certainly there's nothing arduous or time consuming about slipping on two moccasins, but for a reason which I have never been able to fathom, this was a task I loathed. I tried a dozen different tricks to conquer my feeling—singing, making bright chatter, reciting four lines of poetry memorized long ago; reminding myself that this task took but a minute and formerly we had done hours of daily therapy. Nothing worked. When Karen sang out from her room: "I'm ready for my shoes," and sometimes, "my shoes and stockings," my feet might move quickly, but my spirit dragged. I have not had this reaction of overwhelming reluctance to anything before or since. It got to the point where I was gearing myself for the call, and I realized that this was something I had always let Gloria do because I disliked it so much. I now had to discipline myself sternly not to delay, so Jimmy or Rory or Marie would do it. Then, one morning, after two years of failing to conquer or even lessen my repugnance, I found the answer. To put on her shoes or stockings, I found it easiest to kneel on the floor in front of Karen. This memorable morning, as I knelt, the thought came into my mind (through no impetus of mine) —I can make this an act of love and adoration of Him Who has so loved us; I can be a contemplative in action. This was the answer. It was a positive thought that brought with it real joy, rather than a negative device for escape. It was no revolutionary idea, but it revolutionized my life, for no longer were my mornings shadowed by the dread of the summons or the ensuing and persistent feeling of guilt. I recalled the words so recently read at Gloria's wedding: ". . . nor will God be wanting to your needs; He will pledge you *lifelong* support of His graces in the sacrament which you are now going to receive."

July 16 set some kind of a record for heat and humidity. As soon as Jimmy came home he took Karen for a swim. They returned about seven, and while we ate a salad supper on the porch we made the final plans for the church ceremony in celebration of our silver wedding anniversary, nine days hence. Bishop Weldon would celebrate a Pontifical Mass. We were delighted at the number of affirmative replies to our invitations since we had assumed that a Saturday morning in July would lure people to the golf course, the beach or sailing. Frank and Maisie Sheed would be back from England in time, and Dominic Tranzillo, at the organ, would play a Gregorian Mass of his own composition. We had splurged a little and Dominic had assembled from throughout the county a fine choir of male voices.

Karen, looking dreamily to sea said: "And Glo and Russ will be home four days before the anniversary and that's only five days from now."

"How wonderful it will be for your children to hear you renew your marriage vows," said a voice from the doorway.

I swung around and there were Mr. and Mrs. Lea.

"Glo! Russ! What brings you home now?"

"Trouble with the car?" asked Jimmy practically.

"The car is fine."

"You both look marvelous. But you're five days early."

"No we're not. We had a slight change in plans."

"How so?"

Everybody got kissed and Gloria said: "We came home to prepare the best Silver Anniversary Party that anyone ever had."

"You're crazy to interrupt your honeymoon."

"I think they're sweet," said Karen.

"Didn't you think *we* could do it?" asked Marie a little stiffly.

"Not as big a party as we think it should be," answered Russ.

"How big?" I asked apprehensively.

"Just your closest friends," answered Glo evasively.

"How big?" I asked again.

"Only those you would want with you on such a special day."

"How big?" I repeated raising my voice.

"That's no concern of yours," Gloria smiled. "We've made all the plans and you will have nothing to do with it."

"How big?" Now I put the question feebly.

"My, you're persistent. All right then, sixty for brunch."

"Sixty!"

"It will be a breeze. We have it all worked out. Now don't

you want to hear about our honeymoon?"

The next night I found Jimmy standing in the pantry with a list in his hands. "Those kids will have to mortgage the house before they've lived a week in it. Listen to this—sixty pounds potatoes, four hams, four turkeys, salad makings, liquor—" His dismay was lightened by a laugh. "Here's a note in Karen's hand—'The Bishop is bringing the wedding cake.' What can we do to stop them?"

"Nothing."

"I'll try talking to them."

"I already have."

"Maybe they'll listen to me."

"They won't and any more talk will only spoil it for them. Their hearts are set on it."

"As you say," said Jimmy with little conviction.

The following morning I was distracted from my bed-making (as I frequently was) by the view from my window. Far out on the Sound moved ponderous freighters like stiffened dowagers, steam yachts like well-tended matrons, and sailboats like lissome youngsters. The breeze riffled the water and crept through the marsh grass. In the park across the street stood a man calling to Lark who was on our porch. She bounded down the steps and frolicked over to him. He bent over, and as she came up to him , head high, tail wagging, he brought up his fist in a mighty blow under her chin and kicked her viciously in the stomach. She sailed backward with a heart-rending howl of pain. I screamed and the man took off. I tore down the stairs, out of the house, and into the street in pursuit, but as I turned the corner three blocks away he was nowhere in sight. I hurried back to the dog who was limping toward home, whimpering with each step. I picked her up carefully and carried her into the house, then called the police and reported the brutality. The man was not apprehended. Fearing internal injuries I took Lark to Drs. Miller and Clark and they kept her for observation. There was no lasting physical damage but a very real psychological damage. From a gay, loving, demonstrative creature who approached all the world confident of love returned, she became suspicious and fearful. When approached by anyone other than the family, she would stop stiff-legged, trembling, and bark in truly terrifying fashion. She never snapped nor even bared her teeth, but the affrighted stranger had no way of knowing he was safe. We thought that time, patience and kindness from those not too frightened to pat her, would restore her to the delighted dog she had been. I kept her in the house but, with a host of persons coming and going, she would manage to get out. The streets around us were a favorite walk of many elderly folk and Jimmy and I feared that the dog would one day be the cause of a heart attack. A year went by with no improvement and finally the day came when Rory was called upon to decide that Lark must go. Lorraine and Michael Donohue found a wonderful home for her on a farm where today, she has the responsibility for guarding three children, acres to romp and hunt, an adoring family to cherish her, and no strangers walking by the house to renew the old terror. Rory's newspaper route became a solitary and lonely venture as were his walks and expeditions along the shore. Two years have passed but there are still days when I fancy I see her racing across the sand, or hear her pattering up the stairs bringing a message from the first floor. I wonder where Dante would assign the *human* being responsible.

July 25 was warm and clear with just a few mare's tails brushed across a sky that was startlingly blue. During the lengthy Nuptial Mass Kristin was a model of decorum. It was only as we moved off the altar for the Recessional that she violated protocol. As we reached her pew she stepped out and held up her hands. So it was that I walked down the aisle, twenty-five years married, with a babe in arms.

ଚ∾
chapter twenty-six

In August, when the little red house looked like a museum piece on the inside, and a picture post card on the outside, Glo and Russ looked around for some field of service. They were welcomed as volunteers by the Montrose Veterans' Hospital where there were casualties from the Spanish-American War and successive wars up to the Korean War. Many of the men, their families and friends worn by years of effortful contact, had had no visitors for more than a decade. There were patients with both mental and physical disorders. Gloria worked in the physiotherapy department and Russ spent a full day a week working with the men on a radio station, and introducing them to television techniques.

In September, on her 21st birthday, Marie went to Massachusetts to attend a wedding. She telephoned us Sunday to say she'd probably be home for dinner. She did not arrive until after midnight, and of course by then, I had her under a truck or dead in a ditch. My saner husband had gone to bed and to sleep. When Marie finally breezed in I exploded with the anger of relief. "And where have you been, my pretty maid?"

"Oh, I drove home with Ronald Smiley," she answered peeling off her gloves, "and we took a wrong turn." Her laugh ricocheted. "It took us a neat one hundred and thirty miles out of our way." She waltzed over to me. I held myself rigid. "Did you drive one hundred and thirty miles through a wilderness—no telephones?" I asked nastily.

"Oh, darling, you were worried—I'm so sorry."

"I wasn't worried—I was frantic!"

"I should have called."

"You damn well should."

"Forgive me?"

"I'll try, but it will take a few minutes. Put on a pot of coffee."

I sat nursing a tension headache as she winged her way from closet to stove. "You know, Mom, I've been going to the same parties with Ronnie for six years and this was the first time I noticed him—I mean really noticed."

"And—"

"You and Daddy will like him and he's coming next Saturday afternoon."

"Fine. Glo and Russ will be here and you can get a family opinion."

"I gave him the usual instruction about just walking in—that we don't like the bother of answering the door."

It so happened that when Ronnie presented himself for the first time, Glo was alone in the kitchen doing a crossword puzzle. He walked in as directed.

Gazebo screamed: "Shut the door, Stupid!"

And Glo glancing up asked bluntly: "Who are you?"

With praiseworthy aplomb, Mr. Smiley complied with the command and answered the question.

Jimmy hurried through the back door and demanded truculently: "What blithering ass parked his car behind mine?"

So it was that Ronnie was introduced to the family. Marie proved a fair prophet for we did like him, all of us—and immediately. It was a good thing we did for we began to see a lot of Mr. Ronald Smiley.

Fall came with its shadows unlike all others, distinguished by their caprioles. Massed clouds were pierced by a sun that splintered the water with brilliance. Fragrant halos of blue smoke floated above burning piles of leaves and it was time to gather up all the mending, turn on the television and watch the World Series. Then I missed Gloria most of all. As I sewed on buttons I had no one with whom to debate the advantages of a sacrifice bunt or a right-handed pitcher. It's never fun to abuse an umpire alone and there had been great charm in the superb pithiness of Glo's remarks, spoken with great feeling to umpires and players as well. I missed her keeping the box score between stitches and our lovely, heated post mortems. I was tempted to keep Karen home from school but resisted nobly.

It was a comfort to have Joe on week-ends. He had come home from abroad with a suitcase filled with presents, and for Marie—a zuchetto of Pope Pius XII, which one day would be the cap for her wedding veil. We began to suspect that this day might not be too far in the future. Karen and I discussed it; Jimmy kept his counsel with, I think, the idea that if he didn't talk about it, it might take longer to happen, for no father relishes losing two daughters within a year.

When Marie and Ronnie were out one night bowling, Jimmy seemed a little more thoughtful than usual. I suggested we 'dry fire' my 22, the only way to keep in practice if one can't get to the pistol range regularly. We were aiming at the clock on the bookcase when Father Mischke arrived, providing a much better distraction. He was the Provincial of the Crosier Fathers and had just concluded his visitations of their houses throughout the world. He had wonderful pictures to show and incredible tales to tell. Kaasi Slezak stopped in and she and Father talked at length of Indochina where Kaasi had grown up. Just before he left, Father told us of showing his movies to a ladies' society of a church in New England. "I narrated as the film went along," he said, "and explained that when the natives really dressed up for Mass on, say a Holy Day, they would wear a bracelet on the upper arm. Of course, in the movie, the ladies could see that this constituted the major covering of both men and women. At the completion of the film, I invited questions. One good woman stood, and in a voice quivering with indignation (I assumed at nudity in church), inquired: 'Father, do you mean to tell us that you let those women go into church without *hats?*' "

Karen hooted with appreciation and it occurred to me that though physical disability, and restrictions on her time, limited her going out, fate had arranged for much to come to her. The Kerrs, Slezaks, and O'Briens brought close the world of the theatre; the Sheeds, the world of letters and valuable insights developed in their travels around the world; the Amendolas, the world of sculpture. She had the association of authors, publishers, politicians, businessmen, musicians, composers, doctors, teachers, missionaries of many sects. There were people with two strong legs, plenty of leisure, high-powered cars to whisk them about, who had not access to the intellectual riches that were spilled in Karen's living room and kitchen. And there were some glorious debates that raged loud and long. One night when Marie was twelve, I had found her at midnight, sitting on the stairs and weeping. "Oh, Mommy," she had sobbed, "if you and Phil don't stop shouting at each other, you'll never be friends again!"

Many of the associations that were ours were due in part to the special situation that elicited from people an interest and constant kindness that is too often hidden, too often forgotten.

There was a great deal on the credit side of Karen's life. Still we were constantly concerned with the debit of her dependence—the assistance she continued to need with the braces and crutches before she could be mobile. It was apparent to me that more and more Karen, too, was wrestling with this problem. In my deep concern I wondered if she thought that maybe she had come to the end of the road. As the marsh grass turned from saffron to spring green to summer gold, then to the brittle copper of Fall, Jimmy and I thought and talked, thought and talked. We were like those oxen who turn the water wheel, plodding endlessly the unbroken circle. There were many times when one had literally to lift the mind and place it on something else. I thought of a statement of James Anthony Walsh, one of the founders of Maryknoll, "If I didn't believe in God's Providence with all my heart I'd be too scared to get out of bed in the morning."

On a sharp October day, while we were having dinner with Gloria and Russ, they handed me a package.

"Quick! Open it." Rory hung over my shoulder.

"Hurry—please!" Karen urged. "Little boxes are the most exciting."

I undid the wrapping and removed the lid. Nestling in cotton was a gold circlet. As I lifted it, Glo and Russ said: "Congratulations, Grandma!" In the center of the ring was a pair of gold booties.

"When?" I shouted along with everybody else.

"May."

Gloria, of course, would have no one but Dr. Schell (now a sparkling 81), though this entailed a two-hour drive for each visit. "I wouldn't feel safe with anyone else," she explained when it was suggested there must be someone closer to home. We felt safe too, since Russ was an RH positive and Gloria an RH negative, and we knew there wasn't another Dr. Schell.

As time went on Rory took more and more responsibility for Kristin. Marie and I were grateful for our days were crowded. The Superintendent of Schools continued to deny us any assistance on transportation so, still lacking the thirty-five dollars a week for a cab, Marie drove Karen to and from school.

Our thoughts for Christmas were somewhat subverted, not only by a small concern for Gloria, but also for Jean who had the same blood factor and whose baby was due during the holiday season. As it turned out we had days of rejoicing prior to Christmas for on the anniversary of Grace Oursler's death, Jean delivered her fifth boy, Gregory.

Joe spent the holidays with us and when Glo was around, he hovered, though this he would stoutly deny. Although Ronnie did not live with us, he might just as well have. About the only time we didn't see him was when the golf course was free of snow. "I guess if I shot in the low seventies, I'd be out in freezing weather too," was Jimmy's comment, spoken with just a hint of envy.

At the end of March Ronnie asked to "speak to Jimmy." I sat upstairs and typed with furious lack of concentration, hearing Marie's footsteps pacing the floor above me, and made a pretty good guess as to the purpose of Ronnie's talk. I picked up the intercom and buzzed the third floor. When Marie answered, I said with no introduction: "I'm all for it," and hung up.

Ten seconds later she ran into the office and asked in amazement, "How did you know?"

"You're insulting. Anyone with a modicum of intelligence would know."

"How?"

"Well, neither one of you exactly simper—but there are times when you come pretty close to it."

"It's going to be hard on Daddy—two of us leaving in a year."

"He won't think of that."

"I know it. That's what makes it hard for me. He never thinks of himself. Never—" she repeated reflectively. "I think Ronnie is like Daddy. That's why I love him."

One spring day, in the Chapel of Our Lady of Good Counsel, Ronnie and Marie had their Betrothal Ceremony. Their wedding was set for August 29.

Joe took a job in a delicatessen week-ends and Friday nights, to earn the money for his "sister's" wedding present —wedding portraits to be done by one of New York's finest photographers.

It was Joe and Marie who found her wedding dress. Where Glo's had been dainty, Marie's was regal. Together they decided on the fingertip veil and determined the design in which it would be set on the zuchetto.

On May 3, the wedding plans were pre-empted by Kristin's second birthday. When we had moved into Sursum Corda there had been no one under twenty-one on the street. Now, thanks to the Creans, the Kerrs, and the McEneaneys there were eighteen youngsters within spittin' distance. So Kristin's party was a huge success and Hicky (Dr. Schell) did very well at musical chairs. I went out to the kitchen for some more ice cream and found Glo sitting down and looking a little wan. For Glo to sit down during a kid's party was indication of something. About 9:00 p.m. we left for the hospital. Glo insisted that Jimmy go to bed for he had to rise early. Joe, Russ, Karen, Marie, and I played hearts in the deserted hospital lobby, alternately looking at our cards and the large clock at the end of the foyer. While it was still May 3rd and Kristin's birthday, Gloria gave birth to a baby girl. Hicky brought us the news: "They're both fine." To Russ: "I hope you're not disappointed, but I wanted a girl."

"So did I."

The blond angel was named Mary deLourdes, to commemorate the Feast on February 11, on which Glo and Russ had received their word from Rome.

Jimmy had an interesting thought. Were it not for Gloria's super-human efforts in running the house, driving Karen to school and nursing me—we never would have had Kristin. Could it not be that God had sent Mary on Kristin's birthday in recognition of this fact? We thought it likely.

On a scorching June day, Joe graduated from Fordham. As there is a silver lining behind every cloud, so it seems that there is a cloud behind every silver lining. Joe would be living with us for a month, but then he would leave for Florida, fifteen hundred miles away. He had taken a posi-

282.

tion with the Jordan Marsh department store.

We were managing a fair adjustment to the prospect of this separation from Joe, when Russ and Gloria dropped a bombshell. Russ had decided to open his own FM station —in *Florida*. Miami, to be exact. This was the only time in my life when I could pretend to heroism. Following Jimmy's example, I *urged* them on. It would be hard enough to be separated from three children but to have the blossoming grandchild snatched away was almost more than we could bear.

Marie took time from wedding preparations to help Gloria pack some fifty-nine cardboard cartons which the Leas were going to transport in a trailer attached to their car. Their house was rented, and we all had a hand in the final painting, buffing and polishing for the fortunate tenants. Crowded as her days were, Gloria still found time to take Mary deLourdes for several visits to the Veterans' Hospital. When I protested that she was attempting too much in the short time remaining she said: "There is nothing I have to do as important as this. On our first visit men wept when they told me they hadn't seen, let alone held a baby, in forty years."

I was not able to help Gloria as much as I wished since a two-year-old places considerable demands on a mother's time, and most enjoyable time it was. Kristin's night prayers were a particular pleasure; she had grasped that prayer is conversation with God and hers was personal, hearty, and practical, frequently accompanied by gestures. Etcetera, who followed her everywhere with unflagging interest and devotion, always sat on the bed as Kristin knelt beside it. One night after the final Sign of the Cross (which resembled nothing so much as brushing away an annoying fly) Kristin suddenly looked up at the crucifix, put her hand on the cream-colored back of the Siamese and amended: "And Jesus, today I had ice cream *just that color!*"

It was only a month or two later that my wee one almost broke up a church service. The congregation had sung a hymn in honor of Mary, Mother of God, and was now silent for the solemn part of Benediction. Apparently Kristin decided that another hymn to Mary was in order and the silence was shattered by the faulty but recognizable melody and words—"For it was Mary, Mary long before the fashions came."

I privately thought that both Mary and George M. Cohan would have been delighted. The congregation and celebrant certainly were.

As Kristin grew and was allowed more freedom she took the usual number of spills and tumbles. Funnily enough, she would take her sobbing self to Ocean Borne and Peri to be 'kissed and made better.' She would also nap on them as Karen had napped on Shanty for so many blissful years.

Marie and Ronnie had decided that they wanted the very best in marriage counseling, so several times a month they drove to Springfield, Massachusetts, where Bishop Weldon, father that he was, arranged hours from a grueling schedule to help them prepare.

Their wedding day, August 29th, dawned clear and hot, and got hotter with each hour. If Marie was uncomfortable there was no sign. She looked cool and stately as she walked up the aisle behind Karen. More than that, she was breathtakingly beautiful. Her dress was a long-sleeved pure white peau de soie, with a bodice crusting of Alençon lace. The skirt fell softly full in front, then swept back in voluminous gathers to a four-tiered bouffant pouf that spread over the floor behind her in a wide and whispering train. Her hair, more black than brown, was dressed softly in front and arranged in a high chignon. The effect of queenliness was heightened by a pearl coronet set on the zuchetto from which fell a froth of veiling. Her dark eyes glowed, and as she drew closer, I saw a small trembling of the cascade of orchids she was carrying. As she and Ronnie moved to the sanctuary, Bishop Weldon stood facing them, smiling with utmost tenderness.

The day after the wedding, we stood on the observation platform at Idlewild and watched a great silver plane carry Joe away. Driving home, Karen was very white and very quiet.

The next day we waved good-bye to Glo and Russ and Mary as they made a reluctant and final circle of the house and headed for Florida.

"This ought to be a memorable trip," said Jimmy in an effort to lighten our spirits. "A nursing infant, a loaded trailer, a car that has done 98,999 miles, a Labrador, a Newfoundland, and a cat!"

"I can't wait for Glo's first letter," said Rory. *"That* will be worth reading."

Karen said nothing. I knew her heart was aching, not only for the three departures already effected, but the final one that would come only two days from now, for Rory was going away to prep school. They had been unbelievably close for fourteen years and this last wrench was going to tear wickedly at Karen's heart.

Rory was going to Worcester, Massachusetts, to Assumption Prep, unqualifiedly one of the finest prep schools in the country. Here he would find priest teachers who saw, as Newman, the aim of a liberal education—"Nothing more or less than intellectual excellence," to be achieved by a process of training in which the intellect "is disciplined for its own sake, for the perception of its own proper object and for its own highest culture." Here he would find men who put first things first—What kind of a person am I going to *be?*—and only then—What am I going to *do?*

The day before he left, Rory walked the Park and the shore, storing sights and sounds; the wash of water as it hissed through the marsh grass; the strident call of the gulls; the peeching of the terns; white sails clustered like a gaggle of geese, and the beautiful 12-meter *Columbia* like a brush stroke on the water; the sun flirting with the sea from behind scuttling clouds; gray rocks; green trees. That night he roamed the house, finally settling in the kitchen. "I shall miss this room most of all." He gave me a quick peck on the back of my neck. "I'll finish my packing."

Karen managed to smile as Rory threw her a kiss through the train window. She kept smiling until the train was out of sight. Then her face fell apart but she did not cry. Dinner was bleak and strained with Karen exercising great control. Then I made a mistake in timing, a thoughtless, stupid, cruel mistake. When we had finished dinner at the too-large kitchen table, removed the dishes and the cloth, I took out three leaves, making the table much smaller. That did it. It was so final.

Karen broke down. Completely. Utterly.

કે

chapter twenty-seven

After the exodus we were bereft. With three of my assistants gone and Karen in school, I was busier than I had ever been. The twice-a-day round trip to Good Counsel took a big hunk out of hours needed for cleaning, washing, ironing, sewing, shopping, cooking, supervising and reading to Kristin; the care and feeding of livestock, the work of our Foundation, correspondence, and the everlasting call of the telephone. Frequently I was tempted to skip daily Mass and gain forty-five minutes; then reason dictated that I needed all the assistance I could garner and those forty-five minutes were a good investment. Over the kitchen sink I tacked a card on which were the words of Lord Astley before the battle of Edgehill: "Thou knowest Lord, I shall be verie busie this day. I may forget Thee. Do not Thou forget me."

Happily, the Cherns had come to a decision which would make it possible for Karen to see them frequently. On a brisk Fall day they moved their kennels from Vermont to a beautiful estate in New Milford, Connecticut. Jimmy, Karen, Kristin and I were waiting when the cavalcade from Vermont came through the gates on Bear Hill Road, car after car after car, carrying over three tons of Newfoundlands to their new residence.

Every brilliant tree and vine and bush was a reminder of Gloria for she loved the Fall best of all. Jimmy determined to send Fall to his daughter, so we drove to Yorktown and gathered branches and berries of every color and hue and mailed an enormous box *air mail* to Miami. Glo wrote:

When the box of beauty was opened I bawled, of

286.

course. Natives came from all around for they had never seen the glory of hardwoods except in pictures. . . .

Send me detailed news of Kristin, what she says, what she does. I miss Karen so much it hurts all the time. Lordy, I'm homesick. .

I replied:

Kristin is very active and consequently always bruised. She rarely has two sound knees, so night prayers are frequently said in a most unliturgical crouch. She scraped her elbow the other day and when Daddy cleansed it, told him: "God gave Daddies gentle hands." Every time she takes medicine she says: "God bless Dr. Ginia," and every time she sees the American flag she says, "God bless my country." I encourage both prayers. Dr. Haggerty may not need them but the country sure does.

Many of my letters to the South were written in shorthand, it was so much faster. Russ was intrigued and began to decipher them. One day he asked Glo to interpret a symbol that looked like a seagull tilting to starboard. "For them," she answered. He continued his application and became quite literate.

The Leas reported that in Florida nobody wanted to rent to a couple with a child or a pet, so they had bought a houseboat and a beautiful thing it was: twelve feet wide, forty feet long. It had been designed and built by a man and his wife for their days of retirement. The kitchen had a stove and a refrigerator bigger than ours. There was a two-inch-thick, round mahogany table and six captain's chairs. A bath complete with tub, and an incredibly lovely master stateroom with large double bed, bookcases, dressing table and chairs. A second room had double-decker bunks. The boat was completely furnished even to bath linens.

Glo wrote:

. . The fabrics are the finest and colors heavenly.

We are docked at Pier C, and have a lovely park right across the street. Russ walks to work in five minutes. There are around us, home-made boats and quarter-million dollar yachts. For the most part we find that people who live on the water, regardless of the size of the bank account, are simple and friendly.

Just unpacked the last cardboard carton that Marie packed. *What was she thinking of?* Silly question! It was a week before the wedding. Of course we don't have enough closets (who ever has?) but where the devil am I going to store her handiwork:

ski boots
two dozen quart size Mason jars
the branding iron for the goats
woolen underwear
Some pots and pans I *do* need
John Leo's rubbers

Am sending you some smoked sailfish. Even Daddy would not mind Friday down here.

We have decided what we want for Christmas—*KAREN*.

Karen had a card from Russ:

My dear sweet Sister,
Things are really popping down here now. A lot of radio equipment is arriving and I am quite busy trying to make it all go together—an electronic crossword puzzle. Everything I built works. I think my wife is surprised.
See you at Christmas,

Loads and loads of love,
Russ

Joe wrote a long letter to "Dear Everybody". The last sentence read: "My love will always be with *Sursum Corda*. Karen— the first trip to New York, we have a theatre date. O.K.? Thanks for the picture of the kitchen."

Karen and Ed Carver got a little business deal going which would help Karen defray the cost of her flight to Florida. Ed raised purebred Persian kittens, but, due to his commitments, he was not available to show them to prospective buyers. So, as soon as they were weaned, he brought them down to Karen. She inserted ads in the papers and found that the demand always exceeded the supply. Karen spent a good bit of time talking to 'lookers' and deciding whether or not they would be fit guardians. She could be ruthless when necessary.

For the first time since she started school, Karen couldn't wait for the holidays and her reunion with Glo, Russ, Mary and Joe. As her bank account grew so did her eagerness to be off. Jimmy and I, ostrich-like, refused to think of a Christmas with only two children at home.

We had Christmas dinner the night before Karen's departure. There was the customary coterie of friends and the Cherns brought the tree. But Gloria wasn't there to find the corkscrew, or change the fuse which always blew with demoniacal timing while Daddy was carving the bird.

Karen's plane was scheduled to leave Idlewild at 9:00 a.m. I woke while it was still dark, raised myself to glance at the clock, and then looked out the window. The world was white! I jumped up for a closer look and found there was over a foot and a half of snow and it was still snowing heavily. This could be tragic. Our tires were smooth and we had no chains. As early as I dared, I called a friend who was a cab driver, and asked him to take Karen to the airport. He would. I was in Karen's room helping her with last minute packing when he called back. He couldn't even get his car out of his driveway. Karen moaned and buried her face in her hands.

Jimmy got on the phone and called driver after driver. Those who could move were already booked up. Time was racing by. Karen said she felt nauseous. Jimmy said: "I'll drive to the station, load bags, wheelchair and crutches on the train. From Grand Central we'll go to the Air Bus Terminal and take the limousine to the airport." He checked the trains, then the terminal. Time had run out for this solution.

Karen broke into tears of frustration and disappointment and I was trying to find some way to comfort her when Margaret Chern came down for coffee. In a few words we presented the problem. "I'll be dressed in five minutes," Margaret said. "Jimmy, load my car, it has new farm snow treads. Karen, dry your eyes and put your coat on. *We'll make that plane.*" In ten minutes flat, the motor roaring mightily, they backed out of our driveway.

It was a long and anxious wait until Jimmy called from the airport. *"We made it!* The way that woman can drive! She says years of winter driving on unplowed roads in Vermont have given her a knack. A knack!—at one point the road was completely blocked by a tie up of cars and trucks. She blithely ran *off* the road, *through* drifts, and back on after she'd passed the mess. I've never seen anything like it!"

Christmas morning on the way into church Rory commented bitterly, "I don't like *not* pushing a wheel chair."

A few days after Christmas Rory received a telephone call. I was ironing to the sprightly strains of *The Music Man* (I can do a man's shirt in nine minutes flat if the music is right) when my son raced through the kitchen door shouting: *"You'd never guess*—the break I've been hoping for!" He cavorted around the kitchen singing: "Forty-five minutes from Broadway—"

I felt a small stirring of apprehension. For three years Rory had been pleading with us to let him do summer stock. For a variety of reasons we had refused. I disconnected the iron and turned to face him, or rather kept turning to keep facing him as he continued his antics. I started off with a question. "Don't keep me on tenterhooks—spill it."

Keeping to Cohan's melody he sang: "Father Rover does say, they're doing a play—" He caught my expression and hurried on, this time not singing but speaking quickly, "The Olney Theatre, under the auspices of Catholic University—in Maryland—they're doing *Life With Father*—and Father Rover says there's a man in New York I can call for an appointment to read. Would that be all right with you and Daddy? And Jean?" he added thoughtfully.

I must bring this fifteen year old down to earth, and

quickly. "Hold on. One thing at a time. Yes, I'm sure it would be all right with the three of us. But please recognize right now that reading, and getting the part are two different things. Also, you are totally inexperienced and you will undoubtedly be up against some professionals."

Nothing daunted he replied, "I know. I know. But as long as I have your permission—" he landed a kiss on the top of my head and Charlestoned out of the room. In a few minutes he was back. "You'd never guess what Jeannie is going to do for me."

"What?"

"I just called her and she has a copy of the play," he was breathless, "and inasmuch as I have to be in New York tomorrow at 1:00, she suggested I come over at 10:00 a.m. and she will have me read and give me some advice."

"At ten in the morning. Jean? Are you sure?"

"Sure I'm sure. It was her idea."

"Rory, do you realize—have you any idea—"

"What Mom?"

I shook my head. "Greater love hath no man—"

"Oh, I see what you mean. Sort of the middle of the night. She's great, isn't she? Just the greatest."

"She sure is," I concurred with much feeling.

"May I call now and tell the man I'll be there?"

"I know Daddy would say yes," I took a deep breath. "You may."

The phone rang incessantly, but no word from Rory. Maybe he flubbed it and is too dispirited to call, I thought. Or maybe, more hopefully, maybe he did well and wants to make a personal report. Or maybe, and most likely, he was given no indication at all of how he performed. It was time to start dinner and I began to bread a cutlet. The phone rang again. I lifted the receiver and a cultured voice introduced the caller as the gentleman for whom Rory had read. His comments on Rory's ability were sincere and generous. Yes, he definitely wanted him even though at the moment he was not sure how he would cast him. Was I agreeable?

I was.

Rory would leave for Olney a few days after the close of school and stay until July 18. Jimmy said: "We'll all come down for opening night." It was pretty exciting.

We felt that the time for giving Rory an allowance had passed so he would have to find employment for the balance of the summer. He went back to New York the following day and got a job as a messenger-clerk, starting the day after his return from Maryland. With the two jobs he should, by the end of the summer, have enough saved to buy his clothes and enough pin money for the next school year.

Rory's vacation was over and he was pretty miserable about returning to Assumption before Karen came home from Florida. "It's over two months since I've seen her and now it will be another three until Easter vacation. Please have her call me often."

Kristin was no less miserable when Rory departed. Every time a plane went over the house she would ask eagerly: "Kaaki coming home *now?*"

We were standing in the breezeway at the airport, Kristin perched on Jimmy's shoulder, when Karen's plane taxied to a halt. Impatiently we waited for the passengers to alight then hurried up the gangplank. Kristin raced ahead of us to the door, passed the stewardess, and ran up the aisle to Karen. Instead of smiles and shouts of glee, Kristin flung herself on the seated figure, sobbing uncontrollably. Karen wrapped her arms around the shaking shoulders and murmured: "I'm home, darling. Kaaki's home." Kristin squeezed her tighter and it was a few minutes before she knelt up on Karen's lap. "Don't go away—ever—anymore." Her voice still vibrated with subsiding sobs.

It seemed forever (and it darn near was) before the luggage was released and we were in the car. Karen sat with a Newf on each side of her and Kristin in her lap. "Now," said Jimmy pulling out of the parking lot, "tell us everything."

"First I have a present for Mom from Joe."

"Darlin' Zoe," chirped Kristin as Karen handed me a box. "It mustn't be in a draught," she warned as I removed the lid. I looked for some exotic bloom and found an alligator!

"His name is Gigidinella," my daughter told me, "and he's partial to chopped top round."

"He's charming," I said studying the ten-inch form and the unblinking obsidian eyes. "Where do we keep him?"

"In any one of the bathtubs. We certainly have extra ones now."

Karen's report on the South was not finished that night, nor the night after, nor the night after that. One story caused us a great deal of uneasiness. Glo had been to court. Karen told the story: "Glo and Russ don't have a phone on the houseboat so they use the phone on the dock. Early one evening, as Glo passed the booth she saw a man banging and tearing at the telephone box inside. So," continued Karen with relish, "Glo rushed over, tore open the door of the booth and yelled at him to stop. He continued his assault on the instrument. Glo shouted that she had a baby and if she needed a doctor that phone might be her lifeline. The man ignored her. (I got this story from the people on the pier. How I wish I'd been there.) Your dainty daughter, 5', 2", 108 lbs., grabbed the guy, caught him off balance, yanked him out of the cubicle, and when he tried to go back in *she gave him a good beating*. As soon as he could get away from her he fled, but they caught him."

Jimmy said: "That's quite a story." He sighed. "I wish our girl had a little bit of fear."

Karen said: "So do I," and continued, "—and Daddy, the most awful thing! We went for a walk in the park one morning and there were two men, stripped, hanging from trees. I was horrified. Glo says it's not unusual, that they're Castro's G2 men and this is what loyal Cubans do to them when they discover them. They never injure them, just hang them up." Then with a facile leap so typical of our children, she said, "Mary knows all the fishermen and they give her 'goodies'—*raw fish*. She munches it like candy—tiny uncooked tidbits, ugh! It almost made me sick to watch her." Then she added wistfully, "Mary will be walking soon. I wish I could see her take her first steps."

"How's Joe?"

"Fine. He loves his job and he's bought an MG and it's

stunning. He and I 'did' the city and he only ran out of gas twice while I was there. You know Joe."

"We know Joe."

"Daddy," Karen said sweetly, "they want me to come back for Christmas next year."

"Of course," said Jimmy and didn't even swerve the car.

"Of course," I echoed in strong voice and faint spirit.

ह∾

chapter twenty-eight

For the first two weeks after she came home, Karen was in what could be best described as a bubbling state. Jimmy and I began to hope that this return to her old self would be lasting. At the end of the month we realized that for a fortnight, there had been a kind of creeping quietude in Karen. We thought it might be caused by lonesomeness for the Leas and Joe; the return to routine. She'd had two weeks of new places, new faces, new activities and the acceleration of living at the pier with interesting people involved in unusual pursuits. I thought that school and our house probably seemed flat. I could remember feeling that way, a sort of letdown, after a particularly exhilarating vacation. It would wear off.

But it didn't.

As week moved into week, instead of Karen's usual zest, there was a growing indifference; always so voluble, she was increasingly silent. I explored the possibilities of something being amiss at school. All was as usual but the nuns had also noted the change and were concerned. Jimmy and I walked miles and miles along the shore talking, thinking, talking. We kept creating ideal circumstances for confidences, but Karen kept her counsel. The only thing we were sure of was that we shouldn't push. Daily I resisted the temptation to write or call Ed Doll; he couldn't make a diagnosis three thousand miles away and there was no visit planned for the near future. I wrote in my day book instead.

TUESDAY

Karen seems *tortured!* She is pale and listless; has little appetite; her nights are restless. Week-ends she seems to want nothing but to sleep. Could this be an escape? I have all sorts of morbid fears. Dr. Jim Johnson is going to give her a physical tomorrow. I almost hope it is something physiological—that we can deal with.

THURSDAY

Jim says there is nothing the matter physically. That Karen is terribly troubled about something. That although she usually confides in him with the same uninhibited freedom as the rest of us, she was totally uncommunicative. He says we can't push—just be available and loving—and wait.

Is there anything worse than *not knowing*. I think one only really worries, when one wonders. I feel a crumbling of mental effort as I hopelessly knead the situation over and over and over. I'm glad Jimmy is at work 5 days a week and that Karen is busy with homework in the evenings. There must be a limit of endurance—even for him.

Where Karen's moodiness impinges on Kristin's atmosphere I have something to say and the effort she makes is, if anything, more heartbreaking. I'm trying to stick to something I read in Latin a long time ago—

> *Videre Omnia*
> *Dissimulare multa*
> *Corrigere pauca*
>
> To see all things
> To act as though I'd seen but little
> To correct a few

MONDAY

I've asked Karen to read to Kristin a little every evening no matter how much homework she has. This helps. I wonder why. Maybe part of her unhappiness stems from her inability to do much for Kristin when she's on crutches.

Every morning we have to ask if she's ready to have her braces put on. Frequently she sleeps through her alarm. She used to wake before it went off. Left her in wheelchair this afternoon to take care of Kristin. Decided it was a slight risk for possible big benefit. I went to a beauty parlor for a shampoo. First time in beauty salon in fifteen years. Proprietor offered me $300.00 for my hair—price determined by inches. Came home and told Karen and Jimmy that "my hair will cover my cemetery plot." A bad pun but it provoked some nice hilarity. Karen was just toying with her dinner and Kristin, with a Latin lift to her shoulder and extended palm, said to her sister, with pleading, and a rising inflection: "Manga!" More hilarity. What's more blessed than mirth?

My concern is not maternal preoccupation. A.M., Marie, and Jean have commented on the change. Marie said: "She's wrestling with something enormous. She needs time, patience, prayer and more love than ever." She added: "Always be accessible—you don't know when the pot may boil over. Let's hope it's soon." Marie is so wise.

The end of February, there was a beneficent change in our household. Don and Teri Lawlor, contemporaries of Marie's and Ronnie's, but equally friends of ours, came with their two children to stay with us for a while. Don was between jobs having had the courage to give up radio work which he did not like and return to teaching which he loved. He needed several months of intensive study and a place that afforded a measure of quiet and privacy, in order to get his Master's degree. It was a gay evening when we put the leaves back in the kitchen table, set up a highchair for John Michael, and stacked baby food on the shelves for Stephen. There was a definite change, if not recovery, in the atmosphere of *Sursum Corda*. Teri, Don and Karen were beautifully *en rapport* and the advantages to Karen of having two babies in the house were not mixed. She brightened perceptibly but it seemed to us that it was a surface brightening and Jimmy and I perceived that there was no amelioration of the hidden difficulty. Teri, with marvelous sensitivity said: "It's as if the shell is cracking—but only a little, and not enough." I was sure that Karen's *dependence* in the use of braces and crutches was a contributing factor, but this we had faced for some time, and I did not believe that it alone was the cause of the personality alteration which was more acute.

Kristin, her actions and speech, more than anything else, seemed to lift, if not dissipate the shadow that hung so heavily over her sister. Because I'm so forgetful, I would jot down the babe's more unusual comments during the day and give Karen a report in the evening.

On school days, we rose with the dawn and I found the sunrises ample reward for the effort involved. There is much writing on sunsets, and almost none on sunrises which I find far more beautiful, far more dramatic. There were mornings when looking from my bedroom window, the sea and sky would seem to be bathed in blood; and others when the sky would be a vivid hyacinth shot through with crimson and gold, twice-told in the water.

We had our routine that would enable us to leave the house at 7:40 a.m., drop Jimmy at the train, and pull up in front of Karen's building at Good Counsel at 8:15. Kristin, age three, made things easier by dressing herself completely and tidying her room. We said our morning prayers in the car on the way to the station and Kristin's contributions were sometimes distracting, though always wholly reverent. "Thank You, God, for letting the puddles take pictures of the sky and trees." Or, "You know God, my Siamese lets me know when You are going to send rain. He sleeps with his paw over his nose."

One day, after we dropped Karen, she asked: "Will Kaaki have braces in Heaven?"

"No."

"Crutches?"

"No. She won't need them."

"No wheelchair?"

"No. She—"

"She will walk."

"Yes. In Heaven, all bodies will be perfect."

"I'm so glad for her." There was a pause. "And flowers will never die?"

"And flowers will never die."

She and I would listen to the news on the car radio coming back from school and after weeks of reporting on Africa she asked: "Where is Congo?" I told this to Karen: who said: "Buy her a globe and at night she and I will look at the places in the news."

John Michael and Stephen were too little for much companionship, and Kristin spent hours playing with Etcetera. The two would stand at one end of the second floor hallway and Kristin would say: "Get ready—get set—" The Siamese would quiver but not move. *"Go!"* and they would race down the long corridor, then repeat the performance from the other end. Occasionally, to slow Kristin down, Cetty would, while running, nip her gently in the ankle. When she went upstairs, the cat would race ahead so he could reach out and grab her gently through the spindles as she mounted the last few steps. These activities gave Kristin abundant material for her 'report' to Karen. She related stories with more than a touch of ham and almost always elicited a laugh from her audience.

During a visit from the Sheeds, Kristin asked them: "Will you be my Granny? Will you be my Grandfather?" Charmingly they complied and for weeks she announced this new status to anybody and everybody. As the years passed, this relationship became valuable and significant.

Karen's swimming lessons for the past two years had been sporadic, due to the fact that Barbara Cunningham had married Joe Leichtweis (and what a wise choice that was), and they were rapidly building a family. Tracey, their second daughter, was born in March and Karen was godmother. When the baby was two months old, Barbara and her pupil resumed swimming in the pool. Barbara also noted the change in Karen. "It's as if she's *wearing down!*"

We did notice, however, that on the days she went swimming, there was some lifting of Karen's spirits.

News from Florida was frequent and nothing made me happier than when Jim Brennan would walk in and call: "A letter from the kids!"

Darlings All,

The tugboat races were marvelous. I thought of Mother's two great wishes in life—to have a tugboat; to have a mule. Hope A.M. and Bill sail their yawl down here in time for the Lipton Cup Races.

I've saved the best news for the last. *Mary is walking and she walks like a sailor.*

Please send me news of our family of friends. Pat O'Brien was here last Sunday—that helped.

Love you, each of you, very, very much and Oh how we miss you. So glad Joe is here. He 'babysits' for us so we can get out once in a while. He also steals Mary and they go off for a whole day together to 'secret' places.

Oh how I miss you.
Love you, Karen.

With the coming of Spring, the clouds over Karen seemed to lighten a little. I began to hope that she was working toward a solution of her problem, though we still had no inkling of its nature. The three children in the house were a constant source of delight to her, and Teri and Don were loving companions.

I had a cloud of my own that was constant. Instead of calling me to have her braces put on, I had to check Karen several times each morning to find out when she was ready. After much prayerful thought I finally decided that I would stop checking and if the summons didn't come, I'd leave it at that. Week after week went by and the braces were not worn.

One morning, during the Easter vacation, Karen called

to me in the kitchen to put on her moccasin shoes and stockings. Teri and Kristin were upstairs with the babies. Now was a good time to take a step that I believed necessary. "I think you should put them on yourself," I called through the door.

Silence greeted my remark. I lit a cigarette with hands that shook a little. Finally, Karen said in a small voice: "I wouldn't know how to go about it. I have difficulty reaching my feet."

"Sit in the slipper chair. It's low and should be just right. Would you like French toast for breakfast?"

"That would be nice," Karen answered in a way that revealed she didn't care whether she ate or not.

I beat the eggs with unnecessary vigor, and vacillated painfully between doubt and certitude of the wisdom of my edict. I had nothing to go on but instinct, yet so often before it had been a sure guide. Reason can wage a bitter battle with the maternal heart and for the next two hours I went through a battle as bitter as any I had heretofore experienced. From Karen's room came sounds of heavy breathing, exasperated, almost despairing groans, and once a hoarse "Oh, God, help me!"

I made and drank several pots of coffee. I washed the kitchen windows though my eyes were too blurred to see streaks. I felt as though I had an atom bomb inside me that was building up to a tremendous explosion. I began scrubbing the kitchen floor. I could have used a sponge mop with a long handle but I needed more physical outlet than that, so I took a brush and did it on my hands and knees—exploding an agony on linoleum and burying it in a froth of suds. I was rinsing with meticulous care with my back to Karen's door, when I heard her behind me. Casually, oh so casually, I turned and as I did so said: "Best washing this floor has ever had. Doesn't it look nice?" I looked up at her. Her face was flushed, her eyes a little glassy, and there were traces of tears. With calculated disinterest I glanced at her legs and feet. Her stockings and shoes were on. "Well—good for you. Now you need no assistance from anybody, home or anywhere else. How do you feel?"

"Pleased—and exhausted. It took me two hours and ten minutes."

"I can't think of anything better to do with two hours and ten minutes."

"Neither can I," her voice registered a great fatigue—and complete conviction.

I rose from my knees and kissed her. "I'm terribly proud and happy. There's no indignity in asking for help in what God didn't equip you to do for yourself. But I think there is some indignity in asking for help if you *can* do a thing for yourself."

"I know you're right. I wonder how long it will take me tomorrow."

"Every day it will take you a little less time."

"It's going to be expensive," she gave a genuine laugh.

"How so?"

"If I don't rip the stockings with my toenail I manage to do it with a fingernail."

"Good investment."

Teri and Kristin came in. "What's a good investment?" Teri asked putting John Michael in the highchair.

Karen said: "Well, girls, I've done it."

"Done what?"

"Put on my own shoes and stockings."

Kristin said: "You're wunnerful, Kaaki."

Teri's voice was low and tremulous, "You *are* wonderful!" Then she laughed. Gazebo joined in. "I bet I can guess the nature of the investment."

"What?"

"Torn hose."

"Precisely."

"Cheer up. You don't have to be crippled to face that problem. Every woman lives with it all her life." She ran a hand over her gleaming black hair. "Let's get spruced up and you and Don and I will go out tonight. I'll set your hair in a different, more sophisticated style and we'll do something. I don't know what, just something to celebrate."

Karen's laugh tumbled about the room. "You know, kiddo, I feel that a celebration is in order. Those were the two sweatiest hours of my life—if you'll pardon the indelicacy."

"I don't envy you." Teri said with the realism which is the quintessence of sympathy.

Morning after morning, Karen sweated it out. Morning after morning, I sweated it out. And morning after morning I was forced to make Kristin sweat it out for she pleaded: *"please* let me help Kaaki." Teri was a coward and would retreat upstairs when the ordeal began. Forty-nine days later, Karen was putting on her shoes and stockings in 12 minutes flat.

Easter brought Karen a present from the Baldwins in Louisiana, an electric typewriter, and what a change this wrought in her life. "Won't Ed Doll be delighted!" she exclaimed after several minutes of awed silence. Then with an impish grin at me: "I hope that *now,* Ed and I have your permission." With all the subtlety of a Mack truck she referred to the only time I went contrary to a suggestion of Ed's.

I answered with emphasis. *"Now* you have my permission. Your handwriting is good."

At the close of the school year, Karen began typing instruction under Mr. Alvin Graham. Rarely have I met a teacher so gifted. Patient, kind, enthusiastic, he also had that rather rare ability to inspire the pupil with the confidence he felt in her. It was one of our happiest selections. Typing wasn't easy for Karen. Quite the contrary. But we had taken her to our friend, Dr. William Cooper, for an appraisal of manual and digital dexterity, and if he said she could type—she could. Typing requires rather fine finger motions and spastic fingers give reluctant cooperation. Karen and Mr. Graham closeted themselves in her room and worked an hour to an hour and a half a day. Then she would practice another five or six hours. When she was beginning to know the position of the keys and didn't want to look, she would call to me in the kitchen: "Where is the 'f'?"

What we found was very curious, was that my mind didn't know—but my fingers did. To answer her, I would curl my fingers as though above the keyboard and then automatically the right digit would move to the right position. I had to laugh as I remembered how I had been able to concentrate on many dull sermons by dint of placing my hands in this position over my lap and pretending to type the words as the preacher went on—and on.

A.M. volunteered to train Karen in the writing of business letters. She gave her a few lessons, they typed some letters and brought them to Karen to correct spelling, punctuation, phrasing, typing errors, spacing, margins, and grammar.

Joe came to spend his vacation with us and on the weekend of July 4th, we all drove to Baltimore to stay with Rett and Jim Kelly, who, tragically for us, had moved from Larchmont. On the fifth we went on to Olney, met Father Rover and attended the opening night of *Life With Father*, which Rory had the good fortune to play with Laurence Hugo, Ludi Claire, and Joseph Plummer. It would be most unseemly for me to put in print what I thought of my son's performance. I do think it proper to say that the director was pleased, the cast was pleased, and from a few remarks I heard from the audience, I could assume that it was pleased. Pat O'Brien sent him a telegram which read: "TONIGHT A STAR IS BORN." Jimmy and I thought that if our son chose this as his life's work, he would make the grade.

For several weeks Karen seemed happier. The remainder of the summer and fall was a matter of small events and a large parting—

The Lawlors left us for Lisle, Illinois, where Don was to teach at St. Procopius, the Benedictine College—

A.M. introduced Rory to a lovely woman, Virginia McGuire, who took him on as crew in her Rhodes 19. Happily they skipped across the Sound week-ends or almost as happily sat becalmed—

Colin Kerr started a Worm Farm in *our* yard—

One red letter night the three Jims—Dengler, Killilea, Kelly, and I, went striper fishing, caught 22 "keepers," and Kelly caught three at one time—

On October 16, Jean's *The Snake Has All the Lines*, was published—

On October 17, my new book *Treasure on the Hill*, was published—

303.

On October 18, we received word from Florida that had been withheld "lest you worry." Another Lea was on the way. Glo wrote:

> . . . Miraculously, I have found an obstetrician who is another Dr. Schell. He says I will have the baby in January, probably the same week, maybe even the *same day* that Marie has hers. As wonderful as that would be (imagine the joint birthday parties of the future), I told the doctor that I had had Mary on Kristin's birthday and I intended to hold off and have this baby, Feb. 2, on *Daddy's birthday*.
>
> He thinks I'm kidding!

Karen continued to live in what Jimmy described as a "minor key."

ह**>

chapter twenty-nine

Gloria's letters were the only thing that seemed to cut through the thick anguish in which Karen lived.

With real pleasure she read:

> December 10
>
> . . . Joe has been made buyer of the linen department. He will come to *Sursum Corda* for his vacation this summer . . .
>
> Mary calls me "Matey." She is a tender child and is careful about climbing into my "used-to-be-lap." If the baby is a boy it will be named James for his grandfather.
>
> Cannot believe you will be here in twelve days! Joe, of course, will be at the airport with us to meet you. . .

As the time for her departure for Florida grew near, Karen's gaiety was no longer *determined*. The day before she left she received two Christmas presents. Jim Meighan sent her stock in Standard Oil of New Jersey so she would have an income of her own, and immediately we sensed a new pride of independence.

Just before dinner, Richie, of whom we saw too little since Marie had left college, came with the second gift. If I could have looked ahead to the joyous companionship it was to provide Karen I would have been more enthusiastic, for she brought us another pet—a Dachshund. He was sleekly black with brown markings and a critical eye. He was the smallest dog we had ever had—by far. After a week Jimmy said: "He's just a big dog in a little skin." His name, of all things, was Pierre.

The first order of business was to introduce him to the Newfoundlands. While Karen watched from the porch, Jimmy took them on leash to Kerrs' wide lawn and I took Pierre. As we approached the big dogs I spoke soothingly to my small companion, while Jimmy had his pair stand still. From three feet away Pierre charged, not along the ground, but with an impossible leap. He flew at Peri with a lion-like growl and fastened his teeth in her shoulder. Peri yelped in surprise and pain. Nothing, no one, had ever treated her thus. I yelled to Jimmy: "Grab Peri's head and hold it!"

He, wise man, just stood still. Peri's reaction was one of stupefaction, then, turning her massive head, she gave a mighty shrug loosening Pierre's grip. The little dog sailed off to land in a chastened lump in the snow. Peri had not bared her teeth nor even growled. Shakily Pierre stood up and the two big dogs walked slowly over to him. He stood silent and trembling as they leaned far down to touch noses, their plumed tails fanning the air. They walked around him, inspecting minutely this tiny, strange creature—he kept turning as though on a pivot. After a few minutes, their investigation completed, they ambled away, and to our great surprise Pierre trotted in their wake. Soon his slender tail began to describe happy circles. Jimmy and I exchanged a look and unsnapped the three leashes. Now we'll see—I thought. All we saw was two Goliaths and one stalwart

David, a happy triumvirate, racing together through the snow.

Karen's delight was unforced.

The morning Karen was to leave for Miami we received our Christmas letter from Ed Doll. We read it while we waited at the airport.

Dear Friends—

Happy days to you all! May the Holy Spirit cheer and uplift your souls. We out here shall be closer than you think to the kitchen and parlor of *Sursum Corda.* .

I ponder as I wander on the good fortune we have in knowing you all and sharing in your family joys, sorrows, aspirations, commitments. Truly the riches of living derive from one's friends—in sickness and in health. I cherish the time and circumstances that brought us together and am strengthened by your assurances of what we mean to you.

And Kristin! How I wish we might enjoy her enjoyment of this special season. The wonder of life so promising in her. And the expectations of Gloria—so limited our natures in deploring grief which enriches joy. .

Karen: I'm proud to have known you all these years —you have done me lots of good.

May the New Year be good to you in health, and strength to enjoy happiness and sustain sorrow. God love you all as we do.

Edgar

P.S. I have sent under separate cover the present that Kristin asked me for.

The photograph of Ed that followed was inscribed: "To Kristin—and I do tremble when I think Heigh Ho, would she were mine!"

Karen's absence this year did not leave us quite so lonely for Marie and Ronnie were staying with us. Their home in Scarsdale was a good distance from Dr. Schell and the hospital, and there was considerable hazard involved in driving the icy, snowy roads. Once more the house was marvelously, noisily, messily normal.

Karen had again been bubbly when she came home from Florida. Now there was a return of listlessness which increased daily; whatever her problem, her struggle, it was corrosive.

I had written Glo, Russ and Joe at length about the situation throughout the past year, and it had been my hope that while Karen was south she would unburden herself to one of them. Eagerly we awaited word from Miami. Dispiritedly, Gloria wrote that they had all been appalled at the change in Karen which evaporated to a considerable extent during her stay. They thought, however, that her joyousness seemed *deliberate*. No confidence had been given.

For Karen, life was one aching day after another, then a letter from Gloria brought about a remission.

Darlings,

WE ARE COMING HOME IN JUNE
AND
WE ARE COMING HOME FOR KEEPS.

Joys, like troubles, rarely come singly and the day we received this news Marie gave birth to a lovely baby boy.

Anxiously we awaited the call from Russ that Gloria's baby was arriving, for it was now overdue. Our plans were all made; the neighbors lined up for emergencies; Jimmy's bags were packed. He was taking his vacation to go to Miami, take care of Mary, and run the houseboat while Glo was in the hospital. He would also stay with her for a week after she came home, since Russ could not possibly leave his station. Jimmy certainly had plenty of practice. I couldn't count the vacations in the early days of our marriage when I was pregnant and he had had to "rest up" by cooking, cleaning, shopping, washing and ironing. He was experienced—poor lamb!

Glo kept her promise and on February 2, Jimmy's birthday, Evelyn Ann was born.

You never know how much you use a finger until you cut it and it's out of commission. Equally, you never appreciate the thousand services a husband performs, until he's absent. Karen and I advanced our rising time to 5:30 a.m., made the most of every minute in the day, and even then were tidying up loose ends after 10:00 p.m. The roads were so choked with ice and snow that when we could get the car out, a round trip to Good Counsel took a good two hours. The Sound was now so frozen that only in the middle was there a lane of open water through which the big ships could pass, and it looked to us as though they were being pulled across the ice by invisible harnesses. Harbors were ice-locked, coal barges sat off shore and we had to cut down our heat to conserve our fuel supply. We burned driftwood in the fireplaces and kept the big black stove in the kitchen going full blast. The temperature continued to drop (drop—it plummeted to twelve degrees below), and in order to keep pipes from freezing, we let water run at night and set up two electric heaters to throw their warmth on pipes that were most exposed.

The big dogs relished both cold and snow and although they had a snug house in which to curl up out of the weather when there was a fresh fall we would find them outside, two mounds under white blankets. Everyone else was perpetually shovelling like mad to keep access to the street. I didn't have to shovel a path at all—I just sent the Newfs to the street and back five or ten times, and their combined three hundred and twenty pounds packed down the snow in a neat, hard avenue. When you're talking about a snow depth of several feet and a distance of over one hundred feet, this was no mean contribution.

One night, the sky hung dark and heavy and outside there were only occasional spots of brightness from street lights. Ocean Borne was with Karen, Pierre on the second floor with Kristin, and Peri and I sat in the heavily curtained living room.

My reading was interrupted by a deep growl from Peri, who had been sleeping with her head uncomfortably pillowed on my feet. She scrambled quickly to her feet, hackles up, and stood listening and snarling. I listened too, and heard stealthy footsteps on the long stairs up to the porch. I flipped on the outside light, moved swiftly to the door, Peri beside me, opened it and sent her out with the command: "Go get him." She rounded the side of the house barking with horrible ferocity. I ran to the front window, pulled the drape aside and dimly made out a figure racing away through the park, the dog in pursuit a couple of hundred feet behind. I then called the police.

I waited in the living room until 3:00 a.m. for Peri to bark to be let in. Finally I gave up and went to bed confident that the dog could take care of herself unless she were shot—and there had been no report.

When I came down the next morning, Peri was not in the pen and when I whistled at the back door there was no response. I became alarmed and started for the park to look for her, afraid of what I'd find. As I came round to the front of the house I saw her huge black form sitting 'guard' on the top step of the porch. There was no indentation in the snow around her as there would have been had she lain down, and I realized she had been sitting watch all night. When I called her she came, but reluctantly. Thereafter, until Jimmy's return she took her place on the porch each night at dark and sat in vigil until I summoned her in the morning.

Karen and I got a kick out of running our house like two pioneer women under constant assault from the elements. She comported herself cheerfully but I saw a split-level picture and close to the surface was a constant abstraction that verged at times on morose brooding. Even Jean's genius for therapeutic evocation had not prompted Karen to unburden herself. I found that I was taking every opportunity to observe Karen unnoticed. Her eyes, darkly ringed with shadows, had the lifeless dryness of sorrow unwashed by tears. I carried her trouble with her—not knowing what it was. For a year, I had barely resisted trying to force a confidence that would make it possible for me to help. Help—said the heart. You can't—said the mind; you *know* there are times when one's battles must be solitary struggles.

I dreaded Jimmy's return to Karen's pallid interest, or worse, her calculated levity.

Thank heaven, no blizzard halted the delivery of the mail

and after a letter from Miami Karen would be animated for several hours, sometimes a whole day. Her oft-repeated phrase: "Well, the kids won't have to *write* much longer—they'll be here!"

She wrote to Gloria:

I was elected assistant manager of the basketball team. Needless to say I'm delighted.

Kristin dictates: "Tell Glo I love her since I were very little. Grandfather is silly—but not very."

I will soon be twenty-one and I wish to take steps to dispose of my body for autopsy—to serve whatever purpose might be served by a *total* study and the correlation of *all* findings. I want to find a group that holds to Ed Doll's definition of good science—the uncommon observation of the commonplace.

Bill and A.M. will be sailing South soon. What a hole this will leave in my life. They will see you in Florida, then on to the Bahamas.

Richie and Johnny Forsman are going to be married. I couldn't be pleaseder.

Ed Doll has accepted the appointment as "coordinator of the new program of investigation into the nature and treatment of learning disability in children" at the Vanguard school. This should bring him East a number of times a year. I need him.

Kristin has composed her first "po-em" about Frank Sheed.

> Grandfather's sweet
> And cute as a wink
> He can sing, he can dance
> And Boy! Can he think!

You can't imagine what Kristin means to me, especially now.

The months will drag 'til I get my hands on my redheaded niece and my arms around all of you. I varnished the high chair last night.

I enclosed a note of my own with Karen's letter. "Big Secret. Jinny Franze, one of Karen's closest friends at Good Counsel, called to say we must not order Karen's school ring—the girls want it to come from them!"

ॐ

chapter thirty

Kristin was visiting across the street and I was frying kippers with little attention, looking out the window to the sea. We had had a thaw and the ice-locked Sound has been reprieved. For a day and a night a twenty-five mile an hour gale had been raging and the breakwater and beach held tumbled, crazily slanting piles of floes.

Karen made a conversational effort. "You can't cook those when Marie is pregnant. The odor makes her sick." Her voice was toneless.

"Glo says that Mary and Russ eat kippers for breakfast."

Karen was sitting at the kitchen table, a book open before her, yet she hadn't turned a page in a half an hour. "They do."

I put a little more butter in the pan and turned the fish, saying with calculated off-handedness: "You're far from cheery. Is something bothering you?" Why I chose to speak the question, and at this time, I don't know, unless it was due to some inner prompting that mothers not infrequently experience. I was certainly not prepared for Karen's response. Most deliberately I had not looked at her as I spoke, only allowed myself a glance at her face at the interrogation point. I was appalled at what I saw—her face *crumbled* and in that first moment of revealed anguish, her head jerked backward before falling forward as she sobbed raspingly— *"Oh, Mother! Mother help me! I don't know what to do!"*

311.

Her head was bowed over the neat, impersonal lines of print as she cried rackingly.

I moved to her, but not quickly, and put my arms around her saying nothing. I held her close for a little, then walked around the table and sat facing her. I let her cry a while and keeping my voice empty of emotion I encouraged, "Let's work this out *together*—whatever it is." I went to the stove and turned off the fish giving her time to collect herself. I took down the glasses and plates and went back to my chair at the table.

Minutes passed. Finally she raised her head and began to speak in a voice punctuated by tearing sobs, the tears running freely. "It's about—the braces—and crutches—and the wheelchair."

"What about them?"

Tremors tore her body; her speech was spasmodic. "I haven't been wearing the braces and using the crutches every day, but I haven't been able to make a decision."

"Decision on what?"

There was a prolonged hesitation. In her face I read doubt, dread, desperation.

I hoped my studied nonchalance was convincing. "Talking things out has always helped. Let's have a go at it."

"Oh! I want to." Her hands were clasped so tightly that the knuckles were purple. "—I *need* to—but—I'm not sure I have the courage."

"Courage you have aplenty. Now, let's have it. Be blunt—it will be easier for both of us."

She began to speak through tears that still ran heavily, and with the words her face was washed of all emotion save relief. "I can't have it both ways. I either wear braces and use crutches—or I don't. Dr. Moore says I have reached my maximum physical potential. I'm so *dependent* in braces. I have so much more *freedom* in the wheelchair. Now—" she paused and her eyes bored into mine, "—should I give up the braces and crutches—*forevermore?* Should I use a wheelchair *exclusively? Should I?"*

So this was it. This was the cause of a tormented year. "That, my darling, is a decision only you can make."

"But what do *you* think?" Her knotted hands tortured

each other. Her breathing was shallow. Unconsciously she was asking me to make the judgment. I knew what I believed to be best but I could not tell her. I had not the right. "Please. Mommy," she urged, "what do you *think?* I'm not asking you to decide, just tell me what you think."

"It isn't up to me to think one way or the other."

"Please!" She extended her arms to me across the table and moaned, *"Please!"*

My whole being yearned to wrap my arms around her, pillow her comfortingly, and tell her what I thought. But that would be failing her. I clenched my fists at my side and spoke sternly: "This is hardly the time for emotion. You're faced with a decision that must be an intellectual one, so get hold of yourself and start *thinking.*"

She dragged her arms back across the table and let them fall at her sides. "I've been *thinking* for a *year.*" She tried desperately to control her shattered voice.

"Not *thinking—feeling!*" I handed her a handkerchief.

She struggled valiantly to regain composure, wiping her eyes with her fist, a peculiarly appealing gesture. "You're right." Her voice was low. "But I've done some thinking about the twenty years you and Daddy and the kids have worked getting me to walk. To say nothing of the expense."

"You're off base right there." I said crisply. "We did not put twenty years into getting you to *walk.* What ever we 'put in' was to get you to your maximum potential for independence. Walking was never an end in itself—rather a means to an end. What you have to decide, is whether *now,* and in the future, walking will best serve that end."

She spoke through parched lips, "I can't decide *alone.*"

"You must."

She turned her head from left to right as though seeking escape.

I lit a cigarette and kept silent.

"Suppose—suppose I decided to stick to the chair, wouldn't people think me a failure?" Her head drooped in anticipated humiliation.

"You shock me. Since when do we make any decision on the basis of 'what people think'? And maybe, my pretty lass, you'd better give some thought to the definition of 'failure.' "

The blood suffused her neck and face. I had stung her and I wondered wildly if I was being too harsh.

"But if I decided to give up braces and crutches—wouldn't *I* be failing *you and Daddy?*"

"Again you're emoting—not thinking. Examine what I just said about the purpose of all our efforts."

She closed her eyes and was still for many seconds. Without opening them she said in a low voice: "I guess I'm very worried about how Glo and Russ and Joe and Marie and Ronnie and Rory and Jean would feel."

"Always the word *feel*. Your doubts do them an enormous disservice. They're really insulting to both their intelligence and their love."

She shuddered as though with a chill. Well, she'd been sick with this thing for a long, long time.

"Let's use another phrase that might be helpful," I said more gently. "Let's say you must be *scientific*. I remember Ed Doll saying that the business of science is to make the obvious obscure."

"I remember that too." She looked out the window at the wind-whirled snow. "I also remember," she said pensively, "that Ed said 'one should utilize one's assets to offset one's deficits.' "

"Now you're *thinking*."

There was a small lift to the corners of her mouth. "And Father McSorley said the same thing in a different way: 'Concentrate on the residuals instead of crying about losses. Assess assets so you can be realistic about what you have to work with—.' "

"It was either Walter Kerr or Ed Doll who said that our security depends on how successfully we deal with apprehensions."

She turned to look at me and there was the smallest hint of a smile. "I should have been thinking of all these gems of wisdom for the past year—instead of stewing."

"Let me remind you of another gem that has helped me to make many difficult decisions. Years ago, Father McSorley taught us to appraise a total situation by drawing a line down the center of a piece of paper making two columns— *Pro* and *Con*."

314.

"*Now* I remember. I wish I'd remembered a year ago."

"*Now* is all that can be presently profitable." I went to the desk and got a legal pad of lined yellow paper, a pen and a ruler. I put them on the table in front of her. "I have many chores waiting for me upstairs. While I take care of them, why don't you get to work—which means using your mind —and only your mind." I gave a little laugh and kissed her lightly.

Her sigh seared my heart. "O.K." She drew the line down the paper and wrote *Con.*

I went to my bedroom. I had no chores that couldn't wait, but I had an overpowering conviction that now Karen should be on her own with the present clarity of her thinking. Now, today, she must excise the malignant cancer of doubt that caused her illness and her pain. Her excision would be, temporarily, even more painful, and the courage to acknowledge must necessarily anticipate the courage to determine. Any parent's heart is riven with compassion when a child is drowning in pain or sorrow, but how much more intense the empathic suffering when one cannot help, and the child must bear its agony alone—unaided.

I wondered if she would reckon the absorption and concentration required in using crutches, so that the beauties she walked by went unnoticed; that in a wheelchair she would move, deeply thrilled, through a world that had always been there, where she could see the *tops* of trees washed gold by the setting sun.

My mind darted from thought to thought as a dry leaf before the wind. In a wheelchair, Karen could go far afield —and alone. Jimmy and I would have to relive the emotional experiences of Karen's first days outside on crutches. There are some pretty wild drivers in the Manor who might not see her chair if they came around a córner at a fast clip, or might not be able to stop if they did. There would be a calculated risk involved—the ever present *possibility* of accident and injury. On the other hand, there was the *probability* of psychological damage if Karen were unable to go out—alone.

I stood at the window and watched and listened as the gale grew in intensity. The pounding of my heart was one with the drumming surf and I felt pity for the sliding sands at the mercy of the predatory waves. Not all the cacophony in our ears was of the wild water; was not Karen attuned to the coursing dissonance of the raging sea against the indifferent rocks? I dropped to my knees and murmured to myself —"She's not really alone, for God loves this child *infinitely* —that's a great deal more than you do."

I tried to pray but the fervor and intent of my prayer kept pulling my mind back to Karen—she couldn't even walk across a room unless someone locked the braces at the knees and helped her to her feet; she couldn't sit down unless someone unlocked the braces; she couldn't get up if she fell and for that reason could no longer go out alone; she couldn't do for others; she had no freedom. I wanted to rush to her and plead: "The chair, the chair, my darling." I stayed where I was and asked God to enlighten her mind. Had she the strength, conviction weighing, to say: "I choose to walk no more."

Karen's handling of her difficulties had nourished the characters of each member of her family. I had reason to believe that, directly and indirectly, she had nourished others also.

How many times her life was thought forfeit. The pregnancy which the best doctors thought would terminate early; her birth at six months, ten days when she weighed 1 lb. 12 ozs.; the critical weeks and months that followed; the unanticipated, serious complications.

Memories came flooding back—memories that had been wishfully forgotten. Karen's cyanosis as an infant when she was fed, which Dr. Gundy had diagnosed as an allergy; the difficulty which made x-ray of the thymus necessary; the atresia at the cardiac and pyloric end of the stomach which caused projectile vomiting when her formula reached three ounces. More x-rays had been taken and Dr. Gundy had called a consultation. An esophagoscopy was considered and rejected on the basis of Karen's size (eight pounds at four months), and her poor condition; she could not survive the anaesthesia. On December 6, the doctors had told Jimmy and me that inasmuch as her food could not be increased to keep up with her growth, she would, in their opinion, not be alive at Christmas. We had been further warned that there was the hourly danger of pneumonia which could be caused by regurgitation and aspiration.

When all this intelligence had been imparted by the consultants, Jimmy and I had held a consultation of our own. We then inquired of the doctors if there were not some surgical procedure that could be followed. Yes, they could cut off the end of the esophagus, eliminating the trouble spot and try to stretch the rest and make a new connection. However, they again warned that she would not be able to survive the anaesthesia, let alone the surgery. Jimmy and I had then decided that if Karen were going to die anyway we would, at the last possible moment, risk the operation and we had so advised the doctors.

But Christmas of 1940 had come and gone and still we had not received the summons for our fateful decision. As we had moved into the New Year we were sure that every time the telephone rang—this was it. We were as prepared as parents can ever be, for Karen's death.

On January 25 the summons had come. Jimmy and I had a long wait in the corridor outside the x-ray department, while doctors consulted endlessly over plates. Although we had thought ourselves prepared, we both had bouts of vomiting while we waited. After an eternity, we were called into the room where a group of sober men stood in front of a series of illuminated pictures. I don't remember who spoke the words that sent the world whirling and spinning.

"These most recent x-rays show Karen's esophagus and orifices to be perfectly normal."

Another voice had said: "We cannot find any scientific explanation."

And John Gundy had said for the second time since Karen's birth: "This child must have been born for a very special purpose."

On January 26, Karen, who had not been able to handle more than three ounces of liquid, was fed mashed carrots and mashed baked potato with no consequent difficulty. We were asked by the doctors if we would be willing to leave her in hospital, so that other physicians could come and see her —the whole situation being "most unusual." We had agreed.

317.

His problem child safe at last, John had gone away for a few days for the first time since Karen had been born five months before. Jimmy and I were blinded by our joy, as one coming out of a dark tunnel into brilliant sunshine. At first, the shock of relief went so deep that we felt nothing. Then came an almost unbearable ecstasy with the full realization of life newly given.

The joy was short lived for on January 27, Karen contracted the flu. Her temperature soared to one hundred and five degrees and again she was put on "critical." Again consultations, and one doctor urged a transfusion. The opinion of the others was that it would probably kill the baby. We couldn't reach John. Again we decided—she's going to die anyway, let's try it.

There were many serious misadventures during the course of the transfusion which was accomplished by taking blood in a syringe from my arm and then putting it in a vein in Karen's ankle which had been incised. A nurse remarked to me: "It's mighty tricky business. That vein is only as big as a piece of No. 60 sewing thread!"

Following the transfusion, the little body had been peppered with needles for clyses and the fever had mounted higher and higher; searing, unyielding. That wondrous joy of twenty-four hours seemed a chimera, a mirage in the desert of hopelessness.

Fervent prayers of thanksgiving had become once more, fevered prayers of petition.

And, once more, God had willed that Karen should live.

It was not possible to recall the many times that Karen did not die, without speculating on the Reason. I thought that to some it must seem that for many years we had been pelted by a downpour of tragedy. The truth of the matter was, that just as the rain is drawn upward, and returned to us in the caress and beauty of snow, so our "tragedies" had been kissed by the sun, and fell freshly upon us in purity, in beauty, in peace.

As I prayed that Karen might be guided in reaching a right decision, so I knew that her decision could never be isolated in its effect.

Slowly I rose from my knees and slowly went downstairs.

As I came through the kitchen doorway, Karen looked up, her eyes bright, her cheeks pink. There was a look more of *intensity* than of strain.

"I've been busy," she remarked and handed me the paper.

Without looking at it, I asked: "And do you think you can soon come to a decision?"

She took a deep breath and on its exhalation answered: "I already have. And you know, Mom, I could have, and should have decided long ago."

"And what have you decided?" My hand holding the paper began to tremble. I put the paper face down on the table, so its rustling would not betray me. I felt lightheaded and the throbbing pulse on each side of my neck seemed about to burst through the skin.

"I have decided—to use Ed Doll's phrase—that crutches are too expensive."

"Oh."

"I *know* that I am more independent, more useful, without them. I am going to 'graduate' from crutches and 'commence' in a wheelchair!" For all her knowing there was no concealing the uncertainty with which she studied my face.

My heart quivered and tears gushed from my eyes. "You are a young woman of great courage. I am very proud to be your mother!"

"Then you think I made the right decision?"

"*That* no one can say but you. What I can say is that I *believe* you made the right decision."

"And you're crying because you're happy, as you always do." Her face melted and a smile of ineffable joy lifted the corners of her mouth and shone in her eyes. "Oh, Mom, I'm so happy—really happy—and relieved—and hopeful, and the future isn't dark any more."

I turned her list face up on the table. I saw only the three words, before my eyes blurred again too heavily to read anything more:

Con braces and crutches	*Pro braces and crutches*
PRISON	
PAIN	

And scrawled across the bottom of the page in letters three lines high was written

FREEDOM

I ran to her, and held her close. "Daddy is going to be so proud, so very proud, and so very happy!"

She flung her arms around my neck and laughed. The rollicking notes chased the darkest shadows from the deepest corners. "All the tomorrows are bright and promising."

"Very, very bright. Very, very promising."

She tilted her head to look up into my eyes. "No more will I be a drab, slow little sparrow that hops around with his head down." Her laugh was a shout of triumph. "I'll be free, really free. I'll be an eagle with my face to the sun."